ECCLESIASTES

A Reflective Exposition

Thomas
MIERSMA

REFORMED
FREE PUBLISHING
ASSOCIATION
Jenison, Michigan

©2022 Reformed Free Publishing Association

All rights reserved

Printed in the United States of America

No part of this publication may be reproduced, stored in a retrieval system, or transmitted in any form or by any means—electronic, mechanical, photocopying, recording, or otherwise—without the prior written permission of the publisher. The only exception is brief quotations in printed reviews.

Scripture cited is taken from the King James (Authorized) Version. Italics in Scripture quotations reflect the author's emphasis.

Cover design by Erika Kiel
Interior design by Katherine Lloyd, the DESK

Reformed Free Publishing Association
1894 Georgetown Center Drive
Jenison, Michigan 49428
616-457-5970
mail@rfpa.org
www.rfpa.org

ISBN 978-1-7368154-7-2
Ebook ISBN 978-1-7368154-8-9
LCCN 2022946954

Vanity of vanities, saith the Preacher,
vanity of vanities; all is vanity.
—*Ecclesiastes 1:2*

Let us hear the conclusion of the whole matter:
Fear God, and keep his commandments:
for this is the whole duty of man.
—*Ecclesiastes 12:13*

CONTENTS

CONTENTS

PREFACE

This book is an exposition of Ecclesiastes. It began many years ago as a series of sermons on the book while I was on the mission field. It was expanded as I have preached through elements of it more than once. It also was set down as an extended series over almost a decade in the *Standard Bearer*. This present exposition of book of Ecclesiastes is the result. It is intended to be read for spiritual instruction, reflection, and edification rather than as a formal detailed commentary on the book.

The word of God in Ecclesiastes intends to set forth the realities of everyday life under the sun. It looks at that life of men from the viewpoint of what we see in the world about us. It treats our labor and its fruit, our evaluation of that labor, and other various elements of daily life. It looks at the works of men individually and corporately. It covers the politics of men and kingdoms, entertainment, and the stages of life from youth to old age. As it does so, it reflects on these things with a spiritual reflection as to their meaning and value.

As believers we walk in the world by faith as sojourners. It is especially a spiritual evaluation of the life of men or wisdom that Ecclesiastes intends to give, for we walk in that world by faith and not by sight. The world lies under the sovereign providence of God over all things, as creator and as Lord of heaven and earth. The world which God made is now a fallen world, a world under judgment and the curse of God upon sin. This reality subjects that world to vanity, to the reality that nothing of man really abides and endures. In treating this reality Ecclesiastes shows us the terrible bondage to sin which holds the unbelieving sinner.

This word of God also addresses the limitations of our understanding of God's government over all things and the unfolding of his counsel in time. The works of God in his providence and righteous judgment are sensed by one walking by faith, but many things from day to day are hidden from us. That God is righteous and that he judges sin and the works of men, in time as well as eternity, is something we know by faith. We walk by a faith that trusts in God whose promises we know. He is, as God, both righteous and merciful. However, the spiritual wisdom of believers, also that of Solomon, has a finite character. We cannot find out by observation all that God is doing, nor do we see his righteousness in judgment manifested at once. Wicked men live and walk through this life seemingly without trouble and then die, the problem the Psalmist also wrestles with in Psalm 73. Yet we know by faith that it shall be well with them that fear God. Death is the judgment of God upon sin, and all the heaping and gathering of the wicked does not profit.

Because of the transitory character of all things, daily bread and the present enjoyment of it with thanksgiving is a gift and blessing from God to his people alone. The grace of contentment in submission is one that God gives to his people. The wicked and the unbelieving fool are given over by God to the folly of sin; under the judgment of God, they heap and gather, seek their treasure here below, and know not genuine contentment. The wicked strive in sinful pride with God's government to their own hurt. Ecclesiastes sets forth the blessedness of those who fear God and yet comes with a warning to us not to follow the way of the world in covetousness. It addresses especially young people, beginning their labor in this life, with the calling to walk in the fear of God.

The word of God in Ecclesiastes is antithetical, in this sense: that the grace of God is particular for his people alone. Grace is not common or universal. Ecclesiastes assumes that we know the promises of God, the grace of God in Jesus Christ, and his word. It assumes that we come to its wisdom with spiritual understanding to learn wisdom by the Spirit of God though his word. Solomon very clearly has God's word as it then existed before him while he writes. He draws particularly on the early chapters of Genesis in his treatment of man, who is of Adam, and is dust and returns to the dust.

Our Savior in his preaching and teaching does not quote directly from Ecclesiastes. Jesus, rather, takes up the truth and concepts found in the book and expands on them, particularly in many of his parables. The rich fool who will build bigger barns is a good example. As such, Ecclesiastes belongs to an aspect of the fabric of the gospel. It undergirds the knowledge of the world as it is fallen in sin under God's judgment. The world can afford us no salvation; man cannot deliver himself from bondage; under the sun the works of men do not profit; salvation is a work of God alone, which is from above; God must enter into our misery in the person of his only begotten Son to save and redeem us. Under the sun, deliverance is not to be found but only vanity and death. Ecclesiastes points to the need for the work of God's grace in Christ, the true Savior, as the only solution to the fallen world and its vanity.

Part One

INTRODUCTION TO THE BOOK OF ECCLESIASTES

INTRODUCTORY REMARKS

God gave us the book of Ecclesiastes to instruct us in spiritual wisdom as those living in a world fallen in sin and under the curse. He gave it by one who was old and endued not only with the wisdom of age and experience, but with the wisdom which only the Spirit of God can give. The Preacher of Ecclesiastes searches the life of man under the sun in order to give us to see with spiritual understanding the way of that life and its value and meaning in a world subject to vanity because of sin. In many ways the book addresses especially the young person taking his place in the affairs of life and beginning life's journey (Eccl. 11:9; 12:1). Its purpose is not so much to give what is mistakenly called practical instruction or instruction on how to *do* something, but rather to give true practical wisdom by giving us to *see* the realities of life with spiritual discernment. The word of God in the book would give us glasses to see the reality of life under the sun.

With the intention of turning to this word of God by way of exposition, we would, have clear in our minds two issues: first, who the author is and then, second, what the theme of the book is. Both these elements are important. There are commentaries on the book that depart from the plain statement of the book that the Preacher is king in Jerusalem, namely Solomon. Attributing the book to an author after the captivity, as they do, reshapes its contents and its theme. Both elements have been ably explained on the pages of the *Standard Bearer* many years ago: the identity of the Preacher by whom God gave this word by Rev. Cornelius Hanko at the time of the Second World War in the *Standard Bearer*. His article is quoted in full.

II

THE AUTHOR
OF ECCLESIASTES[1]

Cornelius C. Hanko

It has always been a safe and established rule to determine the author of a certain book of Holy Writ, if at all possible, from the book itself. What surer guide could we have than the word of God, which is its own indubitable testimony of its infallibility?

Applying this rule to the book of Ecclesiastes, it hardly seems possible that any one should as much as question the fact that Solomon is its author. The first chapter expresses this very definitely. Its opening statement reads: "The words of the Preacher, the son of David, king in Jerusalem." Although he calls himself the Preacher (*Koheleth* in the Hebrew, *Ecclesiastes* in the Greek, from which the book derives its name), he adds that he is the son of David and king in Jerusalem. Verse 12 adds to this: "I, the Preacher, was king over Israel in Jerusalem." And verse 16 continues: "I communed with my own heart, saying, Lo, I am come to great estate, and have gotten more wisdom than all they that have been before me in Jerusalem; yea, my heart had great experience of wisdom and knowledge." To assure ourselves that this could only refer to Solomon, we need but compare it with 1 Kings 3:12, where the Lord addresses Solomon, saying: "Behold, I have done according to thy

---

1   From the *Standard Bearer*, Vo. 20, issue 5, December 1, 1943.

words; lo, I have given thee a wise and an understanding heart, so that there was none like thee before thee, neither after thee shall any arise like unto thee."

If more proof were needed, we could refer to the second chapter, verses 4–9:

4. I made me great works; I builded me houses; I planted me vineyards:
5. I made me gardens and orchards, and I planted trees in them of all kind of fruits:
6. I made me pools of water, to water therewith the wood that bringeth forth trees:
7. I got me servants and maidens, and had servants born in my house; also I had great possessions of great and small cattle above all that were in Jerusalem before me:
8. I gathered me also silver and gold, and the peculiar treasure of kings and of the provinces: I gat me men singers and women singers, and the delights of the sons of men, as musical instruments, and that of all sorts.
9. So I was great, and increased more than all that were before me in Jerusalem: also my wisdom remained with me.

Comparing this with what is written of him both in Kings and in Chronicles, we can only conclude that no one else but Solomon could be the Preacher, who concludes in Ecclesiastes 12:8–10 by saying:

8. Vanity of vanities, saith the preacher; all is vanity.
9. And moreover, because the preacher was wise, he still taught the people knowledge; yea, he gave good heed, and sought out, and set in order many proverbs.
10. The preacher sought to find out acceptable words: and that which was written was upright, even words of truth.

Considering all this, we can safely conclude that the Preacher is none other than King Solomon, whom the Lord granted riches and wisdom in abundance. We can even conclude that he wrote this book in the evening of his life after he had experienced all that life could offer to one in his position, and after he had tasted the full realities of those things of which he wrote.

Yet, with all this overwhelming evidence before them, the Bible critics, almost without exception, are well agreed that Solomon could not possibly be the author of this book. They quite unanimously insist that some other person, at a much later date, either collected various proverbs of Solomon into one book, or wrote the entire book under the assumed name of the Preacher, as if he himself were King Solomon reproducing the thoughts and experiences of the memorable personage, Solomon.

Entirely ignoring the divine inspiration of the Scriptures and ruthlessly exalting their own opinion above the testimony of the word itself, they reduce this book to the level of a mere piece of fiction.

Their main objection to recognizing Solomon as the author of Ecclesiastes is, as they say, that the style of the book is of a much later date, when the Hebrew language was interspersed with many Aramaic words and expressions. This objection is based on the assumption that Solomon could not possibly have made acquaintance with those Aramaic terms that they find in the book. Yet it hardly takes into consideration that as king, the like of whom could not be found, with all the building that he had done, he must have had exceptional amount of contact with the nations round about. Granting that there are many words in Ecclesiastes not found in the earlier writings of the Old Testament, this is still no reason to deny the testimony of the book itself that it was written by Solomon. The style and language must be that of Israel's great king.

The other objections bear even less weight. It is objected that Solomon would never have said: "I, the Preacher, was king over Israel." He might have said, "am king," but never "was," because he remained on the throne until the day of his death. But this objection is more fancied than real. Must we assume that he could not possibly have said that he was king over Israel unless he had abdicated the throne? The only correct explanation is that he appeals to his rich experience as Israel's anointed king in giving his estimate of life, as he does in the first chapter.

Again, it is objected that Solomon would never have said that he was "king over Israel in Jerusalem," since he had no knowledge of kings over Israel who had not reigned in Jerusalem. The assumption is that only one who was acquainted with Israel's later history would emphasize that Solomon was king in Jerusalem instead of in Samaria. Also the objection is raised that since Solomon had not proceeded from a long line of kings, he could not have spoken of "all that were before me in Jerusalem." These last two objections may well be considered as "begging the question." Taking for granted that the author was acquainted with Israel's later history, it is a simple matter to arrive at the conclusion that this assumption must first be proven. There is, on the other hand, every reason to accept that the theocratic king of Israel, conscious of his high calling and having his throne in the holy city, would not hesitate to mention this in introducing himself to his readers. Nor is it strange that he would say that his wisdom exceeded "all that were before me in Jerusalem," since God himself had said: "I have given thee a wise and understanding heart, so that there was none like thee before thee" (1 Kings 3:12). He is simply stating that God's promise was fully realized.

Having established in our own minds that Solomon is the author of this book, we raise the interesting question, is Solomon also among the prophets? We know that no one could hold any office in Israel unless he was anointed of the Lord. Anointing spoke of the fact that God had ordained and called him to a special office, and that God also qualified him through the Holy Spirit to fill the office to which he was appointed.

We also know that Solomon was anointed to be king over Israel, and that he had been endowed with the special gift of wisdom as theocratic king. The Lord had granted his request when he asked for wisdom to judge the people with an understanding heart, "that I may discern between good and bad: for who is able to judge this thy so great a people" (1 Kings 3:9). This wisdom was not a mere natural gift, or bent, but a special gift of the Holy Spirit to qualify him to the office to which God had called him.

But Solomon received even more than he had asked. Ecclesiastes informs us that this wisdom qualified him to be a preacher as well as a king in Israel. He writes: "Lo, I am come to great estate, and have gotten more wisdom than all they that have been before me in Jerusalem: yea, my heart had great experience of wisdom and knowledge" (1:16). And again: "Also my wisdom remained with me" (2:9). As in his conclusion: "Because the preacher was wise, he still taught the people knowledge; yea, he gave good heed, and sought out and set in order many proverbs" (12:9).

This fact is the more significant because the office was generally imposed on separate individuals in the old dispensation. Though the threefold office of prophet, priest, and king is essentially one office, as is evident from Adam in paradise, in Christ in his threefold office, and in the office of believers today; yet the Old Testament prophet was no priest, and the priest was not a king, according to the general rule. But Solomon presents himself to us as the Preacher-King, who had been endowed with the Spirit of wisdom, not only to rule the people as their king, but also to instruct them as their prophet—a fact which clearly emphasizes that the threefold office as essentially one, even as it was perfected in Christ, the anointed of God, *par excellence*.

The message of the Preacher carries a special appeal to us in our day because it is so exactly the opposite from all present-day philosophies which boast of the wisdom and culture of the world. One keynote rings through the entire book, that all things, outside of the grace of God in Christ Jesus, are subject to vanity. God's curse rests upon the world of fallen mankind, and man himself bows under the bondage of corruption and death. There is nothing new under the sun, nothing that is not branded with death, nothing that is not subject to vanity. Even joy and mirth are empty madness, and natural wisdom brings grief, while all labor is vexation of spirit. The creature runs in a treadmill as in a "vicious circle." All man's skill and ingenuity, his discoveries and inventions, his labor and his progress end in destruction. War—peace—depression—war stalks man's path wherever he turns. All that is and all that cometh is vanity. Vanity of vanities, saith the Preacher, all is vanity.

This is the conclusion of the whole matter: "Fear God, and keep his commandments: for this is the whole duty of man" (Eccl. 12:13).

THE THEME OF THE BOOK OF ECCLESIASTES

B efore turning to an exposition of the book, we would do well to consider its central theme. The theme is the vanity of man's life in a fallen and sinful world. This theme, however, must be approached from a certain point of view. God is sovereign in the life of men. That sovereignty extends to the smallest details of life, so that not a hair falls from our heads nor a sparrow to the ground but by the will of God, as Jesus taught us (Matt. 10:29–30). The vanity of man's life exists because of sin and God's judgment upon sin. God in his judgment has subjected the life of the creation and therefore also of man to vanity (Rom. 8:20). Although hidden from us in the day-to-day affairs of life, God is realizing his counsel and purpose. Life has value and meaning in the light of that purpose which is known by faith in Christ.

The writer of Ecclesiastes is not an unbelieving skeptic but a believing child of God, who walks in God's fear and whose treasure is in heaven. Indeed one of the purposes of the book is to guard us from the folly of a world that seeks its life and happiness here below. As the book is written by Solomon at the end of his life, there is indirectly a testimony to his sorrow for his own sin. This is not expressed directly, as David's confession in Psalms 32 and 51, for that is not the purpose of the book. Rather, like David, he would guide us with his eye in the way of wisdom (Ps. 32:8).

By way of introduction, therefore, it is well to consider what is meant by this idea of vanity that stands at the heart of the book. Rev. George Ophoff gives an able treatment of this theme and a valuable synopsis of the book as a whole. Without apologies, his article is quoted in full.

IV

VANITY OF VANITIES[2]

George Ophoff

W e turn to the second verse of the first chapter of Ecclesiastes and read: "Vanity of vanities, saith the Preacher, vanity of vanities; all is vanity."

Doubtless, no other book in the Bible has suffered so many misapprehensions in a theological point of view as the book of Ecclesiastes. It has been accused of many contradictions within itself, of being inconsistent, of lacking unity and coherence on account of absence of plan and connection. The inspiration of its contents has been attacked. Very early this was doubted on account of the supposed moral levity and skepticism of its teachings—a skepticism that was said to extend to a perfect despairing of all order and aim in human life. But these accusations are untrue. The book is consistent. It has plan and connection indeed. There is not a single contradiction to be found in it. If so, it could form no part of the infallible Scriptures. It was composed not in unbelief but in a flowering faith. Its doctrine is pure, as only the doctrine of the infallible word of God can be pure. And this book, too, holds forth to God's believing people the only comfort in life and death. The truth of these statements is borne out by the sequence of this Bible book.

---

2   From the *Standard Bearer*, Vol. 22, issue 20, August 1, 1946.

ECCLESIASTES

The fundamental thought of the book is set forth in its topic sentence—the sentence with which the Preacher begins his discourse and which reads: "Vanity of vanities; all is vanity." This exclamation appears no fewer than twenty times and is a paraphrase of the superlative idea *extreme vanity*. What may be the thought conveyed by this expression? Not, as some have imagined, that this world is in a state of continual flux, that, as Greek philosophy at one time affirmed, change, movement, is the lord of the universe, even so completely, as to exclude the possibility of an unchanging substratum. Nor would it be correct to place in the room of the term *vanity* the word *sinful* and read: "sinful, sinful, all is sinful." For the sacred writer views the things included in the *all* of the expression "all is vanity" from the angle, not of their sinfulness, but of their *vanity*. The meaning of the exclamation is precisely that all is vanity, that is, empty, idle, useless, futile. But there is this question: what does the sacred writer, the Preacher, include in this *all*? The answer is contained in the following verse. It reads: "What profit hath a man of all his labour which he taketh under the sun?" Thus the *all* in the exclamation "all is vanity" includes all the labor that man taketh under the sun, the whole of his daily pursuits, all his engagements of the hour, of the day; of whatever character and in whatever sphere of life, the sum and total of all man's occupations and strivings in whatever field of human endeavor, in the field of industry, science and invention, economics, philosophy, art and learning. It makes no difference, absolutely no difference; all is vanity, idle, futile. This is truly an amazing appraisal of life, isn't it, of this natural, earthy life under the sun, as man in this present dispensation of the world lives it. It is terrifying in its appraisal, in its depreciation and disparagement of all human endeavor. It provokes the question, "Is it true?" Taking cognizance of the Preacher's grounds upon which he bases his appraisal of all the labor that man taketh under the sun, we shall have to admit, whether we like to or not, that it is true. Let us have regard, then, to the Preacher's grounds for this amazing appraisal of life, encountered in this Bible book. We can only touch upon these grounds. There is no time for delineation.

The first of these grounds is contained in the verse last quoted: "What profit hath a man from all his labour which he taketh under the sun?" The question is rhetorical, and is thus equivalent in meaning to the positive statement: "Man hath absolutely no profit whatever from all his labors which he taketh under the sun." All his labors are profitless, gainless, and on this account, vain, empty, futile. To be sure, the reaction of sinful flesh on hearing this is to decry the statement as absurdly untrue. But let us hearken unto the Preacher and be instructed.

Says the Preacher: all man's labor is profitless, *because* one generation passeth away, and another generation cometh, and, such is the thought conveyed; with the generation that passeth, there passeth also its works, its achievements, its learning, its systems of thought, the thing that men call civilization. All wax old and vanish away and the only thing that abideth is the earth. It all waxes old, becomes outmoded, and thus useless and vanishes away to be replaced with the coming of the new generation, by new works, new systems of thought, a new civilization, which again in turn waxes old and disappears with the waxing old and disappearance of the generation that so recently came. Wrote the columnist Ray Tucker in his daily column of yesterday, I quote:

> The arrival of the atomic bomb struck the braided gentlemen of the American Navy in their solar plexus, for it may mean the eventual abolition of such craft as battleships, cruisers, and destroyers...The fleet of the future may consist mainly of submarines and aircraft carriers. [3]

Indeed, the new waxes old and is forgotten, but, mark you, the new is but the old that again reappears in new dress. It is not

---

3   *The Brooklyn Daily Eagle*, 26 August 1945, 4.

essentially new. Thus it is true, what the Preacher says in the sequence of his discourse,

9. The thing that has been, it is that which shall be; and that which is done is that which shall be done: and there is no new thing under the sun.

11. There is no remembrance of former things; neither shall there be any remembrance of things that are to come with those that shall come after. (Eccl. 1:9, 11)

It all adds up to this: all man's labor is profitless indeed and therefore vain. For in all his endeavors man reaches no lasting goal, attains no enduring purpose; and the new is old; man goes in circles. He is chained to a treadmill. In the language of the Preacher: Like the sun, he riseth, goeth down, and hasteneth to his place where he arose. Man is like the wind, that goeth toward the south, turneth about to the north. It whirleth continually and returneth again according to his circuits; man is like the rivers that run into the sea without ever filling it, and that return again unto the place whence they come. And so full of labor is man, that no tongue can utter it (see Eccl. 1:5-8). Such is man's plight in all his labor that he taketh under the sun; wherefore his labor is profitless and on this account vain.

Secondly, man's labor is profitless and therefore vain, because, says the Preacher, in all his striving, he does not make straight and he cannot make straight, and he cannot even will to make straight, and he may not make straight, the crooked. There is then the crooked. Due to the entrance of sin into the world, and because the curse of God stalks the earth and permeates man's existence, changing his day into night, life—this natural, earthy life—is crooked, disarranged, abnormal, dislocated, hectic, says the Preacher. Wickedness, he saw, was in the place of judgment and iniquity in the place of righteousness. Then, says he, there are all the oppressions that are done under the sun and the tears of such as are oppressed and that have no comforter. Verily, the straight has been made crooked; and, mark you, God made it so, says the Preacher. Can man, then, by all his labors, by all his effort, however mighty, make straight the crooked? Let us state the matter otherwise. Assuredly, the only cure, if there is any—but there is none for the men of man's world—I say, the only cure for oppression; the only cure for wickedness in the place of judgment, and iniquity in the place of righteousness; the only cure for war between the nations; the only cure for graft in government, for corruption in politics, and for dishonesty in business; the only cure for the class struggle between capital and labor; the only cure for the evil of divorce, juvenile delinquency, and crime in general, I say, the only cure for all these evils is the true fear of God in men's hearts. But can man administer this cure? Can he remove his stony heart by giving himself a heart of flesh? Can he establish within him and within his fellow man God's heavenly kingdom and inscribe its laws upon the table of men's hearts? Can he cleanse a single depraved human from his native corruption and create in him a new spirit? Can he shed abroad in men's hearts the love of God? In a word, can man make straight the crooked? If he can, why doesn't he? He cannot. He will not. Thus war will continue as long as the earth endureth, for God will make crooked the straight. Graft in government, corruption in politics, dishonesty in business, all continue as long as the earth endureth. Crime will continue as long as the earth endureth.

Well, then, if man stands utterly powerless over against all these evils, if by all his efforts he can bring in no improvement, what real profit hath man from all his labors that he taketh under the sun? None whatever, says the Preacher, so far is man from having profit from all his labors, that all they yield him is pain and vexation of spirit. We quote him: "Then I looked upon all the works that my hand had wrought, and on the labour that I have laboured to do, and behold all was vanity and vexation of spirit, and there was no profit under the sun" (Eccl. 2:11). Man's labor that he taketh under the sun yields him no true happiness. After having done all, the great void in his life, in his spirit, is still there. Vanity of vanities, all is vanity.

But this is not all. Arriving at the end of his vain days on earth, vain man dies. Says the Preacher,

18. I said in mine heart concerning the estate of the sons of men, that God might manifest them, and that they might see that they themselves are beasts.
19. For that which befalleth the sons of men befalleth the beasts; even one thing befalleth them: as the one dieth, so dieth the other; yea, they have all one breath; so that a man hath no preeminence above a beast: for all is vanity.
20. All go unto one place; all are of the dust, and all turn to dust again. (Eccl. 3: 18–20)

This is the prospect that vain man faces. And says the Preacher, man must then leave his labor with all its earthy gains unto the man that shall be after him. And who knoweth whether he shall be a wise man or a fool? (see Eccl. 18/19). Vanity of vanities, all is vanity. That which befalleth the sons of men befalleth the beast. All turn to dust again (see Eccl. 3:19-20).

No, this is not the babbling of an unbeliever, denying life after death and the resurrection of the dead but the inspired teachings of a preacher of God. Mark the statement: "That God might manifest men, and they might see that they themselves are beasts" (v. 18). This certainly is not the prating of a skeptic but an exclamation of surprise and indignation of a true believer, struck with amazement and sorely vexed by the stupid blindness of the natural man, who will not, in his vain estate, seek after God but who insists that this estate is the only and highest good, and that it will abide forever.

But let us understand the Preacher well. Certainly it is not gnostic heresy and anabaptist philosophy with which we deal in this Bible book. It is not grace that is being opposed here to nature, as if nature, man's earthy estate, all his labor that he taketh under the sun were, as such, depraved, sinful as to its essence, and therefore contemptible. To the contrary, says the Preacher, there is nothing better for a man than that he should eat and drink and that he should make his soul enjoy good in his labors. This also I saw that it was from the hand of God. For God giveth to a man that which is good in his sight, but to the sinner he giveth travail. Eating and drinking, buying and selling, marital and family life as such are not corrupt. Only as the labor of fallen and depraved man is it wicked, indeed thoroughly so.

Nor is it the teaching of the Preacher further, that, whereas all man's labor that he taketh under the sun is vain, the thing for the believer to do is to give up his labor and retreat into monastic seclusion. Though all man's labor under the sun is vanity, man must labor, he must travail. It is calling, duty. Says the Preacher: "Whatever thy hand findeth to do, do it with thy might; for there is no work nor device, nor knowledge, nor wisdom in the grave whither thou goest" (Eccl. 9:10). Man must labor. It is that, says the Preacher, which God hath given the sons of men to do, to be exercised thereby. *This,* says the Preacher, is the conclusion of the matter: "Fear God and keep his commandments" (Eccl. 12:13), or, in the language of the New Testament Scriptures, believe in the Lord Jesus Christ and through him, in his Father the triune Jehovah, and walk all the days of thy vanity as a child of the light. This God's people, by God's mercy and by the power of his grace and under the constraint of a faith that is his gift, also do, in principle. And so all things, thus also this vain earthy estate, and all the crooked that characterizes this estate, worketh together for good to them. And from the vain estate of this sinfully earthy, they even now are in principle delivered. And their works shall follow them. And when the house of this their earthy tabernacle shall be dissolved, and with it their painful earthy estate shall be dissolved, they receive from God a house not made with hands, eternal in the heavens, a house in which nothing is crooked, but in which everything is straight with the straightness of a heavenly perfection. It will be a house in which they face always, not life through the grave, for then they shall have passed through the grave, but just life, life everlasting, life with God in his sanctuary, where they shall see God with heavenly eyes and thus see him as he is, and where he shall satisfy them with his likeness.

Part Two

EXPOSITION OF ECCLESIASTES

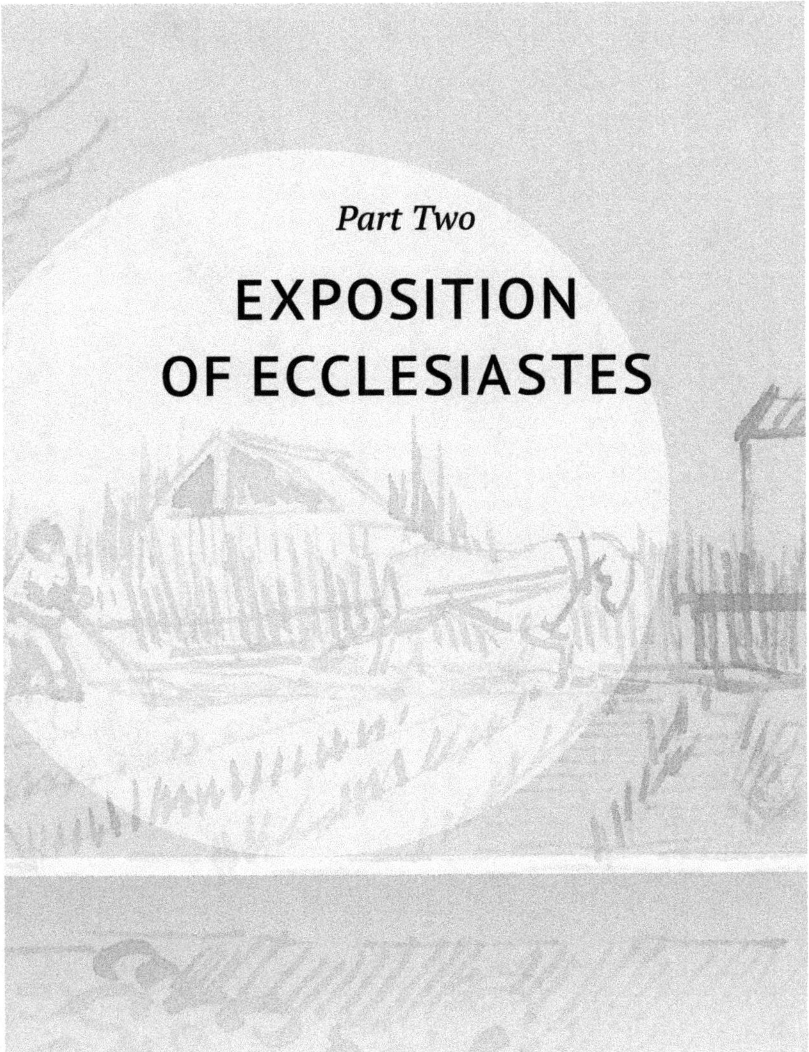

CHAPTER 1

Author and Theme Stated

1. The words of the Preacher, the son of David, king in Jerusalem.
2. Vanity of vanities, saith the Preacher, vanity of vanities; all is vanity.—Ecclesiastes 1:1–2

The opening words of the Preacher are in many respects very striking. His identity, which as we have seen in the introduction is Solomon, is stated as "the son of David, king in Jerusalem." But that identity is initially set in the background. He stands before us first of all as the Preacher and his words. His words are "vanity of vanities; all is vanity." This truth we must hear from the outset. It is from this truth as it is developed that he will lead us to the whole duty of man, the fear of God, and the calling to remember our Creator, particularly in our youth. His purpose is to show us this vanity concretely in the world about us so that we see it, reflect upon it, and indeed wrestle with it, so that the point is driven home.

He therefore steps forth with his words as "the words of the Preacher." The word *preacher* here has the idea of calling or summoning with one's voice. The term draws a certain visual picture, of one stepping forth among the assembly of God's people. He stands before us to show us by his words the reality of the world in which we dwell as it is before us "under the sun" (v. 14). We too must see it, and as it were, experience it and the burden to which he would draw our attention. The viewpoint is of man as he lives from day to day under the sun. More particularly, it is the viewpoint of one who lives by faith in the word of God and his covenant promises and who stands upon the foundation of God's word and his counsel revealed therein over all the affairs of life. It is in the congregation and before the people of God that Solomon speaks his words concerning the realities of life under the sun.

Life under the sun is characterized by vanity. The word has the idea of a breath or vapor. It is used of idols who have no substance but are vanities. It sets before us here the futility and emptiness of life in a fallen and sinful world as it lies under the sun and as such under the curse of God upon sin. That life lies in a world of constant change. It is transitory, constantly in motion, yet does not arrive at or achieve anything under the sun. Nor can the meaning of life and its purpose be found in the world itself under the sun. This is not pessimism but realism. The word of God would lead us beyond the things that are made to the Creator of them all and his fear, for therein alone is the meaning and purpose to be found.

It is the purpose of the book to expound more fully what is meant by vanity: to set before us why all is vanity, vanity in the extreme, or "vanity of vanities."

Of Vanity and Labor

3. What profit hath a man of all his labour which he taketh under the sun?

4. One generation passeth away, and another generation cometh: but the earth abideth for ever.

5. The sun also ariseth, and the sun goeth down, and hasteth to his place where he arose.

6. The wind goeth toward the south, and turneth about unto the north; it whirleth about continually, and the wind returneth again according to his circuits.

7. All the rivers run into the sea; yet the sea is not full; unto the place from whence the rivers come, thither they return again.

8.   All things are full of labour; man cannot utter it: the eye
     is not satisfied with seeing, nor the ear filled with hearing.
     —Ecclesiastes 1:3–8

The text, having raised the subject of vanity, comes to us with
a question: "What profit hath a man of all his labour which he
taketh under the sun?" (Eccl. 1: 3). What does he achieve? What
does he really accomplish? What of that labor abides? "One generation passeth away, and another generation cometh" (v. 4). The
earth endures or abides, but man and his life do not. Man dies and
leaves all his labor and activity. He can take nothing of this world
with him. Death, the reality of it and the outworking of it as the
curse of God upon sin, renders the life of man vain. The word
of God in Ecclesiastes will repeatedly bring up that relationship
between this life, the reality of death, and how it renders the labor
of man vain and empty. The world under the sun was not made by
its creator vain in its beginning, but good. It is sin and the judgment of God upon sin which has rendered it vain. The wages of sin
is death, and therefore all things, even the life of the creature, are
"subject to vanity" and "groaneth and travaileth in pain together
until now" (Rom. 8:20,22).

The creation itself is in constant motion and activity, so that
it also may be said to be full of labor. The sun rises and sets, the
wind "whirleth about continually," "all the rivers run to the sea"
(Eccl. 1: 6–7). Yet in all that motion what destination is achieved?
What is truly accomplished? The sun goes around and around
again, making its circuit in the heavens. The wind does likewise,
turning south or north, blowing continually. The wind never
arrives. It goes in circles. The same is said in the text of the rivers.
They run into the sea, "yet the sea is not full." Not only is the sea
not made full but "the place from whence the rivers come, thither
they return again" (v. 7). Nothing that endures forever is accomplished by the creation. The cycles of the sun and the seasons, the
blowing of the wind, and the flowing of the rivers are full of labor

and activity, in constant change and motion, yet it is vain, it goes in circles.

Now that too is under the appointment of God the creator. The world before the flood was perhaps different in the manner in which God's curse operated. We read of Noah's sacrifice and God's pronouncement:

20. And Noah builded an altar unto the Lord; and took of every clean beast, and of every clean fowl, and offered burnt offerings on the altar.
21. And the Lord smelled a sweet savour; and the Lord said in his heart, I will not again curse the ground any more for man›s sake; for the imagination of man›s heart is evil from his youth; neither will I again smite any more every thing living, as I have done.
22. While the earth remaineth, seedtime and harvest, and cold and heat, and summer and winter, and day and night shall not cease. (Gen. 8:20–22)

By that declaration God himself set the cycles of the seasons in the creation so that the very motions of the creation are not merely the result of some natural process but are a work of God the creator. The effect of that work of God is that "all things are full of labour" and subject to vanity (Eccl. 1:8)

But there is another element to that truth that nothing can be satisfied with fullness. Nothing is ever truly full so that it gives an abiding satisfaction. When an end is obtained, the end should satisfy and endure. As the creation, however, is in constant motion and activity under the sun, nothing in life endures. This is true of man and his life. The life of man in the world is such that his eye is not filled with seeing or his ear with hearing. Enough is never enough, so that a true end is accomplished. Rather the labor of life is a weary burden, because it neither satisfies nor obtains an enduring end. This wearisomeness is set forth in the text in the idea of labor. Yet, as the Preacher will point out later in the book, the deceitfulness of sin is such that the things of this life present themselves as that which *can* satisfy, as that which *will* make a man's life full. Therefore men are given to labor, to heap and gather, not considering whose those things will be. He will also direct us to the right use of the things of this life and their value, which is to enjoy the present gifts of God—in effect, our daily bread—with thanksgiving.

The Thing That Has Been Is Not New

9. The thing that hath been, it is that which shall be; and that which is done is that which shall be done: and there is no new thing under the sun.
10. Is there any thing whereof it may be said, See, this is new? it hath been already of old time, which was before us.
11. There is no remembrance of former things; neither shall there be any remembrance of things that are to come with those that shall come after.—Ecclesiastes 1:9–11

Before we consider the value of things in this life, we must have clear before our minds that the cycles of life render the delusion of sinful man who heaps and gathers to be a vain delusion. For man comes with the false notion that he has achieved something new. He speaks as if "this time things are really different." The reality is rather otherwise: "The thing that hath been, it is that which shall be; and that which is done is that which shall be done: and there is no new thing under the sun" (Eccl. 1:9). He asks: "Is there any thing whereof it may be said, See, this is new? it hath been already of old time, which was before us" (v. 10).

In asking this, the Preacher is asking a question concerning the underlying principle or the essence of things. Development in science and technology has the appearance of something new in its external form. But these developments are not essentially new. Transportation is transportation; that one can travel faster and in greater comfort does not change the fact that transportation is a means to get from one place to another. Increasing complexity in technology from handwriting to printing presses to typewriters to computers is not an essential change. It belongs to the confusion of the early industrial revolution that men equated such changing complexity with a genuine advancement in life itself. But man, the sinner, is still sinful man, though you give him more and varied means to sin. In principle the new thing is just the old repackaged in another form. It truly "hath been already of old time, which was before us" (v. 10). This is even more true of man in his society, governments, and history as they lie in sin. Sin and depravity make the Pelagian idea of human progress a vain hope. The idea that man will solve all his problems by his own efforts or by improving education or the environment or health care is a vain denial of reality: "The thing that hath been, it is that which shall be; and that which is done is that which shall be done" (v. 9).

Moreover, as the text points out, the problem is in our perception because man does not truly remember. Each generation as it rises grows old and dies and is succeeded by another: "One generation passeth away, and another generation cometh" (v. 4). The effect of this is that the knowledge and wisdom born of experience of the preceding generation also passes with it. The result is "There is no remembrance of former things; neither shall there be any remembrance of things that are to come with those that shall come after" (v. 11). Generation succeeds generation: that very succession limits man's perception and understanding. The mistakes of the past are repeated. The kingdoms of the world rise and fall through the same causes of decline, corruption, and the sins of men; yet such is the vanity of man himself that though he knows of the history of the past, there is in him no true remembrance. The same follies in the life of men come again and again in the world.

It is against the background of that transitory character of man's life that all things lead to vanity and futility under the sun.

The Preacher would stand in the congregation of the people of God to teach us wisdom. He would lead us to see the spiritual realities with which these issues confront us, for they are not simply practical matters but spiritual issues. In doing so, he stands in the promises of God in Christ, which are by the true knowledge of God our creator and the reverence of faith that fears him. Of man and all his activity there is nothing new under the sun. There cannot be such, for man is finite and fallen in sin. That which is new can only be of God and that by a wonder of grace. Ecclesiastes stands as part of the background of the gospel. For as it paints a true portrait of the vanity of life it points us to God and the new thing which he alone has wrought in Jesus Christ.

The wisdom the book teaches is spiritual wisdom for a godly seed which the eye of sinful man cannot see. It leads us away from the false seeking of happiness and satisfaction here below, and from the deceitfulness of sin, to the true treasure which is above and to that which alone satisfies. Jesus himself more than once summarizes and paraphrases the spiritual principles of Ecclesiastes in his preaching. He does so when he warns us that the abundance of a man's life does not consist of the things he possesses (Luke 12:15) and when he calls us to seek our treasure in God's grace in him (Matt. 6:33).

The Search of Wisdom

12. I the Preacher was king over Israel in Jerusalem.
13. And I gave my heart to seek and search out by wisdom concerning all things that are done under heaven: this sore travail hath God given to the sons of man to be exercised therewith.—Ecclesiastes 1:12–13

Before we explore the spiritual wisdom which this word of God would teach, the Preacher leads us to contemplate more fully wisdom itself. This is necessary, for wisdom and searching out wisdom is itself also touched with the vanity of this life. It too belongs to the wearisome burden of labor in the vanity of the world.

In a world of constant change under the judgment of God upon sin, all things come to vanity. This is the reality of a fallen world. Nothing satisfies so that it truly fills the heart because the things of this life are not an end in themselves. Only that which God does in Christ can truly satisfy.

To understand this takes spiritual knowledge and discernment. It is in this context that the Preacher, Solomon, stands forth as an instructor in wisdom. God set him as king over Israel in Jerusalem. When anointed as king, he had sought of God the gift of wisdom to rule God's people, and God gave him that gift. It is from that viewpoint that, having set forth the principle of vanity, Solomon would now also stand before us as the Preacher among God's people to teach us wisdom. He sets before us, as it were, his credentials as a preacher and instructor in wisdom, spiritual credentials, of one to whom God had given the gift of wisdom in an extraordinary degree.

That gift was not automatic; it was one which Solomon developed through the exercise of thought, discernment, and contemplation. He tells us as the Preacher: "And I gave my heart to seek and search out by wisdom concerning all things that are done under heaven" (Eccl. 1:13). He says: "And I gave my heart to know wisdom, and to know madness and folly" (v. 17). Wisdom is knowledge applied with skill. As Solomon speaks of it in Ecclesiastes, the focus is on knowledge and understanding put to use in the things of this life. The focus is "concerning all things that are done under heaven." He would set before us certain aspects of a believer's world-and-life view of the things under the sun and our place and calling in them.

That seeking of the things that are done, that searching of them by wisdom, of what is wise and what is folly, involves a serious spiritual effort. It involves study and reflection upon the relationships of life, the place of things—earthly treasures and possessions—and their proper use and end. Solomon has in view man's natural life, its science and discovery, yet with spiritual discernment. By nature we often walk through the world about us without really seeing it. Solomon tells us that he not only observed the things of life, but also "I have seen all the works that are done under the sun" (v. 14), that is, his mind was engaged in analyzing and seeking to understand them.

He did so moreover not only to understand what was wise but also to understand what was madness and folly. His searching had an antithetical character. That does not mean that he entered into all the world of sin around him by walking in sin. The argument is sometimes made that one cannot understand something unless one has directly experienced it. That is not true. We do not need to experience sin to see it as sin. But observing sin and its consequences in the world does belong to a believer's contemplation of the world in which he lives.

Solomon did indeed enter into all the activities of life and labor, and he speaks of it in the next chapter in Ecclesiastes, but what he sought was to know and understand the place of them. Wisdom takes knowledge and puts it to practical use. Yet the wisdom of which he speaks is not mere practical common sense, for he speaks of giving his heart to seek and search. The heart is the spiritual center of a man's life. The heart of a child of God, though he is a sinner, holds within it the fear of God his creator, the reverence of faith, which is the spiritual foundation of true wisdom. That wisdom we are to seek. Its practical use has a spiritual dimension to it.

The world of man is also engaged in searching the things that are done under the sun so as to understand them. Sinful fallen man engages in science and develops technology and art. He develops his man-centered philosophies. He seeks to understand the nature of things: the psychology, form, order, and design of things. Searching out by wisdom, though it be the wisdom of this world, is done by the wicked also. Solomon points this out. It is something given to men. He says, "This sore travail hath God given to the sons of man to be exercised therewith" (v. 13). The text could also be translated "to the sons of Adam."

In forming man of the dust of the ground and giving him the breath of life, God gave to man dominion over the earth as a rational, moral creature. As he was created in the image of God, he could exercise that dominion in the service of God. But man, now fallen, has lost the spiritual substance of the image and the right to exercise that dominion. He cannot in himself serve God for he stands at enmity with God by nature. His wisdom he cannot use aright.

The impulse in man to seek out in the creation the things that are done still remains. We sometimes refer to this impulse in the original state of righteousness as the "cultural mandate." The trouble with the term is that it sets the matter forth as being a commission. Rather, this impulse is something in-created in man's nature, something given to the sons of man. The calling to be fruitful, multiply, and fill the earth was not given to man alone. It was given likewise to the fish and the birds (Gen. 1:22) and is imbedded in the creation itself. That impulse is one "given to the sons of men" by God, though in man, it is given to him as a rational, moral creature.

But in a world that lies fallen under the curse, this impulse is a "sore travail," which God in his judgment hath given to the sons of man (Eccl. 1:13). The wisdom of this world does seek out the order of things and develops the creation. It also seeks understanding and searches out a wisdom. The wisdom of this world, as it is from below and not above, is "earthly, sensual, devilish" (James 3:15). It turns to "madness and folly" (Eccl. 1:17). For fallen man uses his knowledge, skill, and wisdom in the service of sin. He strives with his neighbor for mastery. He walks in covetousness and envy. Jesus may well have had Ecclesiastes in view when he summarized this madness of pride and folly in the parable of the rich fool. He heaps and gathers, as Ecclesiastes will show, and does not ask, "whose shall those things be" (Luke 12:20). Death stands before the fool of this world, as does the judgment.

The Conclusion of Wisdom

14. I have seen all the works that are done under the sun; and, behold, all is vanity and vexation of spirit.
15. That which is crooked cannot be made straight: and that which is wanting cannot be numbered.
16. I communed with mine own heart, saying, Lo, I am come to great estate, and have gotten more wisdom than all they that have been before me in Jerusalem: yea, my heart had great experience of wisdom and knowledge.
17. And I gave my heart to know wisdom, and to know madness and folly: I perceived that this also is vexation of spirit.
18. For in much wisdom is much grief: and he that increaseth knowledge increaseth sor-row.—Ecclesiastes 1:14–18

The Preacher would have us as God's people to see as those who walk through the labor and toil of life and through the same sore travail in a fallen world, "all is vanity and vexation of spirit" for a reason (Eccl. 1:14). That reason is "that which is crooked cannot be made straight: and that which is wanting cannot be numbered" (v. 15). The world does not want to see this or hear it. They strive in the pride of the flesh to make the crooked straight. They believe that man in his wisdom can supply that which is lacking. And when they fail, as they must in the vain madness of the world's wisdom, they are led to despair.

We too need to see the problem. The solution cannot come from man. Only God, the creator and savior of his people, can make that which is crooked straight. It cannot be found under the sun, God's grace, wisdom, and mercy alone can supply an answer. The Preacher would impress this reality of the world about us not to lead us to despair but to seek God our creator. In a world fallen in sin, what is lacking cannot be numbered; you cannot count it all up or reckon it. Man cannot cure it.

The Preacher's example testifies that it is so, as he will show us in coming chapters. He speaks in a manner that reflects on his own understanding. He says: "I communed with mine own heart, saying Lo, I am come to great estate, and have gotten more wisdom than all they that have been before me in Jerusalem: yea, my heart had great experience of wisdom and knowledge" (v 16). Solomon will call to mind his many works and the labor and toil in them. He reminds us of his riches, wealth, and honor in coming chapters. Could Solomon in all his glory and wisdom make that which was crooked straight? Could he by his toil supply what was wanting? The answer is, manifestly, no.

Also he as a child of God, in all his gifts and abilities, in all of his earthly glory and power, could not supply what is lacking. It is not in man to do so. This is reality, not pessimism. Sin, after all, is that which is crooked and bent. Sin is that which is lacking in goodness and virtue. Man cannot take away sin. The effect of sin in a world under the curse of God upon sin is that the whole life of the creation and of man lies in the midst of death. Man cannot cure it. He cannot deliver himself from the vanity of a world that lies in the midst of death.

In this connection he points also to the limitations of wisdom itself, particularly as he will speak of it from the practical point of view of living from day to day in a world that is subject to vanity. He had more wisdom than others. He studied to know wisdom. He says: "And I gave my heart to know wisdom, and to know madness and folly" (v. 17). Did wisdom itself find a cure? Did his study and development of his gifts and exercise of wisdom in his works supply what was wanting? No. Rather he says: "I perceive that this also is vexation of spirit" (v. 17).

Why? He gives the reason: "For in much wisdom is much grief: and he that increaseth knowledge increaseth sorrow" (v. 18). Understanding the vanity of a world lying in the midst of death causes sorrow. Growing in that understanding in spiritual wisdom and discernment increases sorrow. This is true, and the Preacher will show us more fully what he means by this also in coming chapters. This does not mean we should flee from knowledge, for the sorrow of which he speaks works our spiritual good. It leads to spiritual sobriety in a true assessment of life. It leads us to hold loosely to the things of this world and put them in the proper perspective. It must lead us to the cross also where the only answer to a world that lies in sin and death can be found. This sorrow is ultimately bound up with turning to the Lord in repentance that in his grace we might walk daily in the fear of the Lord.

CHAPTER 2

Discerning the Good in the Activity of Life

The second chapter of Ecclesiastes embraces one central thought, which is well represented by the Preacher's initial comment in connection with wine, that by wisdom the Preacher sought to discern "what was good for the sons of men, which they should do under heaven all the days of their life" (Eccl. 2:3). This issue is the concern which the Preacher would bring before us. It is this that he would prove in his heart. He would discern the place of the natural joys of man's earthly life. In taking up the daily activities of life and man's labor, he sought to understand the joy and pleasure found therein, but also their place or purpose, and that from a spiritual point of view as a child of God. This is also the conclusion to which he would lead us in the chapter, as stated in verse 24: "There is nothing better for a man, than that he should eat and drink, and that he should make his soul enjoy good in his labour. This also I saw, that it was from the hand of God."

To lead us to that conclusion, the Preacher sets before us his labor and industry in this life. He first passes it and its joy in review. Then secondly, he sets it in perspective in the light of the vanity of this world. The first element we consider includes the most transitory elements of life: mirth and laughter.

The Question of the Good in Our Labor

1. I said in mine heart, Go to now, I will prove thee with mirth, therefore enjoy pleasure: and, behold, this also is vanity.

41

2. I said of laughter, It is mad: and of mirth, What doeth it?

3. I sought in mine heart to give myself unto wine, yet acquainting mine heart with wis-dom; and to lay hold on folly, till I might see what was that good for the sons of men, which they should do under the heaven all the days of their life.—Ecclesiastes 2:1–10

The word of God here looks at the life of man organically. A child of God stands in the world as a part of it by creation and by nature. Man is a creature of flesh and blood tied to this world. He eats and drinks, being created to do so and to find pleasure therein. He also labors and toils to plant and build. God our creator set the man and the woman in paradise to dress and keep the garden of Eden. The trees of the garden and the green herb were given them for food. Man is therefore a creature of this world, organically bound to the life of the creation. Sin has corrupted that relationship and brought upon man spiritual and moral depravity of nature. The world has been subjected to the curse. Yet man remains man, bound to the organic life of the creation.

Man was made to work and to find delight in his activities as a means to serve God. He still finds delight and pleasure in his activity and strength of life, and this is not in itself wrong. It is the fact that he subjects it to the moral principle of his depravity in the service of sin which works the pollution of sin in all that he does. This organic connection is true for a child of God also, though now in Christ he begins to live a new life.

What is the profit of all these activities, of mirth, of the pleasures of life, wine and the other refinements of life? In speaking of these things the text is not speaking of them as being sinful. It is certainly the case that wicked men use all the activities of life in the service of sin, but evil is not in things nor in the activities themselves. When therefore he speaks of wine, he is "yet acquainting [his] heart with wisdom" (Eccl. 1:3), that is, he is not speaking of drunkenness, but of the place of wine, which God made to gladden the heart, and of food also, as well as the activities of eating and drinking (vv. 24–25).

As mirth and laughter and food and drink are inherently the most transitory, yea momentary, pleasures, he would prove them, or test and try them. What is their value? "I said of laughter, it is mad: and of mirth, What doeth it?" (v. 2) Certainly, the man who makes them an end in themselves, the goal of his life, is a fool. Yet many a child of this world does exactly that to his own ruin. He spends his life for that which does not profit. His laughter is that of a fool. His entertainment is often devoted as much to laughter as it is to uncleanness and violence. He often keeps his evening vigil over it in front of his wide screen idol. His life is an empty one. For that which is a momentary joy becomes, in the bondage of sin, a chain that holds man enslaved to seek after it as if it were the goal of life instead of God.

The Extent of His Labor

4. I made me great works; I builded me houses; I planted me vineyards:
5. I made me gardens and orchards, and I planted trees in them of all kind of fruits:
6. I made me pools of water, to water therewith the wood that bringeth forth trees:
7. I got me servants and maidens, and had servants born in my house; also I had great possessions of great and small cattle above all that were in Jerusalem before me:
8. I gathered me also silver and gold, and the peculiar treasure of kings and of the provinces: I gat me men singers and women singers, and the delights of the sons of men, as musical instruments, and that of all sorts.—Ecclesiastes 2:4–8

The scope of the Preacher's inquiry goes beyond those things that are manifestly transitory: Solomon, besides his official work in building the temple under God's direction, also labored in this life in every aspect of the science and culture of his day. He wrought great works. He did so, not only as king in his office, but as God gave him the means, in every aspect of life in his day. He sets these works before us here, primarily from the viewpoint of his personal interests and labors, that we may see in them our own labors and activities, our work and calling. They are the labor of our hands under the sun.

They included not only his building and planting, but the interest he took in gardens and pools of water. He speaks of the pleasure he found in music and the delights of life that are lawful pastimes and served the needs of the royal court. They belonged to the wonder and splendor of his kingdom as well as to its typical significance. They belonged to the expression of the wisdom God gave him, so that the queen of Sheba stood in awe of even the details of the life of the court (1 Kings 10:4–5).

His activity was with wisdom from God, and he prospered in his labor.

His Portion of Labor

9. So I was great, and increased more than all that were before me in Jerusalem: also my wisdom remained with me.

10. And whatsoever mine eyes desired I kept not from them, I withheld not my heart from any joy; for my heart rejoiced in all my labour: and this was my portion of all my labour.—Ecclesiastes 2:9–10

The labor itself, the design, anticipation, planning, and execution, as well as the sense of accomplishment, was a matter of joy, so that his heart "rejoiced in all [his] labour" (Eccl. 2:10). This momentary joy was, in fact, the true part or portion of his labor. Though fleeting, as with food and drink, it is this which is its true value from the viewpoint of this present life. The joy he found was in the doing of it. To use the figure of the joy of our daily bread, so likewise our daily labor and industry has a certain joy given us by means of it, and that from the hand of God.

It is at the same time a joy that only a child of God can truly experience in a wholesome way. The reason is that in all that labor, gathering, heaping together, and activity, its very transitory character testifies that that joy is not the goal of our life. Our treasure is not to be found in it. Our heart may rejoice in our labor, but we do not set our heart upon it.

For the child of this world, that very ordinary joy is one that he pursues to his own destruction. His god becomes his belly. He is occupied in fretful care, with what we shall eat and what we shall drink. He builds his houses that they might stand forever. He seeks to plant his name in the earth that it may endure. He heaps gold and silver, not for mere delight but as the treasures of his heart. He is in bondage to the things of this world, to the lust of the flesh and the lust of the eye.

Hence the Preacher leads us to the conclusion in verse 26 that God gives to the sinner "travail, to gather and to heap up." It is of God's judgment that the rich fool of this world lays up treasure on earth. To this folly of sin the Preacher will return and vividly illustrate in coming chapters. We have an old man of sin who is inclined by nature to this same spiritual folly. It is grace alone that gives us to eat and drink with joy.

The Transitory Character of Labor and Its Joy

> 11. Then I looked on all the works that my hands had wrought, and on the labour that I had laboured to do: and, behold, all was vanity and vexation of spirit, and there was no profit under the sun.—Ecclesiastes 2:11

He now turns from the passing joy, which God gave him in his labors, to the vanity, or transitory character of it, to put this joy in perspective. "Then I looked on all the works that my hands had wrought, and on the labour that I had laboured to do: and, behold, all was vanity and vexation of spirit, and there was no profit under the sun" (Eccl. 2:11). That same labor of his hands is vanity. It is transitory. It is not an end in itself. It does not endure or abide.

The good is to enjoy the daily blessings of our labor with thanksgiving and contentment in our portion for the day, our daily bread. This is the gift of God (Eccl. 2:26). The passing joys of this life that come to us through our labor and industry are our part or portion in this life. They are not the end of our life, nor are we to find our treasure in them. Having described all his labor and the joy of his heart in it, he therefore turns to its transitory character and its vanity.

Further, all our labor is with worry and care. The increase of possessions and the building of houses, gardens, and vineyards all come with care and toil. Gold and silver do not endure. The entertainment of singers and music—and he has in view a lawful use of these things—are momentary. They are vanity. These good gifts of God and fruit of the labor of our hands have a place in our life. But they are all fleeting, momentary. The joy they afford is a passing one.

How Labor Is Made Vain

12. And I turned myself to behold wisdom, and madness, and folly: for what can the man do that cometh after the king? even that which hath been already done.
13. Then I saw that wisdom excelleth folly, as far as light excelleth darkness.
14. The wise man's eyes are in his head; but the fool walketh in darkness: and I myself perceived also that one event happeneth to them all.
15. Then said I in my heart, As it happeneth to the fool, so it happeneth even to me; and why was I then more wise? Then I said in my heart, that this also is vanity.

16. For there is no remembrance of the wise more than of the fool for ever; seeing that which now is in the days to come shall all be forgotten. And how dieth the wise man? as the fool.
17. Therefore I hated life; because the work that is wrought under the sun is grievous un-to me: for all is vanity and vexation of spirit.
18. Yea, I hated all my labour which I had taken under the sun: because I should leave it unto the man that shall be after me.
19. And who knoweth whether he shall be a wise man or a fool? yet shall he have rule over all my labour wherein I have laboured, and wherein I have shewed myself wise un-der the sun. This is also vanity.—Ecclesiastes 2:12–19

Now Solomon points us to several reasons as to how labor is made vain. He does so in the light of the antithetical distinction between wisdom from God and madness and folly, which lie in sin (Eccl. 2:12). There is in all our labor no true profit, no genuine advancement, even though it be wrought in wisdom. That which is done "hath already been done" (v. 12). All the labor of man and his achievements still bring forth no new thing. The crooked is still crooked. Death and the curse touches everything.

A child of God lives in the world and is part of its organic life. He labors and builds as does the fool of this world about him. The foolish man also builds houses and gardens, gathers treasures to himself. Outwardly, in the things of this life, both are subject to the same principle of vanity. Both the wise and the foolish pass through this life and from it. All our works are touched by death as the curse of God upon sin. Neither are they remembered. There is, however, a profound spiritual difference between wisdom and folly, as between light and darkness, but it is not manifested in the organic life of the world. The wise man has his eyes in his head, sees where he is going, and forms a sound evaluation of things, while the fool of this world is blind and walks in darkness.

Even wisdom in the fear of God, which is better, is still touched by death.

13. Then I saw that wisdom excelleth folly, as far as light excelleth darkness.
14. The wise man's eyes are in his head; but the fool walketh in darkness: and I myself perceived also that one event happeneth to them all.
15. Then said I in my heart, As it happeneth to the fool, so it happeneth even to me; and why was I then more wise? Then I said in my heart, that this also is vanity.
16. For there is no remembrance of the wise more than of the fool for ever; seeing that which now is in the days to come shall all be forgotten. And how dieth the wise man? as the fool. (vv. 13–16)

In speaking in this way, we must keep in mind the viewpoint of the Preacher, as one who is addressing children of God. The contrast is not between intellectual wisdom and worldly wisdom, or common sense over against earthly stupidity and foolishness. Spiritual wisdom, as a gift of God's grace, in its proper fruit gives also to a child of God a measure of practical wisdom that the wise fool of this world does not possess. The unbelieving fool is in bondage to the lusts of the flesh and all covetousness. The wisdom that is from God is from above and sanctifies in grace.

But this also creates a trial for a child of God, a grief that is not only practical but spiritual. He explains this:

17. Therefore I hated life; because the work that is wrought under the sun is grievous unto me: for all is vanity and vexation of spirit.
18. Yea, I hated all my labour which I had taken under the sun: because I should leave it unto the man that shall be after me.

19. And who knoweth whether he shall be a wise man or a fool? yet shall he have rule over all my labour wherein I have laboured, and wherein I have shewed myself wise under the sun. This is also vanity. (vv. 17–19)

We too leave this life and all our labors under the sun. They belong to this life and this world from the viewpoint under consideration. Others will eventually rule over them. This is not a denial of the reward of grace God will give us or of the truth that from that viewpoint our labor and toil are not in vain in the Lord (1 Cor. 15:58). The Preacher, in fact, concludes the whole book with the truth that God will bring every work into judgment (Eccl. 12:14) because there is a reward, though it be not of this world. What is on the foreground in Ecclesiastes 2 is the reality that our labors, from the viewpoint of this world, pass into other hands, and we have no more say in them. Will the works of our hands be sustained and built up or foolishly destroyed?

The Travail of Men

20. Therefore I went about to cause my heart to despair of all the labour which I took under the sun.
21. For there is a man whose labour is in wisdom, and in knowledge, and in equity; yet to a man that hath not laboured therein shall he leave it for his portion. This also is vanity and a great evil.
22. For what hath man of all his labour, and of the vexation of his heart, wherein he hath laboured under the sun?
23. For all his days are sorrows, and his travail grief; yea, his heart taketh not rest in the night. This is also vanity.
    —Ecclesiastes 2:20–23

To another man is given that which was once our portion, our labor and toil. The Preacher not only shows us this fact but also the spiritual burden this reality of life caused him. He uses strong language, that he hated all his labor under the sun, that he despaired or grieved over it.

He looks at all the labor, the toil and sorrow that accompanied all that effort. He calls to mind too the sleepless nights he endured, and yet he must leave it all to another. "For what hath man of all his labour, and of the vexation of his heart, wherein he hath laboured under the sun? For all his days are sorrows, and his travail grief; yea, his heart taketh not rest in the night. This is also vanity" (Eccl. 2:22–23).

Man is inclined to a restless activity that will not let him sleep. There is no peace to the wicked. Yet the trial of heart of which he speaks is not one that besets the wicked only. This same reality besets the child of God in his weakness. The difference is that a child of God has a comfort that is not found in the works of his hands and not dependent upon them.

In speaking in this manner, the Preacher is not rejecting God's sovereign wisdom and counsel in the ordering of our portion in this life and what becomes of the work of our hands. That he also will discuss. Rather he sets before us here the very real struggle and distress that the reality of life in its present vanity causes us. He does so, not to lead us to despair, but to putting the vanity of this life and its labor and toil into perspective. He draws out an important conclusion, which rests upon the fact that all of these things are under the hand of God.

The Spiritual Conclusion: the Good Gift of God

24. There is nothing better for a man, than that he should eat and drink, and that he should make his soul enjoy good in his labour. This also I saw, that it was from the hand of God.

25. For who can eat, or who else can hasten hereunto, more than I?

26. For God giveth to a man that is good in his sight wisdom, and knowledge, and joy: but to the sinner he giveth travail, to gather and to heap up, that he may give to him

that is good before God. This also is vanity and vexation
of spirit.—Ecclesiastes 2:24–26

In reviewing his works and pondering them and setting before
us the struggle of life, the Preacher leads us to a spiritual conclusion, that we may discern what is the good in the activity of life. It
is simply stated: "There is nothing better for a man, than that he
should eat and drink, and that he should make his soul enjoy good
in his labour. This also I saw, that it was from the hand of God"
(Eccl. 2: 24). The transitory works of our hands, the joy of labor
and activity and the fruit of it in food and drink are our portion
from the hand of God as it pertains to this present life. They are
our daily bread. The present enjoyment of them with contentment
is the good gift of God. It is something learned by wisdom in the
school of grace. This is the place of our present enjoyment. And
Solomon is very conscious that God had given him this blessing
also richly: "For who can eat, or who else can hasten hereunto,
more than I?" (v. 25).

What the text says is important for us to apprehend. "There is
nothing better for a man, than that he should eat and drink, and
that he should make his soul enjoy good in his labour. This also I
saw, that it was from the hand of God" (v. 24). This is the good of
the present joys in the labor of our hands and the profit of them. It
is God's gift. It is a gift of grace.

And God gives it only to his children!

"For God giveth to a man that is good in his sight wisdom, and
knowledge, and joy: but to the sinner he giveth travail, to gather
and to heap up, that he may give to him that is good before God.
This also is vanity and vexation of spirit" (v. 26). The enjoyment of
the present gifts of life in contentment are given of God to the man
"good in his sight." To his children God gives "wisdom, knowledge,
and joy." He does not give these gifts to the wicked. The one good
in God's sight is one who stands righteous according to God's verdict before God's judgment seat. His sins are covered, and he has

peace with God. He stands in the righteousness and goodness that are in Christ. The child of this world stands in his sin before God's judgment seat. The sinner in the text is one whom God sees as a sinner, who stands before him in his guilt an transgression as the object of God's judgment in his wrath.

We must not be misled by appearances. The world's rejoicing is that of one who has no rest. It is one who seeks the joys of this life as an end in themselves, and they are bondage to his soul. The labor of his hands works judgment in his life: "but to the sinner he giveth travail, to gather and to heap up" (v. 26). His laughter is the braying of one whose soul is empty of true joy. For joy can be found in God alone; the man without God truly has none. As will be seen in more detail, the book of Ecclesiastes does not teach a common grace or goodness of God to all men, but rather repudiates such an idea. In the things of this life God's grace and goodness are particular; they are for the one "good in his sight" (v. 26).

Not only does the wicked man have no true joy, but all his labor and industry, his heaping and gathering, serve not himself but are made to serve the children of God. God gives travail to the sinner to heap up, "that he may give to him that is good before God" (v. 26). The toils of the wicked are made in God's wisdom to serve the needs of God's people. The spiritual antithesis which the Preacher finds here is an absolute one between the child of God and the child of this world, between one who is good in God's sight and one who stands a sinner—not in common grace but in judgment and wrath the ungodly receive their portion in this life.

CHAPTER 3

The Seasons of God's Sovereign Providence

1. To every thing there is a season, and a time to every purpose under the heaven.— Ecclesiastes 3:1

Having pointed us to the transitory character of life and its vanity under the sun, Solomon turns to the seeming pattern of life in the world. The opening verse states the principle. There is a season and purpose for all things under the sun. The text then presents a series of contrasts that embrace the bearing of children and birth, death and dying, planting and rooting up, and killing and healing.

A Time and Season

2. A time to be born, and a time to die; a time to plant, and a time to pluck up that which is planted;
3. A time to kill, and a time to heal; a time to break down, and a time to build up;
4. A time to weep, and a time to laugh; a time to mourn, and a time to dance;
5. A time to cast away stones, and a time to gather stones together; a time to embrace, and a time to refrain from embracing;
6. A time to get, and a time to lose; a time to keep, and a time to cast away;
7. A time to rend, and a time to sew; a time to keep silence, and a time to speak;

8. A time to love, and a time to hate; a time of war, and a time of peace.—Ecclesiastes 3:2–8

The contrasts encompass the circumstances and affairs of life or purposes under heaven, both of joy and sorrow, activity and labor, gain and loss. Yet this is not a mere description of the things under heaven, for Solomon is speaking not simply of what comes to pass or happens in the life of the world, but of what God is doing. This is not the heathen doctrine of karma.

All of these affairs of life, both the events themselves and the joy and sorrow in them, are seasons or times set by God and in God's purpose. They are his works in the life of men. They are, on the one hand, repeated patterns in the unfolding of time under the sun, so that Solomon can say of them: "that which hath been is now; and that which is to be hath already been" (Eccl 3:15). Yet they are "the work that God maketh from beginning to the end" (v. 11).

It is God who ordains a time to bear and give birth in human life and a time to die. It is he who ordains the season to plant not only crops, but also the works of men, and the time or season to uproot them. He sets the time to kill and to heal, to break down and build up. He is God, the everlasting, sovereign Lord of all. This is the first point Solomon would have us to discern.

It is God who sends the set time of weeping and laughter, of mourning and rejoicing. This is true whether one speaks of the personal life of men, of the times and seasons of the church, or of men and nations. The Heidelberg Catechism echoes this passage when it says that "herbs and grass, rain and drought, fruitful and barren years, meat and drink, health and sickness, riches and poverty, yea, all things, come not by chance, but by his fatherly hand."[1]

The sovereign, everywhere-present power of God, which is his providence, so embraces the life of man that man cannot escape it.

---

1 Heidelberg Catechism Q&A 27, in Philip Schaff, ed., *The Creeds of Christendom with a History and Critical Notes*, 6th ed., 3 vols. (New York: Harper and Row, 1931; repr., Grand Rapids, MI: Baker Books, 2007), 3:316.

Man would ordain when it is time to get and to lose, to rend and to sow. He would determine in his own wisdom the time of love and hate, of war and earthly peace. But these things are not under his hand. The affairs of life come by God's sovereign appointment.

The Government of God Is Not Random

9. What profit hath he that worketh in that wherein he laboureth?
10. I have seen the travail, which God hath given to the sons of men to be exercised in it.
11. He hath made every thing beautiful in his time: also he hath set the world in their heart, so that no man can find out the work that God maketh from the beginning to the end.
12. I know that there is no good in them, but for a man to rejoice, and to do good in his life.
13. And also that every man should eat and drink, and enjoy the good of all his labour, it is the gift of God.
14. I know that, whatsoever God doeth, it shall be for ever: nothing can be put to it, nor any thing taken from it: and God doeth it, that men should fear before him.
15. That which hath been is now; and that which is to be hath already been; and God requireth that which is past.—Ecclesiastes 3:9–15

The government of God is not random. That there is a set time, an appointed time, means that everything comes in its season according to God's counsel and purpose. God has a purpose and a design, a work which he does, that runs "from the beginning to the end" (Eccl. 3:11). That design too is both from the beginning and end of the world, in the absolute sense of the word, and from the raising up, for a season, of a man and then of casting him down into death.

We know that counsel and purpose from the word of God, as

it stands in Christ from the foundations of the world. It is God's purpose to glorify himself in Christ and his church, in the salvation and gathering of his elect. Running through the repeated patterns of life and its times and seasons, there is a straight line, the line of God's counsel. Solomon does not turn here to the contents of that counsel, as his viewpoint is that which is manifested under the sun; rather, he speaks of its sovereign efficacy: "I know that, whatsoever God doeth, it shall be for ever: nothing can be put to it, nor any thing taken from it…that men should fear before him" (v. 14).

God's counsel determines the boundaries of man's life. All things are "of him and through him and to him" (Rom. 11:36). His counsel is unconditional, sovereign, and complete so that "nothing can be put to it, nor any thing taken from it" (Eccl. 3:14). It leads the history of this world through all the seasons of his sovereign appointment to the final end and consummation. Nothing turns that purpose. No man can hinder it. Nor does any work of man add to or subtract from it. The whole life of the world and the history of creation is so under his almighty power that "whatsoever God doeth, it shall be for ever" (v. 14).

God's Works Alone Abide

Those works of God shape the life of men in such a way that God "hath made every thing beautiful in his time" (Eccl. 3:11). Man, by contrast, though he labors and toils, exerting and wearying himself in his labor and task, yet finds that the outcome is not in his hands. "What profit hath he that worketh in that wherein he laboreth?" (v. 9). What does man really achieve? He has nothing of his own but vanity. None of it abides. God's works accomplish their purpose, in his set time, and they are beautiful. They are good, serve his purpose, accomplish his end, and manifest that it is so in their time. They endure. He it is who works all things "for good to them that love" him (Rom. 8:28), and judges the works of wicked men.

The sons of men, sons of Adam, who are creatures of the dust and fallen in sin, have each their task or travail given them. Each has his set time, his place in this life. Man spends his strength in the exercise of it. Yet man is always dust and to dust he returns. He looks for something in all his labor that might endure, deceiving himself that it will endure, but it abides not. There is a reason for this. God also "hath set the world in [his] heart" (Eccl. 3:11). The word *world* is really the word for *eternity of time*. We may say here that this looks at the passing of time as a stream that flows unto that which is eternal. That such is set in the heart of man, distinguishing him also from the animals, means that he is aware of that flow of time, is aware that there is that which abides and endures, but that it is not of man. He knows that there is an eternal end.

God's Works a Witness

Thus man seeks also to find it out, to understand that line as it runs through the repeated pattern of life. He would know from the things that are seen under the sun "the work that God maketh from the beginning to the end" (v. 11). But his very place within time and the transitory character of his place make it impossible that he should find it out. That he is bound in time by the hand of God in all his life, which he cannot control, testifies that men should fear before God (v. 14). He sees also from that which is past and now present, that repeated pattern, that the works of men have consequences; there is judgment. He knows that there is a God who "requireth that which is past" (v. 15).

The apostle Paul sets forth the same thought in his sermon to the heathen in Derbe when they tried to worship him and Barnabas. He says of God as creator, but also Lord of providence, "Nevertheless he left not himself without witness, in that he did good, and gave us rain from heaven, and fruitful seasons, filling our hearts with food and gladness" (Acts 14:17). Paul sets forth the same truth in his more extended sermon on Mars Hill, saying that God

26. hath determined the times before appointed, and the bounds of their habitation;
27. That they should seek the Lord, if haply they might feel after him, and find him, though he be not far from every one of us:
28. For in him we live, and move, and have our being. (Acts 17:26–28)

In both these instances there is also an indictment that man, seeing these things, did not seek after God. The same charge is brought in Romans 1:

18. For the wrath of God is revealed from heaven against all ungodliness and unrighteousness of men, who hold the truth in unrighteousness;
19. Because that which may be known of God is manifest in them; for God hath shewed it unto them.
20. For the invisible things of him from the creation of the world are clearly seen, being understood by the things that are made, even his eternal power and Godhead; so that they are without excuse." (Rom. 1:18–20)

The Proper Spiritual Response

The very sovereign providence of God and man's own life bounded by his will, and the very truth of judgment for that which is past ought to lead men to fear before God. They should lead man to humble himself under the hand of God and to worship. But that does not happen by nature. Therefore, what those things do is to leave man without excuse.

Solomon points out another conclusion from this same truth, that with respect to the things of this present life, this truth of God and his works and the set times of man's life ought to lead man also to a true appreciation of the value of his own labor and what is good in it. "I know that there is no good in them, but for a man to rejoice, and do good in his life. And also that every man should eat and drink, and enjoy the good of all his labor, it is the gift of God" (Eccl. 3:12–13). This ought to be the value of the transitory things of a man's labor and toil: it does not abide. By contrast Solomon says: "I know that, whatsoever God doeth, it shall be for ever" (v. 14).

Yet, as Solomon has already shown, that is not the outcome in the life of sinful man. "To the sinner he giveth travail, to gather and to heap up" (Eccl. 2:26). This truth of God's sovereign providence and disposition sinful man does not want to confess—also many, in the corruption of the Christian gospel, do not want to hear it. Yet man is confronted by it. Man would sew, and it is God's time to rend. He would build up, and it is God's time to break down. He would get and keep, and it is God's time to lose and cast away. God's curse rests upon the ground and the life of man so that all man's labor is subject to vanity. This striving with the power of God—which man discerns, and to which he can neither add nor take away—belongs to the travail of man's life in his rebellion against God.

To his people who walk by faith, God gives a spiritual blessing in the midst of the trials of life, for he gives us to see and confess that the set times and seasons of God's providence come by his fatherly hand, are for our good, and are the blessings of his care and grace. To that child of God is given the gift, not only of food and drink, but to eat and drink with thanksgiving in the fear of God. To him also is given to hold loosely to the things of this life, for he knows the end of God's way from his word, and rather than having all his life and work be made merely subject to vanity, he is made by grace fruitful unto every good work.

The Estate of Men

16. And moreover I saw under the sun the place of judgment, that wickedness was there; and the place of righteousness, that iniquity was there.
17. I said in mine heart, God shall judge the righteous and the wicked: for there is a time there for every purpose and for every work.

18. I said in mine heart concerning the estate of the sons of men, that God might manifest them, and that they might see that they themselves are beasts.

19. For that which befalleth the sons of men befalleth beasts; even one thing befalleth them: as the one dieth, so dieth the other; yea, they have all one breath; so that a man hath no preeminence above a beast: for all is vanity.

20. All go unto one place; all are of the dust, and all turn to dust again.

21. Who knoweth the spirit of man that goeth upward, and the spirit of the beast that goeth downward to the earth?

22. Wherefore I perceive that there is nothing better, than that a man should rejoice in his own works; for that is his portion: for who shall bring him to see what shall be after him?—Ecclesiastes 3:16–22

Man senses that work of God but walks over against it in darkness. This is brought out yet more fully in what he has says in this section of Ecclesiastes 3. Verse 15 ends on the note, "God requireth that which is past," or more literally "seeks what is pursued." In the activities of men, God is a righteous judge. In his counsel and purpose, and in his providence, God judges the works of men in time and eternity. Seeing this is, however, a matter of faith through the word.

What is seen under the sun among men stands in contrast to this truth. "And moreover I saw the place of judgment, that wickedness was there; and the place of righteousness, that iniquity was there" (v. 16). Solomon looked to the place where judgment was to be found, where justice was to be administered in truth. It was not there. Looking to the affairs of men, in court and civil dealings among men, which in Israel were to be according to the law of God, one expected to find justice in the fear of God. But what was found there was a perversion of truth and right, a bending of justice in sin. This is no less true in our day in a sinful world. This was not only in the corruption and perversion of formal judgment, the rule of law, but it was a corruption and perversion found also in the judges themselves. Where uprightness or righteousness in the person of the judge should be found, there was iniquity. They and their judgments were corrupted and perverted. Sin and iniquity lie as stains upon all the affairs of men. When men stand in places of power and responsibility, in the place of authority to render just judgment, iniquity is there. Men defraud their neighbor under a "show of right,"[2] by cunning devices and with lies and deceit.

Solomon does not enter directly into the causes of this perversion of justice. The word of God abundantly testifies of the covetousness of men, of the taking of bribes and influence-peddlling, of the power of rich men to oppress their neighbor. The wickedness of man and his wickedness in judgment fills the world around us under the sun. We should note, however, that Solomon, being king, beholds this not only in the world in general but also as one who rules in the life of the church. In Israel also this perversion of justice was to be found.

Our text does imply a certain spiritual root at the heart of such perversion. It is that men, walking in the arrogance of sin and pride of heart, put from them the truth of God and his judgment. They say within themselves that God does not know. In their darkness they say there is no one above them who will judge what they do as they pursue their prey and persecute the afflicted. Thus it is with the rich man in Psalm 73, of men of power in the earth:

6. Therefore pride compasseth them about as a chain; violence covereth them as a garment.
7. Their eyes stand out with fatness: they have more than heart could wish.
8. They are corrupt, and speak wickedly concerning oppression: they speak loftily.

---

2   Heidelberg Catechism Q&A 110, in Schaff, *Creeds of Christendom*, 3:347.

9. They set their mouth against the heavens, and their tongue walketh through the earth. (Ps. 73:6–9).

God's Judgment in His Own Time

It may seem under the sun that such wickedness of men goes unchecked and unpunished. Solomon himself, though king, is unable to restrain it. Yet, the testimony of God's word, which we hold by faith, stands in opposition to what is seen. Solomon sets before us both what he sees under the sun and what he contemplates in his heart by faith. He shows us his own inner thoughts: "I said in mine heart, God shall judge the righteous and the wicked: for there is a time there for every purpose and for every work" (Eccl. 3:17). God does judge the affairs of men according to his own counsel and purpose. Included in that counsel is that wicked men judge wickedly, for sin must be exposed as sin: "Surely thou didst set them in slippery places: thou castedst them down into destruction" (Ps. 73:18). This too is in the seasons of God's providence. But God will judge the matter with a righteous judgment, that men should render an account before him. He judges between the righteous and the wicked. He did so between Saul and David and between David and Absalom.

The unjust judge is one who is a fool, who walks to his own destruction, but in God's time and not by man's determination. God will bring truth and righteousness to light and wickedness into condemnation. He is truly the righteous judge of all. It is not true that God does not see or know. He does. But that is not immediately apparent under the sun, for judgment is not executed instantly but in its season. That God does judge, is judging even now, and will finally judge in eternity is known by faith. God's judgment serves his counsel and purpose. In that confidence Solomon speaks in his heart of a fact: "God shall judge." Nothing is hid from his sight. His judgment is sure: "God shall judge the righteous and the wicked" (Eccl. 3:17).

Man a Creature of the Dust

Solomon further reflects on this working of God's providence in judgment: "I said in mine heart concerning the estate of the sons of men, that God might manifest them, and that they might see that they themselves are beasts" (Eccl. 3:18). There is in God's sovereign dealings a working of judgment that tests and proves men in the affairs of life, exposing what they are in themselves. Over against the arrogance of men stands the reality that he will die. The wages of sin is death, and man is a creature of the dust. In his pride he exalts himself and works wickedness, corrupting also justice and judgment, in the service of his own pride and covetousness. But he is as the beast of the earth.

What stands on the foreground is the truth of man's creaturely powerlessness. For all his boasting in himself, he "is of the earth earthy" (1 Cor. 15:47). The statement is very direct: he is a beast. Lest we misunderstand the point of comparison, Solomon explains it: "For that which befalleth the sons of men befalleth beasts; even one thing befalleth them; as the one dieth, so dieth the other; yea, they have all one breath; so that a man hath no preeminence above a beast: for all is vanity" (Eccl. 3:19). The beasts of the field were formed of the earth in their creation. They too are of the dust of the ground. Their breath is the breath of a living organism tied to the earth. They too lie under the curse, which came upon the creation because of man's sin. Man, as he is formed of the dust of the ground, in this aspect of his creation, is not different from the beasts. He breathes the same air, eats and drinks, begets offspring. He is tied to the earth and is earthy, a creature of the dust.

Man shares this organic commonality with animals in such a way that he can see it under the sun. It is not hid from him. It answers and rebukes the sinful pride with which man exalts himself. And like the beast also, he dies. He returns to the dust. "All go unto one place; all are of the dust, and all turn to dust again" (v. 20). Solomon has in view the physical reality of death and corruption from the viewpoint of what is seen under the sun. The departure of the breath of a man and that of an animal in death are visibly the same. They both die, and both return to the dust in corruption. From that viewpoint the sons of Adam have not "preeminence above a beast" (v. 19).

Where are the great men of the earth who heap riches to themselves, defrauding their neighbor? Where is the great name, the powerful man, the statesman of the earth, or the man of power and influence? Their names run across the headlines for a season, under God's providence, in the affairs of life, and then the headlines proclaim: they are dead. They carry nothing with them. The result is that "all is vanity" (v. 19). They are like the rich fool in Jesus' parable who heaps and gathers, builds bigger barns, and would then take his ease; "But God said unto him, Thou fool, this night thy soul shall be required of thee: then whose shall those things be, which thou hast provided?" (Luke 12:20).

Yet His Soul Shall Also Be Required

The reality of death confronts man under the sun and testifies against him. But there is more, which cannot be seen with the eye. Man is not a mere beast. He is a creature of the dust and this alone reproves him, but he has also a soul, a human spirit, distinct from the animals. The animal's life is communicated organically by its begetting of offspring. It is of the earth alone, and its life is in its blood. But man was made by a twofold creation. God breathed into his nostrils the breath of life, and man became a living soul or organism. Physically man is like the beast, and yet he is different. But this difference cannot be seen with the eye directly at the moment of death. It too is known by faith and not sight. Solomon therefore adds: "Who knoweth the spirit of man that goeth upward, and the spirit of the beast that goeth downward to the earth?" (Eccl. 3:21). With that distinction comes the truth that it is appointed unto men once to die and afterward the judgment. The Lord will require the soul of the rich fool. He will stand before

God. This truth the wicked of the world do not want to hear in their pride and covetousness. He who walks by faith knows the end of the matter and the distinction between a man and a beast. The spirit of man goeth upward, unto God who gave it and who judges the works of men.

The Way of Spiritual Wisdom

The application of this truth Solomon will make more fully, particularly to the young man and his labor, activity, and walk, "but know thou, that for all these things God will bring thee into judgment" (Eccl. 11:9). Here he would have us to draw a conclusion concerning the activities of life and their place by contrast with the folly of sin. God ordains the seasons of life. To walk humbly with God from day to day in contentment is the true value of the transitory gifts of life. The future is in God's hands and under his dominion. God ordains what happens and befalls us in this life. Not in the life of the world, but in him is our true refuge as the God of our salvation in Christ. The things of the world and the activities of this life are our portion under the hand of God.

Solomon thus draws this conclusion: "Wherefore I perceive that there is nothing better than that a man should rejoice in his own works; for that is his portion: for who shall bring him to see what shall be after him?" (Eccl 3:22). The answer to the question who? is no one, no mere man. The present blessings and rejoicing in contentment are our portion. They are from the hand of the Lord. Tomorrow is unknown to us, hidden in God's counsel. It is in his hand that we should thus rest, content with our daily bread.

CHAPTER 4

Without Comfort

1. So I returned, and considered all the oppressions that are done under the sun: and behold the tears of such as were oppressed, and they had no comforter; and on the side of their oppressors there was power; but they had no comforter.
2. Wherefore I praised the dead which are already dead more than the living which are yet alive.
3. Yea, better is he than both they, which hath not yet been, who hath not seen the evil work that is done under the sun.—Ecclesiastes 4:1–3

"So I returned, and considered all the oppressions that are done under the sun" (Eccl. 4:1). Oppression of a man by his neighbor is a vast subject, considering the many different forms of evil done under the sun. Solomon has pointed out that in the place of judgment evil is found among men. This works the oppression of the neighbor. He calls to mind all the oppression he sees in its various forms, but rather than going into detail, he distills it down to one basic reality: there is the one who is oppressed, and with him are tears—tears of sorrow, grief, frustration, and pain of loss. There are tears in his misery. The oppressor, on the other hand, has power: power over others that is evil and works evil. This distinction between tears and power is not the main thing we must see, however; the real misery of man is more than that. Solomon calls our attention to it: "and behold the tears of such as were oppressed, and they had no comforter; and on the side of their oppressors there was power; but they had no comforter" (Eccl. 4:1).

Both oppressor and oppressed lack a comforter. There is none to console or comfort them, none to stand by them in their life or in their need. They are alone. There is an empty place in man's life because of this; his sin drives him away from his neighbor. This is a fundamental problem in man's misery. If we would tie the elements of this chapter of Ecclesiastes together, its unity lies in man's need for a comforter and the fact that among men under the sun that is not truly to be found.

Through the fall into sin man is become by nature estranged from God, as Paul says to the Colossians, "And you...were sometime alienated and enemies in your mind by wicked works" (Col. 1:21). This separation from God bears the fruit that man is also estranged from his neighbor. His very oppression of his neighbor destroys communion and fellowship. There is no comforter, and can be none, because the love of God alone forms the basis for the love of the neighbor. Except man be reconciled to God, there is no true way of reconciliation with the neighbor. The way of reconciliation must be found in Jesus Christ and the comforter that he gives, which is his Holy Spirit. Man under the sun, who remembers not his Creator (Eccl. 12:1), who does not have God as his covenant God, who has neither God as his shield and comfort nor as the basis to walk with his neighbor. His depravity works a comfortless isolation.

So weighty is this misery of man in oppression and travail that Solomon looks at it and says: "Wherefore I praised the dead which are already dead more than the living which are alive. Yea, better is he than both they, which hath not yet been, who hath not seen the evil work that is done under the sun" (Eccl. 4:2–3). So great is the evil of man without God, the world of man by nature under the sun , that the dead who have passed from this life and its comfortlessness and travail are in a better case. This is not despair nor pessimism but a way of underscoring just how vile are the evil works under the sun and the pain, suffering, and misery they bring in the life of men. The dead endure its suffering under the sun no more. In saying this we must keep in mind the viewpoint of Solomon, which is that which is seen. From that standpoint one who has not yet been born has not yet seen the evil works under the sun and is in a better state than either the living or the dead. His soul has not yet been vexed by the oppression and evil works of men.

This somber reflection on the state of men fallen and alienated from God underscores the misery of man in its wretchedness. Sin is evil. It works evil, and it leaves in its wake tears and sorrow and misery, which is truly a comfortless misery. Solomon is in a sense underscoring what is pointed out in question and answer 2 of the Heidelberg Catechism, that we need to understand "the greatness of [our] sin and misery."[1] This he would show us from the effect of sin as it works misery in man's life. Man's life in sin is without true joy, peace, or comfort, for he is separated from God who is his true life.

The Travail of Man

4. Again, I considered all travail, and every right work, that for this a man is envied of his neighbour. This is also vanity and vexation of spirit.

5. The fool foldeth his hands together, and eateth his own flesh.

6. Better is an handful with quietness, than both the hands full with travail and vexation of spirit.—Ecclesiastes 4:4–6

Having defined the problem, Solomon turns to a further consideration of the travail of men, in which he points us to the way in which man works his own misery. He considers the causes of misery in the life of men and the folly of sin which leads to it.

---

1   Heidelberg Catechism Q&A 2, in Schaff, *Creeds of Christendom*, 3:308.

"Again, I considered all travail, and every right work, that for this a man is envied of his neighbor. This is also vanity and vexation of spirit" (Eccl. 4:4). We are shown man's travail, his labor and toil, his industry. He achieves a right work, that is, he is successful in his endeavor. The point is not right in a moral sense but in earthly terms, under the sun: he labors and his industry is successful. He is an achiever. But "for this [he] is envied of his neighbor." This expression is more comprehensive than the idea of other people's jealousy, though that is included in it. It has the idea of envy or rivalry against the neighbor; that is, it points us to the motives of the achiever as well as the response of those about him. He is the man who gets ahead; he is the one who climbs over obstacles, including his neighbor. He may well be an oppressor. But that struggle and toil leave him isolated and alone, separated from his neighbor through covetousness, both his own and his neighbor's envy. The result is vanity, an empty success, and "vexation of spirit" (v. 6) in all his travail.

By contrast, "The fool foldeth his hands together, and eateth his own flesh" (v. 5). The fool is the man of no industry, the man who is slothful. He is described in Proverbs as one who lies upon his bed rolling back and forth like a creaking hinge (Prov. 26:14). His fences are decayed and fallen and his field overgrown (Prov. 24:31). He does not, and will not, pass his door because there is a lion in the streets (Prov. 22:13). The reality is that he "eateth his own flesh" (Eccl. 4:5). His laziness is such that he devours himself. He too is abhorred of his neighbor, for such is the effect of his indolence.

"Better is an handful with quietness, than both hands full with travail and vexation of spirit" (v. 6). While some would apply this verse to the fool, as if it is his excuse for his indolence, it is better to understand it as an interjection of Solomon at this point in the light of the contrast and the dilemma it poses. Solomon consistently uses the word *better*, that which is the good, or right and fitting, in God's design to introduce his own reflection on the matter before him. The fool has empty hands and is devouring his own hand; the rapacious achiever has both hands full and is hated of his neighbor. What then is the way of wisdom? The better way is a hand filled with quietness, with rest; that is, to labor with a view to one's portion for the day in contentment of heart, which as Solomon has pointed out is the gift of God's grace to his people (Eccl. 2:24). It is bound up with God, our comfort and strength.

The Empty Place in Man's Life

7. Then I returned, and I saw vanity under the sun.
8. There is one alone, and there is not a second; yea, he hath neither child nor brother: yet is there no end of all his labour; neither is his eye satisfied with riches; neither saith he, For whom do I labour, and bereave my soul of good? This is also vanity, yea, it is a sore travail.—Ecclesiastes 4:7–8

In the context of the vain travail of man Solomon returns to his description of the life of men. This is indeed the achiever of this world who has no rest in his hand. Covetousness drives him. He is isolated and alone. His riches do not profit him. He has no comforter, neither does he enjoy the fruit of his labor. Millions must become billions. This is the sinner to whom God, in judgment upon sin, "giveth travail, to gather and to heap up" (Eccl. 2:26).

In his heaping and gathering, he is unable to be satisfied and content. Enough is never enough, and in it also he has no one with whom to have fellowship in his life, neither God nor man. It is a sore (that is, an evil) travail. He is like a rat on a treadmill going only to destruction. He consumes his strength of life in vanity. He has none of the ordinary bonds of life, "neither child nor brother" (Eccl. 4:8). There is a severe warning in this to us as God's people who see this folly in the world about us to flee covetousness and the lust for earthly riches.

The Blessing of Fellowship

9. Two are better than one; because they have a good reward for their labour.

10. For if they fall, the one will lift up his fellow: but woe to him that is alone when he falleth; for he hath not another to help him up.

11. Again, if two lie together, then they have heat: but how can one be warm alone?

12. And if one prevail against him, two shall withstand him; and a threefold cord is not quickly broken.—Ecclesiastes 4:9–12

What is the better way, the way of wisdom? Again Solomon shows us in his reflection. He uses a figure of human companionship to illustrate his point. The figure of human companionship is a simple yet striking one. It draws to mind a range of relationships from the bond of marriage to human fellowship. Striking it is, however, in that Ecclesiastes has shown us that sin destroys such fellowship and leaves man comfortless and alone. In fact, Solomon pronounces woe upon the man without child or brother, who by his own greed and vanity works his own separation in his sin from his neighbor (Eccl. 4:8).

Men in this world have partners in business and other affairs. They enter into the marriage bond as well. Yet the root of sin corrodes those relationships, and when trouble comes, it becomes each one for himself. Marriages break down because of sin. Parents and children are estranged from one another. There is, of course, a semblance of altruism, mutual care for one another, in the activities of men. The human race is an organism and man cannot ignore his dependence on his fellow man. But the semblance of comfort afforded is outward and external, rooted so often plainly in making oneself feel good and in a works-righteousness that has no real foundation. It is so often a using of one another for one's own self-interest. Such camaraderie in times of trouble quickly becomes enmity, mutual recrimination, and distrust. The effects of sin work through all those relationships under the judgment of God.

True comfort, as has been pointed out above, is only in Christ and in his Spirit, the Comforter. In Ecclesiastes 4:9, Solomon is again showing us the better way. His description echoes Enoch's walk with God and the friendship of God's covenant with his people in Christ. That fellowship extends to the life of the church, to a spiritual bond of brotherhood, which the world without God does not have. It extends to the bonds of Christian marriage and family in the life of God's covenant. Then indeed the cord that binds is not a mere human one, and it is not twofold, but it is a "threefold cord" (v. 12). True fellowship with God is the only foundation for fellowship among men in every aspect of life. In this also God's grace is particular, the portion of his people, and the better treasure than the world and its riches.

The Kings of Men and Their Fading Acclaim

13. Better is a poor and a wise child than an old and foolish king, who will no more be admonished.
14. For out of prison he cometh to reign; whereas also he that is born in his kingdom becometh poor.
15. I considered all the living which walk under the sun, with the second child that shall stand up in his stead.
16. There is no end of all the people, even of all that have been before them: they also that come after shall not rejoice in him. Surely this also is vanity and vexation of spirit.—Ecclesiastes 4:13–16

The contrast in the text is introduced by the word *better* (v. 13). This is an indication that Solomon is drawing another conclusion from what he has seen under the sun and drawing also from his own life and experience. He is giving expression to this better, not as a mere human opinion, but as the testimony of God's word. It is important that we keep this in mind.

The point of connection with the preceding portion is with the foolishness of the old king who will not receive counsel because of his stubbornness and the passing vanity of the acclaim of the multitude. Solomon has directed us to the subject of man without comfort in the preceding part of the chapter from an individual point of view. Man personally, because of his own sinful flesh destroys the foundation of communion and fellowship with his neighbor. Here Solomon approaches a similar subject from an organic viewpoint, from the perspective of the life of men in positions of power and in the life of nations and kingdoms.

In considering this, we must also keep in mind this perspective: that behind what happens under the sun is the counsel and providence of God. These are not merely enclosed natural phenomena; they come by the hand of God who ordains the times and seasons in the life of men. There is "a time to break down, and a time to build up;" there is "a time to rend, and a time to sew" (Eccl. 3:3, 7). God is a God of judgment, who judges the wickedness and folly of men in his wrath and also chastens his people according to his own counsel and wisdom, who says to the young man, "But know thou, that for all these things God will bring thee into judgment" (Eccl. 11:9).

A Personal Element

While the description is a general one of the life of this world, there is also a personal element in it. Solomon does not confess his sin directly in Ecclesiastes, but the testimony of that confession or recognition of his sin is there. Solomon was once, in his own eyes, a poor child—not poor in wealth, but poor in spirit— who humbled himself before God and sought the Lord. When God commanded him: "Ask what I shall give thee?" (1 Kings 3:5), Solomon prayed, after reviewing God's dealings with his father David,

> 7. And now O Lord my God, thou hast made thy servant king instead of David my father: and I am but a little child: I know not how to go out or come in,

8. And thy servant is in the midst of thy people which thou hast chosen, a great people, that cannot be numbered nor counted for multitude.

9. Give therefore thy servant an understanding heart to judge thy people, that I may discern between good and bad: for who is able to judge this thy so great a people? (1 Kings 3:7–9)

In answer to that prayer, God gave unto Solomon wisdom to rule and judge as well as riches and long life. In that wisdom he also said: "I made me great works; I builded me houses; I planted me vineyards" (Eccl. 2:4).

But Solomon also married many heathen wives, contrary to God's word. Many of these marriages were political alliances which involved also an increasing resting in his own strength and power. His wives turned his heart to build idol temples outside Jerusalem, sowing the seeds of idol worship in Judah. In the sad history of 1 Kings 11, Solomon is also admonished by the Lord for his sin: the kingdom would be rent because of it and his enemies stirred against him. The wise child that Solomon had been became, in his sinful weakness, an old and foolish king in his government. The grace and gifts of God and wisdom also to see his own weakness remained, but in his rule of Israel he had become "an old and foolish king, who will no more be admonished" (Eccl. 4:13). The root of the matter? The old and foolish king is stubborn in pride. The effect of these sins was that the glory of the kingdom also began to depart.

Against the background of his own sinful weakness, Solomon draws out the contrast. The youth, poor in himself and in the things of the world, but with wisdom, is better than an old and foolish king. To make the contrast sharper, the child is set forth as coming out of prison, from the lowest place, unto honor and glory. But because the old and foolish king walks in pride, his kingdom declines. Its citizens become poor. This is the contrast between the child and the old king, "For out of prison he [the child] cometh to reign; whereas also he that is born in his kingdom [the old and foolish king] becometh poor" (v. 14).

A Repeated Pattern

This is not, however, an isolated case, for Solomon looks at the world about him, the rise and fall of kings and those in authority and power. He looks at the life of men, and there is a pattern here. "I considered all the living which walk under the sun, with the second child that shall stand up in his stead" (Eccl. 4:15). He looks at the child, the second, that is the succeeding or following king, standing in the place of the former foolish king—what of him? What is the pattern among men? "There is no end of all the people, even of all that have been before them: they also that come after shall not rejoice in him" (v. 16).

The pattern is a simple one. The people once rejoiced in the king who, when he was young, was their hope and expectation. He became old and foolish; their expectation failed. In the way of his pride, he lifted himself up, and his rule became the rule of one who is arrogant and stubborn, filled with his own importance, and the citizens of his kingdom become poor.

Now a successor, a child, comes to reign in his stead. The multitudes acclaim him. He will set the kingdom in order. He will be to them a savior. He is the answer. Popularity and hope abound. But this new king too becomes old, and pride lives in his flesh also, for he is man. What then happens? The acclaim turns to disappointment. The expectation of men again fails. The popularity of the new ruler begins to wane. He is, after all, a man. The rejoicing of the one generation leads to the rejection of the next. "They also that come after shall not rejoice over him" (v. 16).

In time the one who is lifted up may well become the oppressor who has power (Eccl. 4:1). He may manifest himself as an unjust judge (Eccl. 3:16). The reality of life under the sun is that man is flesh: he is fallen and given by nature to sinful pride.

When he is exalted in power and left to himself, he will lift up his heart in arrogance and stubbornness to have his own way in willfulness because he is the ruler, the magistrate, the king. The text is not a diatribe against human government. God sets men in positions of power and authority. Our calling is to show due honor to all such. But the text does describe the reality of sinful men in power.

The text also describes the waning glory and honor such men have. The multitudes that seek them, put their confidence in them, and praise them today are the same in every generation, and they "that come after shall not rejoice in him" (Eccl. 4:16). Such men fail, and the expectation of men, their hope, is brought to emptiness, to nothing. It is vanity. Therefore Solomon adds: "Surely this also is vanity and vexation of spirit" (v. 16)—not just vanity, but surely this is also vanity. In the end, this too in the life of the "living which walk under the sun" is vanity (v. 15). Man's life under the sun is in constant change, and nothing genuinely new under the sun arises from man, not even in the rule of men and governments of the earth.

This time with a new leader is not truly different for it is subject to vanity. In the expectations of men and their rulers is to be found only "vexation of spirit" (v. 16), not an abiding rejoicing. The world seeks its comfort in earthly rulers, but it is a comfort that shall fail. Earthly rulers, in their pride, exalt themselves as if they were God to determine good and evil of themselves. Such arrogance in pride God will destroy. For note: earthly rulers and governments come to vanity because God makes it so. He judges among men. To the rulers and judges of the world, who are as gods, the living God says: "I have said, Ye are gods; and all of you are children of the most High. But ye shall die like men, and fall like one of the princes" (Ps. 82:6–7).

Man is dust and he shall fail. Though created in the image of God, yet fallen in sin, he shall also fall from his place of power and die. Man who is dust returns to "his earth" (Ps. 146:4).

The Answer Is Not in Mere Man

3. Put not your trust in princes, nor in the son of man, in whom there is no help.
4. His breath goeth forth, he returneth to his earth; in that very day his thoughts perish.
5. Happy is he that hath the God of Jacob for his help; whose hope i in the Lord his God.—Psalm 146:3–5

There is only one answer to this vanity and vexation of spirit, and that lies in God and in the king who is himself the eternal Son of God come in our flesh and blood: Jesus Christ. To this need Solomon also points us by implication. For in Christ is a king who does not become old and foolish. He governs in righteousness and grace. In him is the fellowship of life eternal, of God's covenant. He gives righteousness and eternal life. His kingdom does not fade, for it is founded in his cross by which he has overcome sin and death. Its glory does not pass away. Its life is resurrection life from above, eternal and blessed forever. For that king we would seek. In him is truly a hope that endures and a rejoicing that does not end. Solomon's kingdom was a fading but prophetic shadow of that kingdom which is to come in Christ.

CHAPTER 5

Ecclesiastes 5: "But Fear Thou God"

1. Keep thy foot when thou goest to the house of God, and be more ready to hear, than to give the sacrifice of fools: for they consider not that they do evil.
2. Be not rash with thy mouth, and let not thine heart be hasty to utter any thing before God: for God is in heaven, and thou upon earth: therefore let thy words be few.
3. For a dream cometh through the multitude of business; and a fool's voice is known by multitude of words.
4. When thou vowest a vow unto God, defer not to pay it; for he hath no pleasure in fools: pay that which thou hast vowed.
5. Better is it that thou shouldest not vow, than that thou shouldest vow and not pay.
6. Suffer not thy mouth to cause thy flesh to sin; neither say thou before the angel, that it was an error: wherefore should God be angry at thy voice, and destroy the work of thine hands?
7. For in the multitude of dreams and many words there are also divers vanities: but fear thou God.—Ecclesiastes 5:1–7

The word of God in Ecclesiastes 5 turns from considering the general vanity of men to their worship of God, for in that worship of God the folly of sin also manifests itself. Before describing that folly, the text turns to an exhortation: "Keep thy foot when thou goest to the house of God" (Eccl. 5:1).

God's house, the temple, was the visible manifestation of God's presence with his people, his covenant dwelling place. It is today the gathering of the body of Christ, the church, which is the "habitation of God through the Spirit" (Eph. 2:22). Entering that house, we enter into the presence of God to have covenant fellowship and communion with him. The holy majesty of God calls forth the exhortation, "keep thy foot" (Eccl. 5:1). The point of that calling is a serious one. Keeping one's foot involves pondering our pathway, having a clear understanding of who we are and who God is as our exalted covenant God. It requires a reflection on him into whose presence we come, before whom we speak, and to whom we bring our worship. That pathway spiritually is the way of the reverence of faith, the fear of God, with which Solomon concludes this section: "But fear thou God" (Eccl. 5:7).

Entering the presence of God as his dependent people, we come not in our own strength or wisdom but as those in need of grace and wisdom, which only God can give. Solomon therefore adds, "and be more ready to hear, than to give the sacrifice of fools: for they consider not that they do evil" (v. 1). Entering the presence of God in worship, desiring communion with him in his house, we come to hear, to be taught of God, seeking his word and his will. This was true for a child of God in the Old Testament as well as for us; the Old Testament child of God needed to be taught the law of God and his promises, and so do we. This is the proper fruit of that spiritual preparation of heart that guides our feet unto the house of God.

The fool, by contrast, does not consider where he is going nor into whose presence he comes. He is not "more ready to hear." The text speaks of the "sacrifice of fools" (v. 1). While that includes a false, formal, or ritualistic kind of worship, it embraces all his spiritual activity in God's house. It embraces not only the sacrifices of bulls and goats laid upon the altar as empty form, but his thoughtless words and prayers, as is clear from the following context that speaks of entering into a vow. The prayer of the Pharisee in Jesus' parable of the publican and the Pharisee, in its pride and self-righteous boasting, is the sacrifice of a fool (Luke 18:9–14).

The word of God therefore adds: "Be not rash with thy mouth and let not thine heart be hasty to utter any thing before God: for God is in heaven, and thou upon earth: therefore let thy words be few" (Eccl. 5:2). The prayer of the publican, "God be merciful to me a sinner" (Luke 18:13), and his attitude, in which he would not lift his eyes to heaven, reflects the truth expressed here. God is infinitely exalted and absolutely righteous and holy. Before him we are mere creatures of the dust upon earth and, moreover, sinners. We are utterly dependent upon him not only for life and breath but for grace and pardon for sin, for his mercy. His heavenly majesty must fill us with awe, even as the wonder that he is yet also our covenant God who condescends to know us in his love in Christ drives out terror and dread.

There was a time in the history of the church in the transition to the Middle Ages, and throughout them, when the exalted majesty of God and of the glorified Christ was so misused that God in Christ was almost unapproachable, except through mediators like Mary and the saints, who would mediate with the Mediator. The Belgic Confession addresses this practice in Article 26, "Of Christ's Intercession." Today the pendulum has swung to the opposite extreme, under the influence of humanistic Arminianism, to the extent that the reverence of faith, the fear of God, has been destroyed in the modern church. The admonition of the text is one we need to hear: "for God is in heaven, and thou upon earth: therefore let thy words be few" (Eccl. 5:2).

The word of God points us to further reason, rooted in the vanity of the world under the sun. "For a dream cometh through a multitude of business" (Eccl. 5:3). After the labors of the day with its busy cares, worries, and stress, one's sleep is often disturbed by the random wandering of the mind in dreams in the night. Such dreams are an empty vanity. In like manner, "a fool's voice is known by multitude of words" (v. 3). In a "multitude of words" the vanity of sin is to be found. The same random wandering of the dreaming mind comes now in the speech of the fool's voice, so that "in the multitude of words there wanteth not sin" (Prov. 10:19). While this is true in general, the point of the text is sharper, for it has in view words uttered before God. Man in his rashness with his mouth, his irreverence before God, reveals himself a fool. He himself is vanity. Much of that which passes for the worship of God in our age has this character. It is senseless and thus profane, like the prayer of the Pharisee, concerned with his own importance, full of man's voice, but with no true fear of God. It is the sacrifice of fools. "But fear thou God" (Eccl. 5:7) is a needed warning for us also.

This truth is next applied to the vow. "When thou vowest a vow unto God, defer not to pay it; for he hath no pleasure in fools: pay that which thou hast vowed" (v. 4). Such vows were a voluntary act of devotion. They were made before God in gratitude for his goodness and grace. Sometimes they were an act of thanksgiving, as in the case of Jephthah the judge, in anticipation of God's blessings. Vows, also necessary ones, such as entering into marriage or when presenting our children for baptism, are profound spiritual acts, which call God to witness. Similar to an oath, the principle of the Heidelberg Catechism in question and answer 102, concerning the oath, applies to them, namely: "calling upon God, as the only searcher of hearts, to bear witness to the truth, and to punish me if I swear falsely; which honor is due to no creature."[1]

Jesus references this passage among others when he warns against rash and profane swearing which characterized the church of that day, and tells us to "let your communication be, Yea, yea; Nay, nay" (Matt. 5:37). The vow was to be a solemn act of gratitude to God, grounded in his promises and blessings, made in consciousness of the truth that he alone enabled one to keep and

---

1   Heidelberg Catechism Q&A 102, in Schaff, *Creeds of Christendom*, 3:344-345.

perform it. This is still the case in our marriage and baptismal vows. The world in which we live has no longer any conception of the seriousness of the oath or vow, not even a superstitious regard. The Christian church likewise, in its tolerance of divorce and remarriage, no longer takes the vow seriously, yet "the Lord hath been witness between thee and the wife of thy youth" (Mal. 2:14).

The abuse of the oath or vow is a serious matter, as the text points out: God "hath no pleasure in fools" (Eccl. 5:4). King Saul troubled the people of God with such an oath, which he placed upon them for his own vain glory. The people were robbed of a complete victory over the Philistines that day and led into sin because of it (1 Sam. 14:24–46). We do well to take the warning of Ecclesiastes 5 seriously. Solomon adds: "Better it is that thou shouldest not vow, than that thou shouldest vow and not pay" (Eccl. 5:5).

Vows were often connected with thank offerings and sacrifices that pointed to Christ, and as such they were serious acts of devotion, faith, and worship. The fool is one who is "rash with [his] mouth" in what he utters before God (v. 2). Solomon warns: "Suffer not thy mouth to cause thy flesh to sin; neither say thou before the angel, that it was an error" (v. 6). The point is that a rash vow leaves one guilty before God. Vowing what cannot be performed or making a careless vow profanes the glory of God. Seeking then to worm one's way out of it compounds the error. The picture is that of making excuses before the priest, the angel or messenger of God, so as to take back the vow, to thus make it void and not have to fulfill it. It makes a mockery of the spiritual character of the vow by seeking to reduce it to a simple mistake. God judges such sin, and Solomon adds: "wherefore should God be angry at thy voice, and destroy the work of thine hands?" (v. 6).

God visits the sin, not only of profane swearing but also of vows made in an empty and vain manner. Vows before God, taken consciously in his presence and resting upon his promises and in his grace to keep and perform them, are blessed— for he who is the witness to them is also the only one who can give us the grace to perform them. The word of God therefore brings both the warning and the calling together here. "For in the multitude of dreams and many words there are also divers vanities: but fear thou God" (v. 7). The fear of God must stand at the heart of all worship, prayer, and the making and performance of the vow. That fear is the reverence of faith, which stands before the majesty of God who is in heaven and sovereign over all things. The life of the world is full of the vanity of sin, but in the presence of the sovereign and exalted God and in his fear there is peace. Drawing near to God in godly fear in Christ, seeking his grace and waiting to hear, we enter into the blessings of living communion with God. Like the publican who drew near to God confessing himself a sinner in need of God's mercy, we also go down to our house justified, righteous before God in his grace for "he that humbleth himself shall be exalted" (Luke 18:14).

Fleeing Covetousness in the Fear of God

8. If thou seest the oppression of the poor, and violent perverting of judgment and justice in a province, marvel not at the matter: for he that is higher than the highest regardeth; and there be higher than they.
9. Moreover the profit of the earth is for all: the king himself is served by the field.
10. He that loveth silver shall not be satisfied with silver; nor he that loveth abundance with increase: this is also vanity.
11. When goods increase, they are increased that eat them: and what good is there to the owners thereof, saving the beholding of them with their eyes?
12. The sleep of a labouring man is sweet, whether he eat little or much: but the abundance of the rich will not suffer him to sleep.—Ecclesiastes 5:8–12

Ecclesiastes 5:7 ends on the note: "but fear thou God." This is the sum of the whole matter. Yet man shows in his folly that he does not fear God when he enters God's house and utters his vows before him. It ought not to surprise us therefore when we see oppression and perverting of justice. He who does not fear God regards not his neighbor. "If thou seest the oppression of the poor, and violent perverting of judgment and justice in a province, marvel not at the matter" (v. 8).

With this observation Solomon introduces several observations concerning human life. Solomon's kingdom was a well-ordered one with chief officers, princes, captains and other rulers, not only in the military but in the levy for the work of the temple and other projects (1 Kings 5:13–18; 9:17–23); this organization continued even into the reign of Ahab (1 Kings 20:13–21). This ordering of the kingdom involved also judges and administrative officials along. The division into provinces and their administration took the form of a hierarchy of higher and lower officials exactly "that the dissoluteness of men might be restrained."[2] The need for it is that man, by nature a sinner, having no fear of God, walks in covetousness and abuses power and authority. It is the responsibility of those who are higher to watch over those under them. But corruption and oppression are still not abolished for they pervade the life of men so that those who are higher are by nature no different. Solomon tells us: "marvel not at the matter: for he that is higher than the highest regardeth; and there be higher than they" (Eccl. 5:8). The king himself sees what is happening in the kingdom and beyond but also that God the eternal king, who is Lord of all, regards it. God will also judge the works of men. He is to be feared.

The second observation he sets before us is the boundary of man's life. "Moreover the profit of the earth is for all: the king himself is served by the field" (v. 9). The picture is that of tilling a field and the earth yielding its increase to the advantage and profit of

---

2   Belgic Confession 36, in Schaff, *Creeds of Christendom*, 3:432.

all who dwell in the land. All live by the fruit of the field. Food and drink are the necessary boundary of man's life, his portion of his labor under the sun (vv. 18–19). However high a man's estate, even that of the king, he is dependent on that most basic necessity of daily bread and the produce of the land.

Yet the root of so much oppression and corruption is the seeking of earthly riches in covetousness, even though the things of this life are but vanity and for a moment. They are not an end in themselves, yet men seek them as if they were the treasure of a man's life. This yields the third observation: "He that loveth silver shall not be satisfied with silver; nor he that loveth abundance with increase: this is also vanity" (v. 10). The things of this life are the necessary portion under the sun. The folly of sin is that it leads man to seek the things of this life as if they will satisfy his soul. Because of sin, the things of this world present themselves to the eye as that which is to be desired as an end in itself, as that which will make one happy. This belongs to the deceitfulness of sin, with which we struggle. But in the heart of a man who does not fear God, this desire brings him into bondage to uncertain riches and to covetousness, the lust for them. Earthly abundance does not satisfy. Enough, whether of gold and silver or abundance, is never enough.

Jesus makes the same point that Solomon is making in the chapter, when he warns us: "Take heed, and beware of covetousness: for a man's life consisteth not in the abundance of the things which he possesseth" (Luke 12:15). He then proceeds to tell the parable of the rich fool who will build bigger barns and to whom God says, "Thou fool, this night thy soul shall be required of thee: then whose shall those things be, which thou hast provided?" (Luke 12:20). Jesus continues: "So is he that layeth up treasure for himself, and is not rich toward God" (v. 21).

Jesus is, in effect, summarizing Ecclesiastes 5 and much of Ecclesiastes 6. The viewpoint, however, is slightly different. Solomon points us to the vanity of covetousness and seeking earthly riches as it is manifested even in this present life. We read: "When goods increase, they are increased that eat them: and what good is there to the owners thereof, saving the beholding of them with the eyes?" (Eccl. 5:11).

He makes a twofold point: first, that as wealth increases so do the demands upon it. The cost of living expands with one's paycheck so that there is no real progress or getting ahead. They simply increase that eat it up. Pursuing earthly riches is a vain treadmill that does not profit. Second, where riches do increase and are heaped up as stored treasure, there is no real good or profit in them. Solomon had great storehouses for treasure and armories. He asks what genuine good did it do to me? All you can do is look at it. To put it in another form, a closet full of shoes, once the latest fashion and style—what good are they? You can wear only one pair of shoes at a time. Heaped gold, if you spend it, is eaten up; if you hoard it, all you can do is look at it.

But that is not the end of the matter. Hoarded treasure needs to be kept, housed, guarded, so that a man can become a slave of his possessions. Jesus says of this,

19. Lay not up for yourselves treasures upon earth, where moth and rust doth corrupt, and where thieves break through and steal:
20. But lay up for yourselves treasures in heaven, where neither moth nor rust doth corrupt and where thieves do not break through nor steal." (Matt. 6:19–20)

Solomon, looking at the vanity of such treasure from the viewpoint of this world under the sun, makes essentially the same point in a slightly different manner. We read: "The sleep of a laboring man is sweet, whether he eat little or much: but the abundance of the rich will not suffer him to sleep" (Eccl. 5:12). The laboring man, by way of contrast to the rich, is poor; he has little. He has the fruit of the hard work of the day, his portion or his daily bread. Yet it was obtained by hard work whether he eats a small meal or a large one; and by implication in the light of verses 18–20, he eats it with thanksgiving as from the hand of his heavenly Father. He is tired from the day's labor and can sleep at night. Jesus said: "Take no thought for the morrow: for the morrow shall take thought for the things of itself. Sufficient unto the day is the evil thereof" (Matt. 6:34).

The rich man, like the rich fool in Jesus' parable, cannot do so. He must either build bigger barns or live in fear of losing what he has because "moth and rust" do indeed corrupt and "thieves break through and steal" (Matt. 6:19). He lives in anxiety and fear, full of fretful care. He tosses and turns on his bed. The very "abundance of the rich will not suffer him to sleep" (Eccl. 5:12). By implication the rich man here is also like that of Psalm 73, a man ruled by covetousness in unbelief. "How are they brought into desolation, as in a moment! they are utterly consumed with terrors" (Ps. 73:19). Fear of loss, fear of being robbed or cheated troubles his sleep. Beholding it with his eyes only adds to his worry. Behind it all stands the reality that he must die and then whose shall those things be?

For the children of God earthly prosperity is a passing thing of this life at best. It is not our treasure. It is a means to serve the Lord and his kingdom, never an end in itself. When it becomes that, through the infirmity of the flesh and covetousness, then we also will spend sleepless nights to no profit. The sinful weakness Solomon describes cleaves to us, hence as he has said, "But fear thou God" (Eccl. 5:7).

Nothing in His Hand

13. There is a sore evil which I have seen under the sun, namely, riches kept for the owners thereof to their hurt.
14. But those riches perish by evil travail: and he begetteth a son, and there is nothing in his hand.
15. As he came forth of his mother's womb, naked shall he return to go as he came, and shall take nothing of his labour, which he may carry away in his hand.

16. And this also is a sore evil, that in all points as he came, so shall he go: and what profit hath he that hath laboured for the wind?
17. All his days also he eateth in darkness, and he hath much sorrow and wrath with his sickness.—Ecclesiastes 5:13–17

In the preceding verse, the text concluded, "the abundance of the rich will not suffer him to sleep" (Eccl. 5:12). Riches for a man given to covetousness bring with them fretful care and worry lest they be lost. In verses 13–17, the Preacher turns to this reality of loss by again describing what is seen under the sun in the life of men. What is seen is a sore or grievous evil, a spiritual sickness. "There is a sore evil which I have seen under the sun, namely, riches kept for the owners thereof to their hurt" (v. 13).

What is this evil? Riches kept for or by the owners thereof. The picture is one of a guarded hoard, like a walled prison, a secured barn, a bank vault, acquired by heaping and gathering and building bigger barns and treasure hoards. The owner is truly rich according to this world. The world about us proclaims that this is a good thing, for riches and wealth give one security, power, and the ability to enjoy life, lifting a man above his fellows. Yet these riches are hoarded "to their hurt" that is, to the owner's own hurt, particularly of his soul, in covetousness (v. 13). The word of God declares, "this is a sore evil," which the text further explains in two ways.

First, "But those riches perish by evil travail: and he begetteth a son, and there is nothing in his hand" (v. 14). The "evil travail" is not specified. It may be a bad business decision, some physical or natural calamity, or upheaval in the world. The precise circumstance is not the point. Trouble comes; the riches are lost or destroyed, or they perish. They are gone, and of them the once rich man now has nothing. He is reduced to poverty. His hand is empty, and his son has no inheritance. Where earthly riches are one's only treasure, the loss of them leaves one with nothing. The man who is not rich toward God gives no spiritual treasure to his children; and if his earthly riches fly away, he is empty handed. His riches are vanity, and he himself is vain.

Solomon does not mean that this loss of earthly riches happens to all rich men, but examples of it are frequent enough, as warnings from God to testify to both the people of God and the world of sin as well of the folly of trusting and seeking after uncertain riches. The man who would keep his riches under the sun has no peace, for an evil travail can and does carry them away. He cannot by his own power truly keep them, though in his pride of heart he deceives himself concerning them. This also besets us, so that the psalmist in Psalm 73 speaks of his battle with this temptation when he says: "For I was envious at the foolish, when I saw the prosperity of the wicked" (v. 3). The rich man of this world, who trusts in uncertain riches is not simply wicked, but spiritually foolish, though he may think that he is the smartest person in the room because of his riches. "Therefore pride compasseth them about as a chain" (v. 6).

Second, regardless of his keeping of his earthly treasure in this world, he himself, the rich man, flies away. This second further explanation is universal and absolute: he shall die. "As he came forth of his mother's womb, naked shall he return to go as he came, and shall take nothing of his labour, which he may carry away in his hand" (Eccl. 5:15). Whatever legacy of the things of this world a man leaves behind him, he himself leaves. He came into the world naked, that is, with nothing, and so also will he leave it. The text as it were piles up the horror of the reality of death under the sun. First, as he came so shall he go; second, he shall take nothing of his labour; third, he may carry nothing away in his hand. He is stripped. His labor is vain and he is empty; he has nothing.

This confronts all of us in the labor and toil of life under the sun. Solomon who had wrought many works feels the weight of it. "And this is a sore evil, that in all points as he came, so shall he go" (v. 16). Yet the issue is not simply death, but that the one who is here described as leaving this life is one who has no fear of God, who has accomplished nothing, of whom nothing of value abides. "And what profit hath he that hath labored for the wind?" (v. 16). His earthly riches and treasures are the wind: empty air that blows away. Seeking earthly riches as the end and goal of life is a vain striving after the wind, after that which does not and cannot profit. Riches cannot deliver from death. Moreover, death as the judgment of God upon sin is such that riches cannot obtain righteousness, pardon for sin, or deliverance before God. The man striving after uncertain riches is a fool striving and laboring after the wind.

Yet the world abounds with this seeking of material riches, with seeking the god of materialism, mammon. It preaches such laboring after the wind, and its song fills our ears as we are also in the flesh and have need of earthly things. We have the calling to labor, to provide for our families. We seek to establish businesses and make them prosper. We are called to so labor in this life under the sun; but if this be the end and goal of our life, if it is first, and not subordinate to seeking the things above, then we also fall into the folly of seeking after the wind. The text calls for some sober assessment of our spiritual priorities. The picture is not one of pessimism. There is positive instruction to be heard in verses 18–20, but we will not rightly understand its blessedness for a child of God, as the gift of God (v. 19), unless we first make a right evaluation of the folly of sin that seeks uncertain riches and labors after the wind.

The word of God then brings the picture of this unbelieving laborer after the wind to its concluding assessment. While a child of God may struggle because of the flesh and the temptations of indwelling sin, the man described here is the rich, unbelieving, and reprobate fool, and the consequences described are of his seeking after the wind. His days are very different from those of the one blessed of God. The wicked man does not "enjoy the good of all his labor" (v. 18). Rather, his days, all his days, have a certain character: "All his days also he eateth in darkness, and he hath much sorrow and wrath with his sickness" (v. 17).

The viewpoint is not one day or a collection of days but the organic whole of his life, the tenor or character of his days, and that particularly in the context of the rich man who heaped and gathered and then lost it all through an evil travail. His days are spent in darkness, darkness of mind, of gloom and disappointment, a darkness that is the consequence of that spiritual darkness without the light of the knowledge of God and his fear. In darkness man heaped and gathered. Enough was never enough. In darkness he lost much sleep worrying over his riches, seeking to guard them from evil travail, and yet the travail came upon him. Riches were his god. Losing them, he now has nothing, and he will die and carry nothing away. He has striven for the wind and obtained empty air.

He ate his meals in that darkness, and the loss of his riches now reminds him of that loss whenever he sits down. He is sick at heart; frustration, anger, and bitterness of soul are his portion. The sickness mentioned is the sickness of his soul without true peace and joy, rather than that of the body. It is a spiritual sickness over the very emptiness of his life. This bitterness of soul is directed at the circumstances that robbed and cheated him of his riches. It is an anger directed not just at men, which may have been the instrument, but at God who is Lord of all. His sickness is a spiritual one, not a physical one.

It is out of that bondage to covetousness and that darkness rooted in man's depravity that grace brings us as children of God and gives to us the light of life, even eternal life. That blessing gives us to eat and drink with a well-founded joy; "This is the gift of God" (v. 19).

His Portion, the Gift of God

18. Behold that which I have seen: it is good and comely for one to eat and to drink, and to enjoy the good of all his

labour that he taketh under the sun all the days of his life, which God giveth him: for it is his portion.

19. Every man also to whom God hath given riches and wealth, and hath given him power to eat thereof, and to take his portion, and to rejoice in his labour; this is the gift of God.

20. For he shall not much remember the days of his life; because God answereth him in the joy of his heart.— Ecclesiasties 5: 18–20

A profound contrast is introduced in this text: all is not darkness; rather, the light of grace shines upon the life of a child of God. The rich fool seeking uncertain riches, the wind of Ecclesiastes 5:16, has nothing in his hand. He is man by nature, in the darkness of sin and death, walking in the folly of unbelief. "And all his days also he eateth in darkness, and he hath much sorrow and wrath with his sickness" (v. 17). This we see in the world around us, though only by faith through the word. Solomon now addresses us: "Behold that which I have seen" (v. 18). He has in view another man, another portion, a work of grace, a gift of God, which is truly blessed. This too is seen under the sun but with the eye of faith in the light of the word of God.

Riches may be there: "Every man...to whom God hath given riches and wealth" (v. 19). Solomon may have himself in view— but the blessedness is not dependent on material riches; his true treasure is the fear of God. The laboring man (for the idea is that of a child of God who may be small in the eyes of the world) possesses it also, for his sleep is sweet (v. 12). This is the thing which is seen: "it is good and comely for one to eat and to drink, and to enjoy the good of all his labour that he taketh under the sun all the days of his life, which God giveth him: for it is his portion" (v. 18).

That it is "good and comely" (v. 18) sets the matter before us as a principle of life under the sun. What is fitting, given the very transitory character of life, is that one enjoy the fruit of his labor in its temporary character, not as a matter of self-indulgence, but as that which is fit and right according to God's design for man's earthly life. What is in harmony with man's nature as a creature of the dust, of flesh and blood, is that he eat and drink the fruit of his labor with enjoyment that, by implication, includes thanksgiving. It is his portion for the day, his daily bread. That is the purpose and design of food and drink, of the things of this life, of material wealth and well-being. It serves a transitory goal and passing purpose.

It is exactly the point that this the covetous man cannot do. Not satisfied with silver and gold (v. 10), he is given over to fretful care over earthly riches, keeping and hoarding that which is transitory, "the wind" (v. 16). He eats in darkness. That which is the good, fitting for his station and character of life, escapes him "all his days" (v. 17). The issue is the spiritual attitude of one of entering into the true blessings of life under God's care. The rich man would be in charge of his own portion. He would determine its boundaries, have it under his power and in his own hand. He would keep and hold, and yet an "evil travail" (v. 14) comes upon him, and it is taken from him, so that he dwells in bitterness and darkness of soul. Unbelievers sense this when they talk about simplifying life; but they are unable to do so because, being in bondage to covetousness, they can only live for the life of this world as an end in itself.

The description is not only of one or two occasions of contentment but of a whole pattern of life: "to enjoy the good of all his labour that he taketh under the sun all the days of his life" (v. 18); that is, not one day but "all the days of his life." It is to work and labor in the vanity of this life. It is to toil at one's calling from the Lord in the sweat of one's face, with toil that is wearisome, repetitive, and in itself vain, for it passes away. It is to work, eat, sleep, and go to work again, whether in business or in cleaning the supper dishes. But in the midst of it, the believer is content, possessing an enjoyment of life that is not dependent on material circumstances and things. It is that which is good and comely, that is, beautiful:

to be blessed with the proper enjoyment of life that is fitting for man's nature. Such labor and toil, yea, even that repetitive labor which is transitory, is that "which God giveth him." Why? "For it is his portion!" (v. 18).

Now, in principle, God gives to each one his labor, calling, and vocation. The measure of our days is in God's hands. Also the wicked receive their place in this life, their talents and gifts, their circumstances and opportunities but the text is describing something more. The idea of blessing, we might say, is of one who walks in that will of God, who walks by faith in the fear of God and his design for human life, also after the fall, where he must labor in the sweat of his face as a creature of the dust who returns to the dust. To that believer is given the grace of contentment. The bitter unbelieving rich man, whose treasure is here below, does not possess the joy of contentment "all the days of his life," here below.

To whom is this given? To the unbelieving rich fool? Not at all. To all men by some common grace? Such a notion would be to fail to understand the text entirely. God gives to him "that is good in his sight" (2:26), that is, to his justified, believing children, this blessing. Do we possess it by nature or of any merit? No. Have we attained unto it perfectly? No, but it is a matter of constant prayer, for both the portion for the day and the grace of contentment. But this portion is given to them that fear God, and it is for them alone. "This is the gift of God" (Eccl. 5:19). God works it by his providence and by his grace in their hearts. It is a blessing of salvation, which delivers from bondage to covetousness. Only one whose treasure is in heaven can so eat and drink with such joy, because he tastes the blessedness of a portion from the hand of his heavenly Father, his portion for the day. Understand well, this also is a blessing that is in Christ, who has delivered us from the darkness of sin and death, the bondage of corruption, also the bondage of covetousness, and brought us into the light of life which is eternal.

This is really Solomon's confession: "Every man also to whom God hath given riches and wealth, and hath given him power to eat thereof, and to take his portion, and to rejoice in his labour; this is the gift of God" (v. 19). Such was Solomon himself, not only as one to whom God gave riches and wealth, but also as to whom he gave the power to eat thereof, for as he will point out, to some he gives such gifts but no "power to eat" of them (Eccl. 6:2). These earthly blessings, which pass away and belong to this present vanity as a portion under the sun, are also a gift of God. This gift, in contrast to the rich fool's darkness and bitterness, is very really a gift of God, even though it is only a portion for this present passing life. It is a profound wonder to stand in this present life, to eat and drink of that portion with thanksgiving in contentment of heart and rejoice in that portion. The world does not possess this blessing. It is by grace, as a gift of God in Christ. Its foundation, which ultimately rests in the cross of Christ, is given us of God as a gift and portion for the day, by which we receive every creature of God with thanksgiving (1 Tim. 4:4–5). The world of darkness lying in covetousness does not know it. Even in food and drink and the eating and drinking thereof, God's grace is particular!

"For he shall not much remember the days of his life; because God answereth him in the joy of his heart" (Eccl. 5:20). Thus does Solomon draw out the reason for this blessing. The years of life pass in the transitory vanity of this present life. They fade away. Fretful care, worries over uncertain riches, fruitless toils for what is only an earthly and vain end characterize the life of wicked men. God gives to his people a different blessing. The passing of the years, yes, also with their trials and sorrows in the things of this life, are passing years that are not remembered. Why? Because riches lost or gained are not our treasure. God is the source of the real joy of heart in daily life under the sun. God answers the prayers for our provision and for the grace of contentment and makes what are the passing moments of life, which are temporary, blessed in him. God does this! He is the author also of this true joy, though it be but the passing enjoyment of life in the vanity of this world. To have peace with God and live under his almighty fatherly care makes all the difference. The result is the opposite of a worldly man's bitter regrets and remembrance that brings no joy. "For he shall not much remember the days of his life; because God answereth him in the joy of his heart" (v. 20). It is God's doing. He is the author of this blessing of peace and contentment even to old age "because God answereth him in the joy of his heart" (v. 20).

CHAPTER 6

"An Evil Disease"

1. There is an evil which I have seen under the sun, and it is common among men:
2. A man to whom God hath given riches, wealth, and honour, so that he wanteth nothing for his soul of all that he desireth, yet God giveth him not power to eat thereof, but a stranger eateth it: this is vanity, and it is an evil disease.—Ecclesiastes 6:1–2

The word of God introduces a new observation of what Solomon, the Preacher, has seen under the sun (v. 1). This observation stands in contrast to that which he has just shown, that which is "good and comely" (Eccl. 5:18). What is good, as a gift of God under the sun in the vanity of this present life, is to eat and drink, to enjoy the good of one's portion. That portion is transitory and its present enjoyment in contentment its proper use. This, however, he has shown is a gift of God, a singular blessing, not only in outward circumstances but of grace, in which God answers a man in the "joy of his heart" (v. 20). This blessing is a gift of God unto his people.

To the one who is evil in the sight of God, the wicked man, is given rather the travail to heap and gather. He is in bondage to covetousness. This results in the evil that Solomon has "seen under the sun" (6:1). This evil is the consequence of his sin and depravity, of his walk in covetousness, and of his desire for earthly riches as an end in themselves. It is thus in harmony with man's state as he lies fallen in the midst of sin and death and under the curse of God upon sin.

This evil must be understood then both as the fruit of sin and as a judgment of God upon sin that comes upon fallen man. It is an expression of God's wrath, a working of the curse of judgment in the life of men. That judgment of God does not come upon the world only as an eternal judgment. God judges among fallen men in time as well as in eternity; it is a temporal as well as an eternal judgment. Through the fall into sin, the world was subjected to vanity, to the misery of sin and its consequences, to evil "seen under the sun" (v. 1).

In the opening verses the Preacher states what this evil is, as it is seen among men, and he will develop more fully what is intended as he unfolds it in the chapter. First, however, he would call our attention to it as something that can be seen and noted under the sun. The reason to attend to it is this: "it is common among men" (Eccl. 6:1). It is seen more than once. It is seen in the life of the world among men on every side. It is common or heavy, a thing that multiplies in the life of men under the sun.

What is this evil, or misery, common among men? "A man to whom God hath given riches, wealth, and honor, so that he wanteth nothing for his soul of all that he desireth, yet God giveth him not power to eat thereof, but a stranger eateth it: this is vanity, and it is an evil disease" (v. 2). It is well to ponder this picture and what is said, for it speaks of two gifts. The one gift which is given is outward and external and readily seen. The other gift is not given nor seen in the same way.

A man to whom God giveth or upon whom God bestows riches, wealth, and honor—who would not desire such a portion? Material riches and the wealth and abundance which they purchase is a portion given among men by God's providence. With it comes also among men honor, a place of dignity, a position of power and respect. There is a certain order to the words used from riches, to wealth, and to honor, for that is the sequence among men in the vanity of this world.

Does that mean that this outward circumstance is given only to the wicked? No, for he has spoken of a child of God, who likewise has received wealth and honor, but with the gift also to eat of his portion and rejoice in it (Eccl. 5:19). Solomon himself was such. But here he has in view the children of this world, the man described by Asaph in Psalm 73:7: "their eyes stand out with fatness: they have more than heart could wish." It may well be that Solomon had that psalm also before him as he ponders with us what he sees under the sun.

The man he has in view has it all: riches, wealth, and honor, "so that he wanteth nothing for his soul of all that he desireth" (Eccl. 6:2). In earthly terms, he lacks nothing. He has everything heart could wish. He wants or lacks "nothing for his soul," that is, for his life in this world. *Soul* refers here to the needs of body and mind in earthly terms, the reference is not to the spiritual needs of his soul. He lacks "nothing for his soul of all that he desireth." His portion is such that all that he desires in this life, in this world, from food and drink to the pleasures of life, whether wholesome or sinful, he has the means to satisfy.

God in his providence gives these things to him. Note well, it is the Lord's doing. The man himself may deem it his own doing. He may boast of his own achievements, his own labor and accomplishments, but it is under the hand of God. "God hath given" (v. 2), God gives to each his portion in this life. If a man prospers in his way in the things of this life, this too is of the Lord.

But what is described here is not grace. Grace is not in things. Grace is not measured by riches, wealth, and honor in the world. Solomon sees one who is "known that it is man" (Eccl. 6:10), that is, one who is born of Adam, a creature of the dust who shall return to the dust.

That brings the second element before us, which is not always as clearly discernible but is also seen under the sun: that God's gift of riches, wealth, and honor is a judgment of God upon the covetousness of men, a work of his divine displeasure, not of grace.

For this man under consideration, though he have all these things, "yet God giveth him not power to eat thereof" (v. 2). He is not given the gift "to eat and drink, and to enjoy the good of all his labour" (Eccl. 5:18). He is not given "power to eat thereof, and to take his portion, and to rejoice in his labour" (v. 19). "This is the gift of God" (v. 19), and he does not have it! It is not given unto him by the hand of God. The reference is not to a physical problem, such as a medical condition which makes him unable to eat, though that may not be excluded, but to an internal problem, a problem of the heart. His covetousness and bondage to the things of this life deny him the power to eat and enjoy.

It might not always seem so. It did not seem that way to Asaph as he struggled with this in Psalm 73. Inwardly, however, as Asaph learned when he contemplated the end of the wicked: "they are utterly consumed with terrors" (v. 19). God sets "them in slippery places" and casts "them down to destruction" (v. 18). Their end is one of eternal misery and, in this life, fear of losing all they have, for it is their only treasure. Solomon, however, adds a certain element to our understanding here. Because such a man "is not rich toward God" (Luke 12:21) also even in this life, he does not truly enjoy the blessings of the things which he possesses. The very covetousness of such a man means he is never satisfied. "He that loveth silver shall not be satisfied with silver; nor he that loveth abundance with increase: this also is vanity" (Eccl. 5:10).

He has all that his soul could desire, lacks nothing of all that his soul might want or desire, and yet truly enjoys none of it because the love of God is not there, neither in his heart toward God nor in God's attitude toward him. He may have houses and lands, have banquets and all abundance, may even seem to have more than heart could wish, but "better is a little with the fear of the Lord than great treasure and trouble therewith. Better is a dinner of herbs where love is, than a stalled ox and hatred therewith" (Prov. 15:16–17).

The wicked from that viewpoint do not even truly enjoy the things of this life. The pleasures of sin, of the world and its covetousness and abundance bring no true joy. Covetousness is bondage: "The way of the wicked is an abomination unto the Lord: but he loveth him that followeth after righteousness" (Prov. 15:9).

"God giveth him not power to eat thereof, but a stranger eateth it" (Eccl. 6:2). A stranger or foreigner comes into his place and takes and eats the substance of his labor. Many of the commentaries, which make the book one written by one living after the time of the captivity, instead of by Solomon, apply this text to the state of Israel and the devouring of their substance by foreign powers. While this might be an illustration, yet the text is speaking about the life of individual men and of a thing "common among men" under the sun (v. 1). Such a view really misses the point of the text. It is seen in the world to this day that the wicked in their covetousness devour one another,that one labors and another, and that a stranger, comes in his place. Earthly riches make themselves wings and fly away. They are vanity. It is true in every age, as Solomon has said: "There is a sore evil which I have seen under the sun, namely, riches kept for the owners thereof to their hurt. But those riches perish by an evil travail: and he begetteth a son, and there is nothing in his hand" (Eccl. 5:13–14). God's judgment upon the covetousness of men rather confronts us. "God giveth him not" (Eccl. 6:2).

Seeing these things as children of God we may well tremble: "How hardly shall they that have riches enter into the kingdom of God!" (Luke 18:24). It is by grace alone. Covetousness and God's judgment upon it bring the world to empty vanity. Pondering the circumstance described, we read of it: "This is vanity, and it is an evil disease" (Eccl. 6:2). It is a grievous misery, and in that sense, a disease of the soul of fallen man and the folly of sin in which he lies in the midst of death. It is God, in Christ alone, who delivers from such misery and gives both our portion in this life and the gift of joy therein. But he gives also an eternal treasure in a joy that fades not away.

The Better Lot of One Stillborn

3.   If a man beget an hundred children, and live many years, so that the days of his years be many, and his soul be not filled with good, and also that he have no burial; I say, that an untimely birth is better than he.

4.   For he cometh in with vanity, and departeth in darkness, and his name shall be covered with darkness.

5.   Moreover he hath not seen the sun, nor known any thing: this hath more rest than the other.—Ecclesiastes 6:3–5

It may be well, at this point, to recall the direction in which Solomon would lead us. He has in view especially young people who are at the beginning of life's pathway and to whom he would say: "Remember now thy Creator in the days of thy youth" (Eccl. 12:1). He would also direct us to "the whole duty of man" which is centrally to "fear God" (Eccl. 12:13). This section beginning in chapter five concerning covetousness and its bondage is a warning, especially then to young people.

That warning is framed by a picture, at this point, of the man given to covetousness who seeks his treasure in this world. That man is in bondage under the judgment of God's wrath against sin. Riches he may be given, but God withholds from him the true joy of life, the gift of contentment: "God giveth him not power to eat thereof". He walks in an "evil disease" of soul; a grievous misery is his existence (Eccl. 6:2). It is this reality Solomon would develop further to underscore it.

Solomon underscores his point in a striking way: "If a man beget an hundred children and live many years, so that the days of his years be many" (v. 3). He draws a picture before us of long life and the begetting of sons and daughters, yea, even a hundred children. In verse 6, he expands on this idea of long life by a number twice a thousand (or 2000), that is, one who lives twice as long as Methuselah (Gen. 5:25–27). Solomon evidently wants us to contemplate the genealogies of men recorded in Scripture, particularly those before the flood, though not limiting them to that period.

Such men did live, not only in the line of Seth, but also in the line of Cain. They had very long earthly lives, their days were many, and their children were many so that a hundred would not have been impossible. Contemplating those long lives with their many years, we might well be inclined to desire such long days in the earth. Solomon himself, when he asked of God wisdom, could have asked such a gift instead, and God gave it to him in measure, even though he did not ask for it.

But what of it? If the "days of his years be many, and his soul be not filled with good" (Eccl. 6:3), is it a blessing or a curse? If a man's soul be not filled with good, what profit is it? If a man's soul is not filled with good, then it is filled with the restless evil of sin. He may have earthly riches and long life, but his soul enjoys no true good. Rather than being "filled with good," it is empty, barren of true joy, having no contentment, no peace with God. In the context, he lacks the gift or power to eat of that which he possesses in joy of heart. Because he is wretched, the prolonging of his days is no blessing. Solomon adds, "and also that he have no burial" (v. 3); he has then not even the honor and dignity of a grave in his end.

The time in view here, in the light of the thought of many days, is not that of the captivity of Israel or the return from exile, as many commentators would have it, but the time of wicked Lamech and his sons Jabal, Jubal, and Tubal-cain, who lived long lives in the era in which they lived. They drowned in the flood. They had no burial, in the sense of the honor and dignity of laying one to rest. They were swept away as were all the seed of Cain. They had earthly riches, the pleasures and powers of the world were under their hand, yet they perished in God's judgment. Can it be said of wicked Lamech and his history and that of his sons that his soul was filled with good? Their long years were vanity and their souls empty of good. Nor did they have a burial, but rather they were erased from the earth, like Jezebel after them.

Thus Solomon exclaims: "I say, that an untimely birth is better than he" (v. 3). This is a rather sober thought. The reference is to a child conceived and born prematurely, to a miscarriage or to a child who is stillborn. Several things may be said from the text concerning the subject itself. The one born untimely, though miscarried, is nevertheless a person who comes into the world, passing from life through death. His birth is an untimely one. The viewpoint of the text is not, however, concerned with their eternal state after death. Solomon's focus is on what is seen under the sun and not that which is hidden from us. God's covenant promises in other places address the eternal state of the children of believers who die in such a manner. Rather he says of them: "this hath more rest that the other" (v. 5). That is, one whose birth is untimely has more rest than the one who has long life and begets many children but whose soul sees no good. The grave, in whatever form that takes, as seen under the sun, is a form of rest, for it is the end of the labor, toil, and travail of life. The description of such a child here is that of a person, of his birth, though untimely, and that as a person he has rest from this life. It certainly implies that such a person shall have his part in the resurrection at the last day, though that is an implication and not the focus of the text.

We must note carefully the point of comparison found in the text and what is set before us. The point of comparison is to draw a relation between the physical reality of one whose birth is untimely and the spiritual reality of one who, on the other hand, lives many days in many years but whose soul is not "filled with good" (v. 3).

Of one whose birth is untimely we read: "For he cometh in with vanity, and departeth in darkness, and his name shall be covered with darkness" (v. 4). The state of one whose birth is untimely is that of darkness in the physical sense, of obscurity. He never has a place in the labor and toil of this present life in the world; his name in this world, its life and activity, is covered with darkness. He is not known among men. His place is taken away before his birth. The text does not remove the possibility that he has a name before God, nor is the darkness spoken of that of God's wrath as such, but of his place under the sun.

The effect is also described: "Moreover he hath not seen the sun, nor known any thing" (v. 5). He has not seen or known the world under the sun nor walked through the years in its vanity. He passes briefly though this world, into the sleep of death and rest which comes at the end of life's journey.

The point of the text is that his portion, his lot, as one whose birth is untimely, is better than the man who has many days and years but whose soul is not filled with good. He has also "more rest than the other" (v. 5). It is not to the sorrow of one untimely born that we are to look but to the horror of one who lives many years with the riches, wealth, and honor of the world, with a house full of children, and yet in it all his soul is not filled with good. He is a wicked man.

The wicked man also comes into the world in vanity and darkness, but it is the spiritual darkness of sin and death. In that darkness of sin he labors and toils: "But the wicked are like the troubled sea, when it cannot rest, whose waters cast up mire and dirt" (Isa. 57:20). And for such, "There is no peace, saith my God, to the wicked" (v. 21). The wicked walks in darkness, at enmity with God, and will not come to the light. He labors and toils for the vanity of this world, because he himself is vanity and in vanity he came into the world. Never is he filled with good. He sees the sun, the glory of God's works under it, passes his days upon earth under the light of the sun, and the truth of God is not hidden from him. But his soul is in darkness and he follows after vanity. He too knows not any thing. Intellect, craft, or skill he may have, but true spiritual knowledge he does not have. It is a world in the folly of sin in which he toils. Its learning, for all its complexity, is still spiritually in darkness. Of that which fills the soul with good the wicked man also knows not any thing. It is not given him of God.

He seeks to leave his name in the earth, giving to lands and houses his name, seeking a memorial after him. But death carries him away. His name and place, though they endured through many years of labor and toil, are taken from him. God himself erases that name and place, and when man passes into the darkness of death, his name is covered in darkness, and his place remembers him no more.

What rest, even in the grave, does such a man have, who has labored all his life with the ceaseless activity of sin for the vanity of this world? All his treasure is lost to him. The stillborn has more rest than he. And if he has not even a burial, not even that dignity is left him. "For the face of the Lord is against them that do evil, to cut off the remembrance of them from the earth" (Ps. 34:16).

By way of contrast how blessed are God's children: "The Lord redeemeth the soul of his servants: and none of them that trust in him shall be desolate" (v. 22).

The Bread of the Mouth and the Soul

6. Yea, though he live a thousand years twice told, yet hath he seen no good: do not all go to one place?
7. All the labour of man is for his mouth, and yet the appetite is not filled.
8. For what hath the wise more than the fool? what hath the poor, that knoweth to walk before the living?—Ecclesiastes 6:6–8

We have seen that God gives to the man who is good in his sight, to his people, to eat and drink in contentment with their portion under the sun. This gift of God is not yet perfected in them because of sin and the infirmity of the flesh, but it is nevertheless a work of grace. To the wicked, held in the bondage of covetousness in various ways, this gift is denied in God's judgment. Solomon has spoken of the man who has may things in this life but "his soul be not filled with good" (Eccl. 6:3).

He now turns to that man to whom is given long life, for this was mentioned before and is considered desirable in the world.

The example he uses is that of one who lives more than twice the length of life given Methuselah: "Yea, though he live a thousand years twice told", a long life indeed, but in the bondage of covetousness, it is a long life characterized by the statement, "yet hath he seen no good" (v. 6). Not only is his soul not filled with good internally, but the good is really withheld from him altogether so that he sees it not. It never comes into his view.

Ungodly man may seek what seems good in his own eyes. He may heap and gather. He may seek after abundance and earthly riches, but his work is driven by a covetousness that finds its treasure below and seeks its satisfaction in earthly things. Such earthly treasures can never satisfy, to fill the soul with good. There is never enough, so that he never has an abiding joy and peace. We may be inclined to say, how can this be? The answer lies in the nature of covetousness: "He that loveth silver shall not be satisfied with silver; nor he that loveth abundance with increase" (Eccl. 5:10). To such a man in his bondage, enough is never enough. He is enslaved to heaping and gathering. Long life does not change this.

Not only so, but we also read: "do not all go to one place?" (Eccl. 6:6). He shall still die. He still comes in the darkness of sin and departs in darkness. He lives for this world and its vanity without seeing the good, which can only be known in God, and death at length carries him away. He goes to the grave, and his portion under the sun is taken from him. "The hoary head is a crown of glory, if it be found in the way of righteousness" (Prov. 16:31), but when it is found in the way of sin, worldly-mindedness and covetousness, it is not a glory but a horror to behold. The old unbelieving fool is one whose long life actually profited him nothing in this life. But he then also goes to the grave in shame and has nothing which he carries away with him. The stillborn, previously mentioned in the preceding verses, has more rest than he.

The Preacher directs us to a reason for this, bound up with the essential vanity of this world under the curse: "All the labor of man is for his mouth, and yet the appetite is not filled" (Eccl. 6:7). His appetite, literally his *soul* in the original, is not filled. The figure of the mouth and thus the appetite, the hunger of the body, reflects the reality of man's life and its vanity. Man works to eat that he may work again to eat again. Never does he, nor can he, lift himself above that cycle to some abiding good that satisfies. He is never truly filled so that the need and desire are quenched. This is the reality of man's life under the sun. If then he knows not the grace of contentment, he is most miserable.

Now this reality of the very empty vanity of earthly life, this need of life driven by the mouth, touches the child of God also. Under the sun we too must labor to eat and then labor again. Solomon raises this point also: "For what hath the wise more than the fool? what hath the poor, that knoweth to walk before the living?" (v. 8). The one who is wise is, after all, one who fears God, for that alone is the beginning of wisdom. The poor in the text, who "knows to walk," is one who holds God's word, walking by faith in the light of that knowledge. He knows how to walk. He may be poor in the things of this world, but he is first of all poor in spirit (Matt. 5:3). Yet he also must live in this world, labor for the needs of the body, and is held in the same circumstances of human life under the sun. Outwardly his life under the sun is bound by the same limits of the vanity of this present life as the life of fool.

Does that mean that there is no difference? In material terms, the organic reality of human life is the same for both the wise and the fool. Spiritually, however, there is a profound difference. The fool labors all his life for the bread that perishes, and in the end he himself perishes. He serves not God but mammon. The spiritual state of the covetous soul, held in the lusts of the flesh, is never satisfied even as his mouth never has enough and the appetite, the lust of his soul, is never satisfied. Since the cravings of his mouth and that of his soul are one and the same, the covetous man is held in bondage to the flesh.

In God's grace there is a better portion given unto the children of God. It is not measured by earthly things or circumstances. It is to have the bread of eternal life and to drink of the fountain of the water of life in Jesus Christ by faith. Our Savior, who by his Spirit gave also this word in Ecclesiastes, refers to the idea of it on more than one occasion. The text asks a rhetorical question: "For what hath the wise more than the fool?" (v. 8). The answer, which the text itself later gives, is this: he has the knowledge of God, the creator, the covenant God (Eccl. 11:9; 12:1). He has the fear of God and keeps his commandments by faith, walking a pathway that is by grace. He has Christ, the end of the law, for righteousness (Eccl. 12:13–14).

Jesus takes up this point of Ecclesiastes by way of contrast and directs us to himself as Immanuel, God with us. "Labour not for the meat which perisheth, but for that meat which endureth unto everlasting life, which the Son of man shall give unto you: for him hath God the Father sealed" (John 6:27). Jesus makes the same point under the figure of water when he speaks to the Samaritan woman.

13. Jesus answered and said unto her, Whosoever drinketh of this water shall thirst again:
14. But whosoever drinketh of the water that I shall give him shall never thirst; but the water that I shall give him shall be in him a well of water springing up into everlasting life. (John 4:13–14)

Jesus speaks of a believer who is fed by that living bread by faith in Jesus Christ and who drinks of that water of life. To that believer the answer to the question "what hath the wise more than the fool?" (Eccl. 6:8) is two-fold. In the outward circumstances of life they appear the same. The fool may even seem to prosper and be better off. But both the wise and the fool die and leave this life. The one is not above the other in earthly terms. Spiritually, however, the believer, who is wise in Christ, has a better portion, for his portion is not founded on outward circumstances.

Though known only by faith and not founded on the things of this present life, his spiritual blessings extend even to the things of this present life. For, though a child of God also labors for the needs of the body, it is given him in a measure to eat and drink with contentment of heart. He serves God and not mammon. Because he has been given "the meat which endureth" and "the well springing up into everlasting life," it is also given him in earthly things, "power to eat thereof, and to take his portion, and to rejoice in his labour; this is the gift of God" (Eccl. 5:19). It is such a gift of grace because it serves a life that seeks the things above. It is a gift in this present life to one who has eternal life.

Better Is the Sight of the Eyes

9. Better is the sight of the eyes than the wandering of the desire: this is also vanity and vexation of spirit.
10. That which hath been is named already, and it is known that it is man: neither may he contend with him that is mightier than he.
11. Seeing there be many things that increase vanity, what is man the better?
12. For who knoweth what is good for man in this life, all the days of his vain life which he spendeth as a shadow? for who can tell a man what shall be after him under the sun?—Ecclesiastes 6:9–12

"Better is the sight of the eyes" (Eccl. 6:9)—with these words Solomon introduces a conclusion to this section of Ecclesiastes, chapters five and six. His concern is that we spiritually take the warning regarding covetousness to ourselves. The sight of the eyes is that which stands before us this moment, under God's providence, as our portion of the day. It is what is given us, seen and known, the profit of the day's labor, our daily bread. It is the good, that which is fitting, and to be enjoyed as the blessing of the day. It is also that which the wicked man, given to covetousness, is not given to see. For though he live twice as long as Methuselah, "yet hath he seen no good" (Eccl. 6:6).

The problem is in man's soul. In discontent, he wanders in heart and mind. His soul roams about, covetousness always leading him away from what is immediately before him to all that he desires and lusts after. The wandering, or roaming about of the desire, the lust of men, brings with it only vexation of spirit, or more literally a striving after the wind which is thus one of futile frustration. Therefore, "Better is the sight of the eyes than the wandering of the desire: this is also vanity and vexation of spirit" (v. 9). Where discontent and covetousness rule, there can be only an empty futility, which striving is ultimately with God.

Solomon then returns to the point, which has been made before, of God's design in creation and now his judgment after the fall as an explanation of this futility: "That which hath been is named already, and it is known that it is man: neither may he contend with him that is mightier than he" (v. 10). This explanation takes us back to man's creation. It contains two conjoined elements. The first is the meaning of the name *man*. It refers to the first man, whose name was Adam, the Hebrew word derived from the word for *dust*. This emphasizes that man is of the earth earthy, a creature of the dust. Being fallen in sin, he receives its wages, "for dust thou art, and unto dust shalt thou return" (Gen. 3:19). The result: "Therefore the Lord God sent him forth from the garden of Eden, to till the ground from whence he was taken" (v. 23). Because this is so, all man's days are bound in a world subject to vanity. This is the judgment of God upon sin. Apart from the grace of God in Christ, he cannot return to paradise or enter into glory. He lies in the midst of death. Leaving aside the question of his eternal reward, man, in himself, in this world under the sun, can be only a creature of the dust, returning to the dust from whence he was taken. Covetousness leads him to pursue what is vain.

Yet man, who is dust (Adam), strives with this reality, for the text continues, "neither may he contend with him that is mightier than he" (Eccl. 6:10). Shall the dust contend with the Almighty, the creature with the Creator? But that is exactly what Adam did in his rebellion in the fall. The lie of the devil was "ye shall be as gods, knowing good and evil" (Gen. 3:5). In rebellion man sets himself in the place of God, in pride he lifts himself up to strive with God who is "mightier than he." This arrogance shows itself, of course, in many ways: in sin and rebellion, in lawlessness, in vain boasting in himself. Man seeks to change times and laws and seasons as if the life of man, the world, and all things are in his own hand. He would be his own lawgiver. Here, however, the focus is on the pride of man who so thinks he is in control of his life upon earth that in the wandering of his desire, in covetousness, he may contend with God and determine his own portion. The rebellion and pride of man rejects the confession: "O Lord, I know that the way of man is not in himself: it is not in man that walketh to direct his steps" (Jer. 10:23).

The fool says otherwise. He says, "I will build bigger barns and enjoy my ease," until, as Jesus himself illustrates, "God said unto him, Thou fool, this night thy soul shall be required of thee: then whose shall those things be, which thou hast provided?" (Luke 12:20). Nebuchadnezzar's boast in himself expresses the same spirit of exalted pride: "The king spake, and said, Is not this great Babylon, that I have built for the house of the kingdom by the might of my power and for the honour of my majesty?" (Dan. 4:30). The judgment of which he was forewarned came upon him. The Lord smote him, gave him to eat grass like an ox, and took his understanding from him until he was compelled to confess the Most High, the Almighty,

34. whose dominion is an everlasting dominion, and his kingdom is from generation to generation:
35. And all the inhabitants of the earth are reputed as nothing: and he doeth according to his will in the army of heaven, and among the inhabitants of the earth: and none can stay his hand, or say unto him, What doest thou? (Dan. 4:34–35)

Covetous man walks in that same spirit of Nebuchadnezzar. In his wandering desire after earthly things, he seeks not what is before him nor acknowledges that it is from God but will be his own master. His own will, his own plans and desires will rule according to his own imagination. The future is, in his blindness, deemed to be in his own hand, and yet it is not so. Man is a potsherd, a broken piece of clay pottery. God says to him: "Woe unto him that striveth with his maker! Let the potsherd strive with the potsherds of the earth. Shall the clay say to him that fashioned it, What makest thou? or thy work, He hath no hands?" (Isa. 45:9). Yet the covetous man denies that sovereign power of God, not only over great issues in his life, but in the wandering of his lust also over the very present reality of daily life as well. He says: "to day or to morrow we will go into such a city, and continue there a year, and buy and sell, and get gain" (James 4:13). To which the word of God in James, who may well have had Ecclesiastes 6 in view, answers: "Whereas ye know not what shall be on the morrow. For what is your life? It is even a vapour, that appeareth for a little time, and then vanisheth away. For that ye ought to say, If the Lord will, we shall live, and do this, or that (James 4:14–15).

Solomon makes the same point. He first reminds us: "Seeing there be many things that increase vanity, what is man the better?" (Eccl. 6:11). By *things* he has in view earthly things, earthly abundance. He has said: "When goods increase, they are increased that eat them" (Eccl. 5:11). Earthly riches, the things of this world, belong to vanity. When they increase, then vanity also increases, and man is not better off. He has still no profit in anything of abiding value. Nor can the riches truly satisfy. It is not in the things themselves that man covets and desires, to do so. It is not in their nature, in the stuff of this world under the sun, to give abiding profit or satisfaction that endures.

Solomon then adds: "For who knoweth what is good for man in this life, all the days of his vain life which he spendeth as a shadow? for who can tell a man what shall be after him under the sun?" (Eccl. 6:12). The life of man is as an insubstantial shadow moving over the ground that vanishes away; he is a vapor, as James puts it (James 4:14). He does not know what the morrow will bring. He may think it is in his own hand. He may deny there is a sovereign potter, deny that God has a hand in his life, but he is a fool in bondage. He does not know what is for his own good. Neither does he determine the course of his own steps. His wandering desire leads him to the delusion of his own power when he is actually but a vapor, a moving shadow on the ground, frail, weak, and brief. Not only is that which he pursues vanity; he is himself vanity. In the flowing stream of life he has no idea what the next bend in the river will bring, for he cannot see beyond the curve of the river. It may be placid water, or it may be whitewater rapids and destruction. His control of the future is a delusion and an attempt to strive and contend with his maker.

In pride man says within himself, I will have this or that, I will get this or that, turning from what is before him to his own imagination, relying on his own power. Yet he does not even know what the next day or hour may bring, even in daily matters of this life and his place in it. He is truly a shadow in himself. "For who can tell a man what shall be after him under the sun?" (Eccl. 6:12). The text certainly includes the fact that he shall die and then what? But the addition "under the sun," suggests that Solomon has in view the fact that also, even in this life while "under the sun," man does not know what comes after, even on the morrow.

Therefore, "better is the sight of the eyes" (v. 9), that which is for today, our daily bread. Prudent provision for the morrow we may make, for the point is not to be profligate or a poor steward of God's gifts as God's people. But it is always, "If the Lord will, we shall live, and do this, or that" (James 4:15). To walk thus requires the grace of God to humble ourselves under his hand, to flee from covetousness, and to receive that which he wills for us which only is good. This is the gift of God.

CHAPTER 7

A Calling to Lay Our End to Heart in Wisdom

1. A good name is better than precious ointment; and the day of death than the day of one's birth.
2. It is better to go to the house of mourning, than to go to the house of feasting: for that is the end of all men; and the living will lay it to his heart.
3. Sorrow is better than laughter: for by the sadness of the countenance the heart is made better.
4. The heart of the wise is in the house of mourning; but the heart of fools is in the house of mirth.
5. It is better to hear the rebuke of the wise, than for a man to hear the song of fools.
6. For as the crackling of thorns under a pot, so is the laughter of the fool: this also is vanity.—Ecclesiastes 7:1–6

"A good name is better than precious ointment; and the day of death than the day of one's birth" (Eccl. 7:1). This verse begins a new section in Ecclesiastes. Solomon has considered the vanity of life under the sun, man's works, and the terrible bondage to covetousness which subjects man's life to vanity. While he continues to describe what is seen under the sun, he would also lead us to some conclusions concerning these things in the following chapter.

Solomon introduces a point of comparison which may at first glance strike us as strange, since he declares that the day of one's death is better than one's birth day. In doing so, he is not, however, making a sweeping statement but is rather calling us to a certain spiritual reflection, to contemplate a sober reality. He does this by first comparing a good name and precious ointment and then, in what follows, explaining more fully his point.

A good name is a man's reputation. It may be viewed both as it stands among men under the sun and as it stands before God. It is not something given at birth but is the fruit of one's course of life, one's speech and dealings among men. We are called as believers to "walk honestly toward them that are without" (1 Thess. 4:12). One, for example, who is to hold office in the church, is to be of "good report of them which are without" (1Tim. 3:7). A good name is the fruit of a godly walk of a life in integrity in the world, though we may suffer reproach for Christ's sake.

Such integrity is the fruit of grace, for it is the fruit of a walk of faith founded in Christ and his righteousness and manifested in the fear of God in an upright walk in the world. It is truly precious. The world may have an appearance of it, for a season, but the bondage of covetousness works its destruction.

This good name is compared to "precious ointment" (Eccl. 7:1). The word *ointment* today conveys the idea of a medicinal salve or lotion of some sort, which is not the idea here. The term refers to a fragrant spice, oil, or perfume, a heady but temporary fragrance which belonged to celebration in the Middle Eastern context. It fills the senses with its power and energy but is fleeting in character. Such spice is costly and precious. It is thus the beloved comes to his bride, "perfumed with myrrh and frankincense, with all the powders of the merchant" (Song of Sol. 3:6).

The good name is better because it is something firm, of lasting worth, the fruit of a walk in integrity, while the perfume of an ointment is a passing thing, a fleeting joy. It is this comparison that is on the foreground here. The day of one's death is a fundamental reality, a sobering one. It stands at the end of life's journey. It is the "end of all men" (Eccl. 7:2). The day of one's birth, while a joyous occasion, is nevertheless a fleeting thing. By it we begin life's pathway in the vanity of this world under the sun. It is a moment in time, a beginning, and we pass beyond it.

It is thus that Solomon further explains: "It is better to go to the house of mourning, than to go to the house of feasting: for that is the end of all men; and the living will lay it to his heart" (v. 2). The feasting and rejoicing of men in this life is, again, a passing thing. He is not speaking here of excess and its evil, as in 1 Pet. 4:3. There is a lawful rejoicing in which the beloved takes his bride to the banqueting house in love (Song of Sol. 2:4). But his point here is that all such feasting, even in lawful celebration, is a transitory vanity. The fool does, in the lust of the flesh, seek it as a goal or end in itself, as his god is his belly. But even in its lawful use in celebration and rejoicing, it is like the day of one's birth— a passing event. It is like the passing fragrance of an expensive perfume that does not abide.

The reality of death, which comes upon all men, is that one enters an abiding, permanent, and eternal state. It is the end of our earthly sojourning and the destination of all men under the sun. It is the sober reality of life in a fallen world. Entering the house of mourning, the living will learn wisdom. It gives one pause to soberly reflect on the meaning and end of one's life and the pathway we are on; "The living will lay it to his heart" (Eccl. 7:2). It works a spiritual good not found in the house of feasting.

Therefore, Solomon adds: "Sorrow of heart is better than laughter: for by the sadness of the countenance the heart is made better" (v. 3). The issue is the heart, out of which "are the issues of life" (Prov. 4:23), and the spiritual state of that heart. Laughter is, again, a passing thing with little abiding value. Laughter does not instruct the heart, while sorrow, in the presence of grief, works a sober understanding. Sorrow that vexes the spirit works grief, but it points to the character of this present life as subject to vanity, calls to mind its end, and questions the foundation on which that life is built. It leads a child of God to his Lord, to seek his Savior, and to seek the things which are above. Feasting and laughter are the world's way of drowning out the reality of death and the questions it occasions. Such reflection in the house of mourning, though in sadness of countenance in grief, makes the heart better. Solomon is speaking, therefore, of that which works wisdom.

Thus he says: "The heart of the wise is in the house of mourning; but the heart of fools is in the house of mirth" (Eccl. 7:4). The world with its laughter, its banqueting, and its entertainment seeks to evade the reality of life. The heart, the spiritual center of a man's life, is also that which shapes his thoughts, desires, and affections. The heart dwells in the house in which it is shaped. The fool's heart is *in* the house of mirth. He does not simply go there; his life is shaped by its passing foolishness, which does not consider the end of his way. The fool seeks to dwell in the house of mirth and feasting.

The heart of the wise frequents the house of mourning, not because it is morbid, but to learn wisdom, which the end of life teaches. For the same reason, "It is better to hear the rebuke of the wise, than for a man to hear the song of fools" (v. 5). Instruction and rebuke teach wisdom. By the word of God we learn the fear of God and true wisdom. The house of mourning is, in a way, a visible expression of that word. It is a form of rebuke which speaks against that which is sin and folly in this life and drives folly away. Rebuke teaches wisdom. Better to hear that word from one who has understanding and learn spiritual wisdom and discernment than to listen to the song of fools.

The song of fools is the expression of the fool's heart, "for out of the abundance of the heart the mouth speaketh" (Matt. 12:34). His song reveals the foolishness of his mind and heart before God and in the world. His song is the expression of his spiritual emptiness and foolishness; likewise his laughter. This is a sobering reflection on what passes for music and entertainment in our day, in all the different means such media is delivered in our digitally-connected and electronic world.

He uses a concrete figure to further ground what he has just said about the song of fools. "For as the crackling of thorns under a pot, so is the laughter of the fool: this also is vanity" (Eccl. 7:6). He is not speaking of true joy or rejoicing, but of the laughter of a fool. It is like the noise made by burning thorns in a fire. They crackle. They are loud in the noise they make. They flame up and burn quickly so that they are gone almost instantly. But they produce no heat that will warm the pot. As a means to heat a pot and to make it boil, thorns are useless. They accomplish nothing.

The point is so also is the laughter of the fool, of the world without God, and its song. "This also is vanity." To then fill one's life with such empty vanity is also folly. It will not teach wisdom in the fear of God. The cackling of the fool's laughter is as empty of true joy as the crackling of thorns under a pot is of real heat. It is useless and vain, serving nothing of any profit. The point of the text should raise the question, too, where do we turn our ear to hear? What is it we seek out that we may listen to it and make it our own? Do we seek "the rebuke of the wise" or the "song of fools"?

The implied warning to be sober and seek wisdom is particularly for those who are young, who are beginning their walk along life's path. This life has an end to it, which comes to all men. "Remember now thy Creator in the days of thy youth" (Eccl. 12:1).

Patient in Spirit in Trial

7. Surely oppression maketh a wise man mad; and a gift destroyeth the heart.
8. Better is the end of a thing than the beginning thereof: and the patient in spirit is better than the proud in spirit.
9. Be not hasty in thy spirit to be angry: for anger resteth in the bosom of fools.
10. Say not thou, What is the cause that the former days were better than these? for thou dost not enquire wisely concerning this.—Ecclesiastes 7:7–10

Ecclesiastes 7:7 seems at first glance to begin a new subject by its opening statement, "Surely oppression maketh a wise man mad." Solomon, however, continues to consider the end of life, our pathway unto it and the need to lay it to heart, which he began at the opening of the chapter. The word *surely* in the original is the word *for* and parallels verse 6: "For as the crackling of thorns." The translators rightly discerned, however, that there is a shift in the thought here, from one form of folly to another, which they indicated by the use of that word *surely*.

Solomon turns from the empty laughter of a fool and the house of feasting to consider oppression and affliction. The one is vanity; the other is a sober aspect of life under the sun in a fallen world. In Ecclesiastes 7:3, the word translated *sorrow* has the root idea of vexation or anger, whether of God or men, which leads to sorrow and grief, and of God's judgment upon sin to death. Death is God's ultimate rebuke to the folly of sin. It is this sorrow or vexation under the sun which Solomon further considers.

"Surely oppression maketh a wise man mad; and a gift destroyeth the heart" (v. 7). The text is enigmatic, as it can be understood as referring to the oppressor or to the effect of oppression, to the recipient of gifts and bribes or to the effect of injustice. As the subjects are oppression and the gift, it should perhaps be understood as referring to both. Oppression is the way of folly as much as the laughter of the fool. For by it one who is deemed wise, when he turns to oppression, is made a fool, literally made to howl, as when David feigned madness (1 Sam. 21:10-15). He is brought to grief. The fruit of oppression is grief and vexation of spirit. Similarly, a gift or bribe destroys not simply justice but the heart and understanding of the one who receives it. It works spiritual self-destruction, leaving misery and vexation in its wake. The result is that the way of man bears the fruit of misery under the sun. Man, the sinner, is so often the source of his own misery or that of others, both because of sin and God's judgment upon it.

"Better is the end of a thing than the beginning thereof: and the patient in spirit is better than the proud in spirit" (Eccl. 7:8). The word *better* in English brings out the comparison intended, though the word itself is one that means *good* or *fitting*. The real outcome of a thing or the pathway of a man and his activity, including its internal principles, is shown by its end, the results and consequences. When man sows the folly of sin, he reaps its consequences. It is at the end that the fruit of a faithful pathway, a course of action, and its impulse is revealed. The beginning of a thing for man is such that the end is unseen as far as man is concerned, since he knows not the future. What afflictions, trials, missteps shall come are hidden at the beginning of a thing. It is when the end of the path is reached that the way is seen and understood.

The result is that "the patient in spirit is better than the proud in spirit" (v. 8). The text uses two figurative words, *long* and *high* or *lifted up*. To be patient in spirit is to be long in the figurative sense of being slow, steadfast, and enduring. Patient endurance in one's spirit, which keeps the end in view, is the better part. The end is ultimately that which God, and not man, determines: "A man's heart deviseth his way: but the Lord directeth his steps" (Prov. 16:9). Being patient in spirit is a work of grace, for it is characterized by humility and a walk by faith that confesses: "If the Lord will, we shall live and do this, or that" (James 4:15). It also has an eye to the true end before God, "For God shall bring every work into judgment, with every secret thing, whether it be good, or whether it be evil" (Eccl. 12:14). That he speaks of the spirit in man, and not simply patience, points to our internal life and the spiritual principles of our internal activity. "Patient in spirit" (7:8) is not simply steadfastness in obtaining an earthly goal. It is a spiritual virtue arising out of our relation to God, waiting upon his will and submitting ourselves unto him.

"Proud [high or lifted up] in spirit" (v. 8) is the spiritual opposite, rooted in man's flesh. It is that internal activity by which a man lifts himself up, exalting himself in his determination to do something. In pride he is haughty, as if he were in control and as if it were in his own hand to accomplish his purpose. This is the way of the natural man and of the old man of sin by nature. Proverbs says of him: "Every one that is proud in heart is an abomination to the Lord: though hand join in hand, he shall not be unpunished" (Prov. 16:5). In like manner: "Pride goeth before destruction, and an haughty spirit before a fall" (v. 18). Such pride is self-willed, self-serving, and covetous. It leads to turning to oppression and bribes, to taking shortcuts to obtain a goal, and it leaves misery in its wake. It leads also to anger, frustration, and vexation of spirit when a man's way is hindered. Its end is destruction.

So Solomon warns: "Be not hasty in thy spirit to be angry: for anger resteth in the bosom of fools" (Eccl. 7:9). The anger or vexation spoken of is not so much that of someone with a short temper, though that is not excluded, but that of one who is hindered in his way, quick to be frustrated, vexed, and angry when his will is halted by God's providence. It arises out of self-will and is the fruit also of oppression. When trials and difficulties stand in the way a man desires to go, he is soon angry. While his neighbor is often the immediate object of his anger, it is the hindrance in his way that occasions his vexation. His anger is really directed against God's hand in his life. He would be in control of his life, but God blocks his way by affliction or trouble. Such anger rests in the bosom of one who is a fool in heart. It is the spiritual disposition of his soul in rebellion against God and striving with him, so that man truly seeks to exalt himself above God.

The result of such vexation is the anger of one who says in his heart, "Why is God doing this to me?" He accuses the Lord of providence and strives with his will, seeking rather to have his own way. The warning of the text therefore continues: "Say not thou, What is the cause that the former days were better than these?" (v. 10). The questioner is really calling God's government and justice into question and setting himself up as judge of God's dealings. Such is the outworking of pride in the heart of man, who does not humble himself before God. When things go his way according to his desires, his pride is lifted up, and he ascribes his success to himself. But let circumstances turn against him, let affliction or trial come, and he is quick in anger and vexation to question God's knowledge, justice, and righteousness. God is at fault, not himself. Such pride is rooted in self-will, which considers not his own sin nor that he is but a creature of the dust.

As we are tempted to ask just such questions in the infirmity of the flesh when we are led in ways of trial, the text not only gives a warning ("Say not thou"), but also a first answer to the questioner: "for thou dost not enquire wisely concerning this" (v. 10). This rebuke arises in some measure because of injustice and oppression in a wicked world, so that it is difficult to see how the end can be good. In the verses that follow a more complete answer is given, but to receive it spiritually there is first the need to bring to a halt our natural rebellious questioning, which is that of a fool and not wisdom. Questioning God's government is not the way of wisdom; it is not asking wisely. The question presumes to know the end before it is reached, to discern from outward circumstances the hidden purposes of God, and to examine them. It is the way of pride and of a spirit hasty to be angry or vexed. It has in it the idea also that I deserve the former days, which I esteem better than the present.

Rather, the way of wisdom is that of a "[patience] in spirit" (v. 8) that rests in the will of God from day to day, for his ways are higher than our ways and his wisdom deeper than our finite understanding. The assurance given us in what follows in the passage is "for he that feareth God shall come forth of them all" (v. 18). But that fear of God means, presently, that with patient and humble spirits we walk through the trials that are sent, when the end is not yet plain and when troubles seem to multiply. It is exactly then that patience is needed, and endurance of faith in hope. It is in such trials that our calling is to walk by faith and not sight.

Nor is it any different for the end of life's pathway. For the end of earthly life itself, which is in the house of mourning and its sober reality, calls indeed for patience in hope of things not seen as yet. Our calling, therefore, is to walk in the same manner now, in the present trials and troubles of life. This takes a wisdom which spiritually appropriates the fear of God, the reverence of faith in God. "Wisdom" rooted in the fear of God "giveth life to them that have it" (v. 12).

Wisdom Giveth Life

11. Wisdom is good with an inheritance: and by it there is profit to them that see the sun.
12. For wisdom is a defence, and money is a defence: but the excellency of knowledge is, that wisdom giveth life to them that have it.
13. Consider the work of God: for who can make that straight, which he hath made crooked?
14. In the day of prosperity be joyful, but in the day of adversity consider: God also hath set the one over against the other, to the end that man should find nothing after him.—Ecclesiastes 7:11–14

After calling us to be patient in spirit in the midst of trials and vexation along the path of life and activity, Solomon now turns to the role of wisdom (v. 11). One who is soon angry, proud in spirit, and questioning God's ways walks the way of spiritual folly and works his own spiritual hurt. Wisdom, which is the fear of God, for that is the aspect of wisdom in view, is profitable in a certain way which he will explain.

"Wisdom is good with an inheritance: and by it there is profit to them that see the sun" (Eccl. 7:11). The text could better be rendered: "wisdom with an inheritance is good." While it is possible to understand wisdom *as* the inheritance, that is, in the sense of a spiritual inheritance, the contrast in the next verse is between wisdom and money and would suggest he has in view first an earthly inheritance. He is speaking too of "them that see the sun" (v. 11).

Material gifts or treasures have a place, but wisdom, with them, is truly profitable. What is profitable is, in a figure, that which goes over and beyond. It excels and thus profits or benefits. Wisdom is good, a blessing of God, and in that sense, it is also a spiritual inheritance of more value than an earthly one alone. Indeed, without wisdom, knowledge, and understanding, an earthly inheritance will not truly profit at all. Wisdom profits because it leads us beyond what we see with the eye to a walk by faith, in a humble spirit with patience.

How so? "For wisdom is a defence, and money is a defence: but the excellency of knowledge is, that wisdom giveth life to them that have it" (v.12). The idea of a defense draws a picture of a shadow that is a refuge, protection, and defense in trial and trouble. As the shade of a tree protects one from the burning rays of the sun, so figuratively a shadow is a protection and defense. Money, earthly riches, certainly fills that function in some measure under the sun. They may well serve to smooth the way of someone through many of the earthly troubles of life; "The rich man's wealth is his strong city" (Prov. 10:15). But such money cannot order all things, nor deliver from death, the end of life's way, nor answer all the troubles even of life under the sun.

Wisdom in the fear of God is more profitable; it goes beyond what earthly treasure can do. It excels or profits because it gives life. It too is a defense and protection to them that see the sun. The expression "giveth life" (Eccl. 7:12) is one word which means to make alive. Here it must be understood that it is God who quickens and works by wisdom to impart life in his grace. When we walk in the fear of God, "God is our refuge and strength, a very present help in trouble" (Ps. 46:1). In his shadow as our faithful heavenly Father, the believer is safe in a way that no earthly refuge can afford. But that refuge is known only by faith in the fear of God. The wisdom of faith, which is a gift of God, imparts life in communion with God, grace in time of trouble, a spiritual refuge. It answers not only present trials but also the end of our earthly sojourning in death and the house of mourning. It is a spiritual possession beyond an earthly one.

That is something no earthly inheritance can do. Earthly blessings, "the day of prosperity" (v. 14), are but for a moment and transitory. Wisdom, which gives life, sustains a meek and patient spirit in trouble and quickens in the hope of an eternal life which is beyond the vanity of this world seen under the sun. To underscore that point Solomon adds a question: "Consider the work of God: for who can make that straight, which he hath made crooked?" (v. 13). God is God Almighty. He determines the times and seasons of life according to his counsel and wisdom. He upholds and governs heaven, earth, and all creatures, as the Heidelberg Catechism puts it, "so…that herbs and grass, rain and drought, fruitful and barren years, meat and drink, health and sickness, riches and poverty, yea, all things, come not by chance, but by his fatherly hand."[1]

It is the fool who seeks by his own strength or by his wealth to make that straight which God has bent or made crooked. He who is but dust will impose his will upon the world, upon his own life, and order his own way. Yet he fails and will always fail because he is not God. The answer to Solomon's question, "Who can make that straight, which he hath made crooked?" is this: no mere man. God's works order the life of all creatures, their time and seasons. He sets boundaries which no man can change. It belongs to the folly of sin and the spirit of antichrist to try to change times and laws and seasons. Yet that which God works stands. It comes to pass.

As we live in a world that increasingly strives with God Almighty, we need to note well what the word of God says here. God is God, righteous in judgment and merciful unto them that fear him. For the idea of the text is not that of fatalism or a shrug of despair. Rather, standing before that wonder of the sovereign majesty of God, we acknowledge him to be God, even our

---

1   Heidelberg Catechism A 27, in Schaff, *Creeds of Christendom*, 3:316.

God. We also, with wisdom that an understanding heart gives, acknowledge ourselves to be his creatures under his care. Yea more, we confess ourselves to be his children adopted of grace in Christ. We would walk in the care of his grace, humbly under his power and in the shadow of his protecting care that gives life to them that fear him.

Solomon then applies this consideration in the following verse by setting prosperity over against adversity, for both shall come under the sun. "In the day of prosperity be joyful, but in the day of adversity consider: God also hath set the one over against the other, to the end that man should find nothing after him" (v. 14). The contrast is not simply between two single days but, as a figure also, the contrast of seasons or times of life marked by good or evil from the viewpoint of our life in the world. As such, the idea is broader than prosperity in terms of earthly abundance but includes when things go well with us in our course of life. The day may include times of prosperity, health, or circumstances that we find desirable under the sun. In such a day the text says not simply "be joyful," but it uses a word that means "to be good," so that it includes the idea of a fitting response of thankfulness and contentment as well as a joyful heart. We are to offer up a fitting response for our portion for the day and God's provision when our labors also are fruitful and attain the end toward which we labored. These are gifts or blessings of God. They are under his sovereign disposition. They are not due to our own merit as the world in pride so often ascribes to man.

But Solomon would also have us understand there are also days of evil, of trouble and distress, of adversity. In such an evil day, whether a single day or a season of life, we are to see or consider God's design. He has set the one over against the other. These days too come from his almighty hand, according to his counsel and purpose. This is the instruction also of Job in his troubles: "What? shall we receive good at the hand of God, and shall we not receive evil?" (Job 2:10). Thus Job also says: "the Lord gave, and the Lord hath taken away; blessed be the name of the Lord" (Job 1:21).

It is this consideration Solomon would also have us see. It is easy when things go well with us to take them for granted. When the way is evil in character in earthly terms, a day of trouble and trial, then to say, "this is God's work in his providence" and receive it with a patient spirit is the way of wisdom. It is the way also to contentment in heart. There is much hidden from us in God's purpose and works. He points us to one aspect of God's purpose in such ups and downs in life: God so works to this end, "that man should find nothing after him" (Eccl. 7:14). That is, that man, not knowing what the morrow may bring, what comes after him, and thus what the future holds, should be reminded that he is man, a creature of the dust as was Adam his father. It should, in fact, drive him to humble himself before God in whose hand is his life and turn in the fear of God to him as Lord of all. For finding that his days are not in his own hand, he must turn to God in whose hand is his life and breath. Wisdom in the fear of God does so, while the folly of sin in man is that he walks after his own imagination in pride of heart. The word of God would teach us the knowledge of the wisdom, whose excellency or profit is that it gives life to them that have it.

He That Feareth God Shall Come Forth of Them All

15. All things have I seen in the days of my vanity: there is a just man that perisheth in his righteousness, and there is a wicked man that prolongeth his life in his wickedness.
16. Be not righteous over much; neither make thyself over wise: why shouldest thou destroy thyself?
17. Be not over much wicked, neither be thou foolish: why shouldest thou die before thy time?
18. It is good that thou shouldest take hold of this; yea, also from this withdraw not thine hand: for he that feareth God shall come forth of them all.—Ecclesiastes 7:15–18

Reflecting further on the sober reality of our life, its trials, and God's government, Solomon returns to that which he has seen. "All things have I seen in the days of my vanity: there is a just man that perishes in his righteousness, and there is a wicked man that prolongeth his life in his wickedness" (Eccl. 7:15). That which he has seen evidently gives him pause. He has said: "Consider the works of God: for who can make that straight, which he hath made crooked?" (v. 13). He is not here considering everything he has seen, but all that belongs to the contrast he now introduces. A just or righteous man perishes while a wicked man prolongs his life.

How can this be in the light of God's righteousness? Solomon speaks of this, too, in connection with the character of each man's walk. The righteous man perishes. He does so even as he walks in righteousness or in the sphere of uprightness. He dies. By contrast, the wicked man in his wickedness continues. He does evil, works wickedness; and yet, from what can be seen under the sun, he prolongs his life. He does not die. Judgment does not come immediately upon him. How can this be?

Solomon puts this sober observation in the context of his own life: "in the days of my vanity" (v. 15). Man is both a creature of the dust and subject to the curse of God through the fall and returns to the dust. His life is frail, fleeting, and transitory under the judgment of God upon sin. The world was subjected to vanity through the fall. His own life also is subject to the transitory character of life in a world under the curse of God upon sin. God, in all that he does, is righteous, but his righteous judgments are a matter of faith in the fear of God. God's ways are higher than our ways. They are both sovereign and transcendent. The divine purpose is unfolded in time and history, and we may observe it; but that does not mean that in the things we see, we can fully understand or find it out. We are to walk by faith in the light of God's word.

In that connection it must be kept in mind that he speaks of what can be seen. Our translators bring this out by rendering the word *righteous* by the word *just*, "a just man." This is not speaking of the man as he stands in heart and conscience before God, but as he appears to us, a just man. In the light of that broader principle of God's providence, there is one element that can be brought to our attention, and it is to this particularly that he would call our attention in verses 17 and 18; that is, when what is seen is self-destructive, so that a just or wise man not only perishes but destroys himself. He is the cause of his own trouble. Likewise, when the wicked walks the way of a fool, he works his own death. Both are rooted in a certain excess. In the light of the conclusion—"For he that feareth God shall come forth of them all" (v. 18)— this excess is not rooted in the genuine fear of God. It is rooted rather in the flesh in both cases and in the pride of life. Solomon is not, in what follows, advocating a kind of golden mean between virtue and sin. Both are, in fact, sin, and he would guard us from them.

The first speaks of false virtue: "Be not righteous over much; neither make thyself over wise: why shouldest thou destroy thyself?" (v. 16). Righteousness is set forth here from the viewpoint of our walk, an upright walk. To such a walk the justified believer is called in the love of God and is to be rooted in the fear of God, which keeps his commandments by faith. To be over-righteous, however, is a different thing. It is to multiply righteousness, to make it beyond what is commanded. It is self-righteousness. It is the walk of the Pharisee, with the internal appraisal rooted in a trust in one's own virtue, righteousness, and works. It is not the gift of justification—righteousness without works in Christ—nor a humble upright walk in the way of sanctification. It is the spiritual problem of Israel under the law: "For they being ignorant of God's righteousness, and going about to establish their own righteousness, have not submitted themselves unto the righteousness of God" (Rom. 10:3). The root is a spiritual problem of having a "zeal of God, but not according to knowledge" (Rom. 10:2). This problem is not limited to the New Testament era nor the rise of Phariseeism after the exile. It is the problem of the church under the law in the Old Testament and is still with us in the New

Testament dispensation. It is the temptation to turn from resting in God's gift of imputed righteousness to trusting our own works and our own inventions. It is rooted too in sinful pride that looks down on others. It belongs to the self-righteous virtue signaling of an unbelieving world.

Similarly, wisdom is a gift of God, which Solomon rightly sought of God. But it could so easily become a seeking after wisdom out of sinful pride for its own sake. One of the things Solomon wrestles with in Ecclesiastes is that wisdom was elusive: "I said, I will be wise, but it was far from me" (Eccl. 7:23). He applied himself to wisdom: "I applied mine heart to know, and to search, and to seek out wisdom, and the reason of things, and to know the wickedness of folly, even of foolishness and madness" (v. 25). The pursuit of such wisdom has certain dangers to it, so that it ceases to be seeking wisdom from God and becomes making "thyself over wise" (v. 16); that is, it becomes an end in itself, a matter of sinful pride, something misdirected and vain.

A holy zeal after God and understanding can become a spiritual problem when it is corrupted by the flesh and sought out of pride of heart and apart from God. Then such zeal becomes what is sometimes called 200 percenterism, a false enthusiasm and a misguided arrogance, which works destruction personally in one's spiritual life but also in the life of God's church. It is the way of being wise in one's own conceit. The Pharisees of Jesus' day who trusted in their own works and regarded themselves as above the publicans and sinners are only one example of this. This false zeal in a good cause is perhaps a temptation particularly to those who are young. So Solomon's admonition in what follows applies to this also: "It is good that thou shouldest take hold of this; yea also withdraw not thine hand" (v. 18). There may be here also a confession of Solomon's own battle with sin and his weakness, though that is an inference and not the main point.

By contrast the text says: "Be not over much wicked, neither be thou foolish: why shouldest thou die before thy time?" (v. 17).

He is not advocating that we sin a little bit but not to excess. He is rather pointing out a certain characteristic of sin, that it, as rebellion against God, it has a self-destructive impulse in it. When one yields oneself to sin, sin becomes the sinner's master; the sinner is in bondage. This he has already shown with the bondage to covetousness in the heaping and gathering of the foolish rich man.

He adds to that warning the parallel thought: "neither be thou foolish" (v. 17). The folly of sin, the way of one yielding himself to sin, is a self-destructive foolishness which endangers not only the soul but also, in its recklessness, the body and life itself. The wickedness he has in view is truly foolish in its recklessness, so that it leads to death, an early death according to the measure of man's life. Pride of heart and the seeming fact that one gets away with something for a season or appears to receive no harm leads to the delusion that "I can do this with impunity." The present thrill of some sin grows dull, and one seeks it now in a more exciting and risky form. The risk itself becomes part of the thrill. This is the way of the folly of sin and the deceitfulness of sin. Therefore, Solomon asks, "Why shouldest thou die before thy time?" (v. 17). The end of sin is destruction; one walking in the risky thrill of sin is hastening to his own destruction, even a premature death according to the time of life.

This twofold warning he would press upon our mind: "It is good that thou shouldest take hold of this; yea, also from this withdraw not thine hand" (v. 18). Take hold of it and, having done so, do not let go of it! The calling to spiritually appropriate this warning is needful; we are inclined by nature to say, "That does not apply to me or this aspect of my life," and to let go of spiritual instruction. We have such warnings in mind, carry them spiritually, and then in some temptation we open our hand and drop them, forgetting all that we know in the temptation of the moment.

The antidote, and what is true wisdom, is "for he that feareth God shall come forth of them all" (v. 18). We are not to be deceived by a false zeal or self-righteousness, neither by the temptations of sin and the folly of excess. For a season they may appear to prosper, but their end is destruction and even death. Hence the emphatic "take hold and do not let go" of the text. The conclusion here gives a reason for hanging on to this instruction. The text pictures, as it were, a path with dangers on either side. To "come forth of them all," all of these dangers of sin, takes the fear of God. The one who walks in either of these errors—being "righteous over much" and being "over much wicked" (v. 17)— will fall, but the one who fears God *shall* come forth of them all. The fear of God, in meekness, keeps one both from being lifted up in himself in self-righteousness and from the reckless folly of sin. The reason given is also a word of assurance in the battle with sin, he "shall come forth;" his passage is safe. The fear of God is the principal thing, for it gives true wisdom in the pathway of life. Indeed, this is the conclusion to which he would have us come at the end of the book: "Let us hear the conclusion of the whole matter: Fear God, and keep his commandments: for this is the whole duty of man" (Eccl. 12:13).

Wisdom Guards in the Way of Spiritual Reflection

19. Wisdom strengtheneth the wise more than ten mighty men which are in the city.
20. For there is not a just man upon earth, that doeth good, and sinneth not.
21. Also take no heed unto all words that are spoken; lest thou hear thy servant curse thee:
22. For oftentimes also thine own heart knoweth that thou thyself likewise hast cursed others.—Ecclesiastes 7:19–22

The word of God is a light in a world of darkness and sin. The knowledge of that word, directing us unto God himself, also shines on the works of God in creation, providence, and the life of the world around us. It gives wisdom as a spiritual gift, which serves as a guide through the temptations of pride and the lusts of the flesh. The internal principle of wisdom is the fear of God, that humble reverence of faith, which seeks to walk after the will of God. It is thus that "he that feareth God shall come forth of them all" (Eccl. 7:18). The path of life is fraught with many temptations; through them wisdom is a guide.

"Wisdom strengtheneth the wise more than ten mighty men which are in a city" (v. 19). The wise man strengthened by wisdom is one who fears God and holds the light of his word by faith. It is the word which imparts wisdom that makes one spiritually strong. The text uses a comparison of ten men in a city, ten being the natural number of completeness. The ten men are mighty earthly rulers. The idea of the text implies that they make the city strong by protecting it from the enemy without and maintaining order within. A city blessed with such mighty men is safe and secure, well-founded, and rightly governed in the world.

Wisdom from God, however, gives a greater strength, for it affords a spiritual foundation beyond the life of the world: a guide through the dangers of sin and temptation. It keeps one from the way of pride and folly. It governs the spirit with humility and discernment. It, in effect, stands beside the one who is wise and makes him stronger than the mere earthly power of the ten mighty men in a city.

The reason for this, and the need of it at the same time, is found in the explanation given: "For there is not a just man upon earth, that doeth good, and sinneth not" (v. 20). A man righteous before God, whose walk is upright and godly, is yet a sinner. He is just in his dealings "upon earth" and does good. Solomon himself, in his judgment upon the throne, was such a man who ruled with wisdom and ordered the coming and going of his kingdom likewise, so that the queen of Sheba stood in wonder at the wisdom and order of his kingdom. In this Solomon was a type of Christ.

For all that, and our text is an indirect confession on Solomon's part, he was still a sinner. For all the glory of his kingdom and wisdom, Solomon had many sins, particularly his heathen wives and condoning their idolatry, and as he grew older, the stubbornness of his temper. Wisdom gives strength to see one's own sin and humble one's pride before God in repentance. It leads to a spiritual reflection on one's own sin and weakness.

Wisdom is a means to restrain, to guard and to guide in the way, but grace alone in Christ takes away sin. The Heidelberg Catechism in question and answer 114 mirrors the idea of the text in connection with the law of God,

> Can those who are converted to God keep these commandments perfectly?
>
> No; but even the holiest men, while in this life, have only a small beginning of this obedience, yet so that with earnest purpose they begin to live, not only according to some, but according to all the commandments of God.[2]

Wisdom strenghthens the man who is a sinner to keep him from the folly of his own sinful human nature. It guards him in the way from the corruptions of the flesh and works a sober reflection on his own infirmity after the flesh. This is Solomon's own reflection, which shapes his conclusion at the end of Ecclesiastes: "Fear God and keep his commandments...For God shall bring every work into judgment, with every secret thing, whether it be good, or whether it be evil" (Eccl. 12:13–14).

It is in the light of that reality of man's sin and depravity by nature that Solomon then illustrates the value of wisdom and the reflection it occasions by directing us to the sin against the ninth commandment into which we also fall. "Also take no heed unto all words that are spoken; lest thou hear thy servant curse thee: For oftentimes also thine own heart knoweth that thou thyself likewise hast cursed others" (7:21–22).

The illustration is well chosen, for this sin is found in everyone. Often, it lies hidden in the mind and heart. Rather than pointing

---

2   Heidelberg Catechism Q&A 114, in Philip Schaff, *Creeds of Christendom*, 3:349.

to a great or manifest gross sin, Solomon points to one close to home. His palace and court were filled with many servants going about their business. Sins of pride, frustration, and anger were a constant reality in such an environment, much like a modern corporate office with a large staff. Today we would also have to add email and other means of communication such as social media to the idea of "words that are spoken" (v. 21).

Walking those halls of the palace, Solomon would hear his servants' voices, speaking to themselves under their breath, murmuring to one another, complaining, sometimes openly venting their anger, sometimes speaking softly in frustrated bitterness. There were times when, indeed, they cursed him over things small or great. The echo of their voices reached him down the corridors. He heard or sensed what was being said, alone or in the group down the hall.

The way of wisdom was to pay "no heed unto all the words that are spoken." The way of wisdom was to pass by without turning his attention to it, "lest thou hear thy servant curse thee" (v. 21). Love exercised in wisdom covers a multitude of such sins, while pride seeks a confrontation and its own glory.

The reason given is rooted in the spiritual reflection, and therefore restraint, that wisdom gives as a guard against the self-willed impulses that seek one's own glory. Wisdom leads one rather to search one's own heart, to recognize the root of sinful infirmity, which likewise lies in one's own flesh. "For oftentimes also thine own heart knoweth that thou thyself likewise hast cursed others" (v. 22). That knowledge, the self-knowledge of the heart, is the fruit of discernment wrought by wisdom as a grace of God.

The servant and his master are both alike sinners, and sin arising from within comes out of our mouths. The mouth of a fool is often found with us to our shame. The counsel here is not to ignore sin, when it is serious, but to take to heart, our own infirmity when we see the weaknesses of others, that we may confess our own need of grace and forgiveness and walk in patience, meekness, and forgiveness with others.

It is a sober reflection that "for there is not a just man upon earth, that doeth good, and sinneth not" (v. 20).

The Limits of Attaining Wisdom for Sinful Man

23. All this have I proved by wisdom: I said, I will be wise; but it was far from me.
24. That which is far off, and exceeding deep, who can find it out?
25. I applied mine heart to know, and to search, and to seek out wisdom, and the reason of things, and to know the wickedness of folly, even of foolishness and madness:
26. And I find more bitter than death the woman, whose heart is snares and nets, and her hands as bands: whoso pleaseth God shall escape from her; but the sinner shall be taken by her.—Ecclesiastes 7:23–26

"All this have I proved by wisdom: I said, I will be wise; but it was far from me" (v. 23). Solomon reviews what he has sought out, proved, and tested by the wisdom given him of God. He has set before us, in chapter 7, the sober reality of death and sorrow, the folly of sin and pride, the sovereign providence of God, and the strength which wisdom gives including the knowledge of one's own sin. But in seeking after wisdom and understanding, he also reached a limit. He has proven much; but when he sought to be wise, he could not attain unto its perfection. He was yet a man, a creature of the dust, and also a sinner.

We must put what Solomon is saying in the context of his own life and conduct as king over Israel, his rule from the throne, and the life of the palace. There was much wisdom displayed in the ordering of the kingdom, the building of the temple, and his other works. First Kings records these works extensively in its opening chapters. When the queen of Sheba saw that order and plied him with hard questions, she was in awe of what she saw and heard of Solomon's wisdom (1 Kings 10:1–10). There was also his enterprise and business sense, his navy, commodity trading, and the wealth of Israel, which was its fruit, in gold, silver, and every luxury. He was indeed wise by the gift of God. But in these things, perfection of wisdom was not attained; there was an undercurrent of discontent even among his servants in the palace and in the kingdom with men like Jeroboam. Prosperity itself cannot truly satisfy because of the bondage of man to covetousness (see Eccl. 5 and 6). It can work discontent because enough is never enough to man, who is by nature given to envy. That discontent would grow into rebellion. Solomon's own stubborn sinfulness, under God's chastening, would fuel it.

If in the ordering of the kingdom much wisdom was attained, in Solomon's own life, we may say his personal life, there were also many sins. He himself confesses the fact of it: "For there is not a just man upon earth, that doeth good, and sinneth not" (Eccl. 7:20). The statement is both an observation of life in general and a personal confession. What then? Solomon sought to be wise and found that he could not attain unto complete or perfect wisdom for all of the measure of wisdom given him. Wisdom is a divine attribute. It is God's ability to form all things and work all things together for the realization of his counsel and purpose, unto the revelation of his own glory and grace in Christ. God's wisdom is beyond the understanding of man. Solomon says: "It was far from me" (v. 23).

He now adds: "That which is far off, and exceeding deep, who can find it out?" (v. 24). The fountain of true wisdom is in God, and man cannot attain unto it. Solomon has said: "Consider the work of God: for who can make that straight, which he hath made crooked?" (v. 13). God's ways are higher and deeper than our understanding. Agur in Proverbs 30 speaks the same language: "Surely I am more brutish than any man, and have not the understanding of a man. I neither learned wisdom, nor have the knowledge of the holy" (Prov. 30:2–3). The apostle Paul makes the same confession: "O the depth of the riches both of the wisdom and knowledge of God! how unsearchable are his judgments, and his ways past finding out!" (Rom. 11:33).

Solomon likewise confronts the limits of his own understanding. He has said in the beginning of Ecclesiastes: "And I gave my heart to know wisdom, and to know madness and folly: I perceived that this also is vexation of spirit. For in much wisdom is much grief: and he that increaseth knowledge increaseth sorrow" (Eccl. 1:17–18). Here he repeats the same idea: "I applied mine heart to know, and to search, and to seek out wisdom, and the reason of things, and to know the wickedness of folly, even of foolishness and madness" (7:25). He has said in himself, "I will be wise." He has given every effort to be wise and to search out wisdom. The object of that study was, "What is wisdom and its way?" Because of sin, that study included also its spiritual opposite, which is folly and madness.

Solomon sought to be wise, but it was a wisdom tainted by the flesh. There was an element of fleshly carnal wisdom that cleaved to his desire. His searching and seeking was not a mere abstract exercise, for Solomon had his own sins to wrestle with. He multiplied wives, not so much out of lust, though that is not excluded, but he took heathen princesses to form political alliances and secure the external peace of the kingdom. In an earthly sense this was the way of the world's wisdom. But it was a false wisdom that led to folly on his part.

When he speaks of knowing the wickedness of folly, even foolishness and madness, he is not advocating *doing* wickedness. His desire was to be wise, but he was still a sinner. He speaks therefore of seeking to understand this reality of sin, as it is part of the reason of things and as it cleaves to him also in his own life. He is somewhat like Paul at this point in Romans 7, "I find a law, that, when I would do good, evil is present with me" (v. 21). Solomon sought not only wisdom as from God but also to know his own sin and the reality of sin around him. Sin is foolishness and madness because it is contrary to God's law and design for man's life and well-being. This too was beyond Solomon's understanding. His confession is similar to Jeremiah 17:9: "The heart is deceitful above all things, and desperately wicked: who can know it?" The answer to the dilemma Jeremiah gives as well: "I the Lord search the heart, I try the reins, even to give every man according to his ways, and according to the fruit of his doings" (v. 10). The Lord alone knows the heart. But that means for man, also for Solomon, "That which is far off, and exceeding deep, who can find it out?" (Eccl. 7:24).

Solomon illustrates this limitation of his own wisdom by speaking of his own personal experience. "And I find more bitter than death the woman, whose heart is snares and nets, and her hands as bands: whoso pleaseth God shall escape from her; but the sinner shall be taken by her" (v. 26). Because he speaks of finding— and that personally, not just by observation—that which he says is "more bitter than death," we may understand that he is speaking of his own experience. Death is the judgment of God upon sin. The bitterness of which he speaks is not, however, physical death, but the state of his heart when he looks at the matter before him. It worked a sorrow in his experience that was to him "more bitter that death" itself, a spiritual grief of heart comparable to the sorrow of death and loss. That grief was the effect of his relation to women. He is not speaking, however, of any kind of woman; he is not speaking of women in general; but he is speaking of one who has a specific character, "whose heart is snares and nets, and her hands as bands." She is an ungodly woman, an unbeliever. The description is that of his heathen wives who caused his heart to err, and who led him to serve or make room for their idols.

His intention is not to discuss his sorrow over his sin. That belongs to David's history and Psalms 32 and 51.

Rather it is to give a warning to the young man who is drawn to the unbelieving daughters of this world. Nor is it to be limited to young men. While that is the illustration in Solomon's case, what he says is also a warning to a young woman in her being attracted to unbelieving young men. It further applies to whatever draws us away from the Lord within the life of the church in a sinful world. His picture is of a woman whose heart, in the deceitfulness of sin, is like one who lays a snare and net to capture a bird. The snare is deceitful, cunningly laid, out of a heart that is a trap of sin, to ensnare one who is heedless and lacking discernment. That trap certainly uses sex and sexuality, but Solomon has a broader view than simply the seventh commandment. It is a trap that preys upon the mind in order to deceive, preys upon the emotions to draw, and seeks to hold by hands that become bands, which are the chains of bondage. Nor is there any need to introduce the idea, as some commentaries do, that the author is speaking allegorically of the woman as a personification of worldly philosophy. He speaks concretely. He is seeking to warn young people, by his own bitterness of heart, to flee from such relationships and not be ensnared by them. He intends that they should remember their Creator (Eccl. 12:1) and not fall into this, his sin.

What makes the warning a sober and serious one is not only Solomon's sin and sad history but what he adds: "whoso pleaseth God shall escape from her; but the sinner shall be taken by her" (7:26). There is a judgment of God manifested in this matter. He who walks in the fear of God, taking heed to his word, walks in a way that is pleasing to God. Because our wisdom is limited and our understanding of our own sin imperfect, it is clouded by the subtle deceitfulness of sin. We are called to "flee...youthful lusts" (2 Tim. 2:22). But it is God's grace that keeps us from that and other ways of sin. God chastens the sin of pride and the one who departs in the way of his own sinful imagination. The sinner is like a heedless bird who does not regard the danger and the warnings given.

The sinner shall be taken and ensnared, and with the ensnarement comes sorrow of heart, bitterness "more bitter than death"

(Eccl. 7:26), for it works often the ruin of life and joy. Such was the case with Solomon's sin. He laid the root of sin in the life of the palace; the consequences would rend the kingdom after his death in the days of his son Rehoboam. The blessings of God's covenant in marriage and family life are at issue, and Solomon's sin undermined both in the life of the church and kingdom. The idolatry of his unbelieving heathen wives, the temples built for them outside the city, would work through the life of the nation. The idolatry introduced into Israel would ultimately lead them into the captivity in Babylon. Solomon when he is old speaks to us: "Learn what I learned to my grief, bitter as death, and walk not in it." Pride supplanted wisdom because of sin. Solomon for all his wisdom did not have perfect wisdom or understanding. In Jesus Christ, the Word and Wisdom of God made flesh, alone is perfect wisdom to be found.

A Spiritual Inventory

27. Behold, this have I found, saith the preacher, counting one by one, to find out the account:
28. Which yet my soul seeketh, but I find not: one man among a thousand have I found; but a woman among all those have I not found.
29. Lo, this only have I found, that God hath made man upright; but they have sought out many inventions.
—Ecclesiastes 7:27–29

In the preceding verses, Solomon spoke of the limits of his wisdom and understanding of God's works and spoke concerning man of sin and the deceitfulness of sin. This latter he found especially in the bitterness that came from his union with heathen women, "whose heart is snares and nets" (Eccl. 7:26). This bitterness of heart was rooted in his own sin. This leads him at the conclusion of the chapter to a spiritual inventory in which he wants us to see what he has seen and behold what he has discerned. He himself wrought many works by wisdom but found those works in themselves led to vanity. He sought out the ways of God, his providence and judgment, and they were deeper than he could attain. His own sin and weakness likewise were marked by foolishness and madness, even as it was in the world around him among men under the sun. He says of all this: "That which is far off, and exceeding deep, who can find it out?" (v. 24).

He now continues: "Behold, this have I found, saith the preacher, counting one by one, to find out the account: which yet my soul seeketh, but I find not" (vv. 27–28). Like one counting coins or change in a counting house to figure out the total, he would add up the sum. He is looking at what he has seen and found in all his labor and activity, in the order and life of the palace, in the city of Jerusalem. It is the inventory he has set before us in the whole course of the book of Ecclesiastes thus far. He would give it now as a summary of what has gone before and have us see it as a personal inventory rooted in his own experience. While it is a summary, it is not the sum. Throughout he has been concerned to give us not an abstract survey but a clear sight of the issues of life under the sun. He speaks with the authority of experience and long reflection. What he has particularly been seeking with diligence throughout are wisdom and understanding. The problem is that he does not achieve a complete grasp of it. He says it is that "which yet my soul seeketh, but I find not" (v. 28). He cannot fully attain to the sum of it all, for it is of God and deeper than his understanding to find it out. Man's wisdom and understanding is limited by the fact that he is man, a creature, and also a sinner. Some measure of understanding he has found but not complete wisdom. There is always more that is deeper than his thought.

Rather this survey results in this inventory: "one man among a thousand have I found; but a woman among all those have I not found" (v. 28). Reckoning up the figure to find out the account, he finds the wisdom from God was a rare thing among men: only one among a thousand men in his experience. And among women? Not one among all those. He effectively found none, which, given his heathen wives, is to be expected. Keeping in mind that his search took place in his life and among those around him, given his relationships, this is not surprising. He is not making a blanket statement about women or men but speaks of those with whom he dwelt and among whom he sought to see and know. The women were heathen women with the superstitions of idolaters. The men included the members of his court and officers of his kingdom, who were often motivated by political desires for power, wealth, and personal advantage. The result is to be expected. Even the one among a thousand men is of such a kind that he says of this survey, "I find not." He found something quite different from what he had thought to find.

The reason is that God alone is the giver of true spiritual wisdom and understanding. Wisdom is only from above. It is not found in man (Adam) and his seed by nature, because we are all fallen in sin. The conclusion of the matter Solomon plainly states, as the result of his spiritual accounting: "Lo, this only have I found, that God made man upright; but they have sought out many inventions" (v. 29). The text, as in other places in Ecclesiastes, speaks of *man*. In the original, it is *the man*, so that the reference is both to Adam, our first father, and to man, Adam's seed after the flesh. The name *Adam* has in it, as well, the idea of man's creation from the dust. He is dust. God created Adam, a creature of the dust, and mankind in him.

God made Adam upright. His whole nature was good, fitted in conformity to the divine will, righteous and holy. It was pure. The result is that he was made with wisdom and possessed knowledge and wisdom from God. He was created able to serve God so that his knowledge and perception of the world around him informed him of the will of his creator. He could discern and understand God's design in the making of all things, including their purpose, value, and place. Adam showed this in the naming of the animals in Genesis 2. He was given the wisdom or skill to apply that knowledge in the service of God with perfect, though finite, human understanding. There was in him no darkness of sin. Foolishness and madness, self-destructive folly, was far from him. He was made upright and given gifts of wisdom. The world also was free from the stain of sin. It was not yet subjected under the curse of the fall to vanity.

"But they have sought out many inventions" (Eccl. 7:29). This is the sad history of the fall. Solomon has turned to the early chapters of Genesis before, for example in Ecclesiastes 3:20 and Ecclesiastes 6:10. The period of the fall, the development of sin, and the flood shed light upon the vanity of life. In confessing "there is not a just man on earth, that doeth good, and sinneth not" (Eccl. 7:20), he leads us to the truth of total depravity of fallen man by nature, who seeks out many inventions of sin. He leads us to the confession that also sin cleaves to us, so that the old man of sin is present in the children of God. He, in effect, assumes we know and understand this history.

In reflecting on this reality, he would lead us here not to an abstract consideration of the matter but to see the consequences as they work out in history. He does this both to confirm the truth of that depravity by nature and to understand its effects in madness and folly. As he has sought out wisdom, so man by nature seeks out sin. He uses here essentially the same term for seeking out a thing. Fallen man's mind, his natural wisdom and desire after the flesh, now lead him to devise inventions of his own. They are evil inventions, far from uprightness in their origin in thought, design, and motive, not just in their external form. The light of wisdom, which was in man by creation, has been changed into darkness; a skilled use of the creation and development of it he still has, but now in the service of sin. It is, under the judgment of God, subject to vanity as a result.

Nor is it a matter of a few things; the matter is one of many inventions. The history of wicked Lamech and his sons Jabal, Jubal, and Tubal-Cain, the seed of Cain and the serpent, is here brought to mind (Gen. 4:20-24). God made man upright, but what became of it through the fall? Sin developed, and man became the gatherer of earthly riches, heaping and gathering them as did Jabal. He gave himself in his music and art to the service of sin as did Jubal. He developed technology and the sciences, discovered iron and brass as did Tubal-Cain. He walked in oppression as did wicked Lamech, the murderer. Even the woman "who heart is snares and nets" (Eccl. 7:26) echoes Lamech's wives and daughter. Lamech is the original polygamist, a sin which Solomon carried to new depths, contrary to the law of God (Deut. 17:17). The contrast is between the God-created uprightness and these many inventions of men. The evil is not in things, but in man the thinker, developer, and inventor who labors in vanity in the service of sin and bondage to it.

This is the summary. What also became of them? They were destroyed in the judgment of God in the flood. What has been the history of the works of men? At the tower of Babel, the city of Sodom, the land of Canaan under the Amorites, Egypt with its plagues, the Red Sea, Jericho— the history is one of judgment and destruction. These are works wrought in vanity. What then of Solomon's own works? What of the glory of his kingdom? He has wrestled throughout Ecclesiastes with the issue that he must give his works to the one who comes after, and who knows whether that one will be wise or foolish? But more than that, there is the fact that stands at the end of the book, and it is to this that Solomon would lead us: "For God shall bring every work into judgment, with every secret thing, whether it be good, or whether it be evil" (Eccl. 12:14). This is the testimony of God's judgments in history, already now in this life and certainly in the final judgment.

As a preacher, Solomon by this sober assessment is leading the reader step-by-step to the conclusion he will set before us at the end, "Fear God, and keep his commandments: for this is the whole duty of man" (Eccl. 12:13). That conclusion is well-founded, for "Lo, this only have I found, that God made man upright; but they have sought out many inventions" (Eccl. 7:29). This is the only conclusion possible, that which "only have I found" and to which alone one may come in a world fallen in sin and in itself under judgment. This is what is to be found by nature under the sun. Salvation and renewal, forgiveness, righteousness, and eternal life can come only from above and by a wonder of grace from God alone. True heavenly wisdom, that walks in the fear of God, is also from above, a gift of God's grace.

CHAPTER 8

The Blessing of Wisdom

1. Who is as the wise man? and who knoweth the interpretation of a thing? a man's wisdom maketh his face to shine, and the boldness of his face shall be changed.
2. I counsel thee to keep the king's commandment, and that in regard of the oath of God.
3. Be not hasty to go out of his sight: stand not in an evil thing; for he doeth whatsoever pleaseth him.
4. Where the word of a king is, there is power: and who may say unto him, What doest thou?
5. Whoso keepeth the commandment shall feel no evil thing: and a wise man's heart discerneth both time and judgment.—Ecclesiastes 8:1–5

The conclusion reached in the preceding chapter is that wisdom, which is of God, true spiritual wisdom and understanding, is a rare gift of God in a fallen world. Fallen man walks after his own carnal wisdom, which is the folly of sin. The problem is "God hath made man upright; but they have sought out many inventions" (Eccl. 7:29).

To this must be added that God's wisdom transcends man's understanding, even the understanding of those that fear him, so that as Solomon sought out wisdom and understanding, he was compelled to say: "That which is far off, and exceeding deep, who can find it out?" (v. 24).

The way of wisdom for man is to seek it first of all in God's word: God's revelation of himself, his will, and his law teach wisdom. The wise man is instructed of God therein. The path of wisdom leads one who fears God away from himself and his own imagination to submission in humility before God. In that walk in the word and will of God is to be found God's blessing. This leads Solomon to a certain admonition or counsel to keep that word of God with reverence, for God maintains his word in his sovereignty and judgment.

He approaches this admonition by way of a rhetorical question: "Who is as the wise man? and who knoweth the interpretation of a thing?" (Eccl. 8:1). Solomon declares repeatedly in the book of Proverbs that wisdom is the principal thing to be sought after, to be desired more than gold, and is the gift of God. To have this gift is to be a wise man who "knoweth the interpretation of a thing," that is, discerns and understands the meaning of things.

The blessing of wisdom is twofold. First, "a man's wisdom maketh his face to shine" (Eccl. 8:1). The shining of God's face is a figure of his turning upon us in favor, rooted in his grace and love. Here the figure is, in a sense, a reflection of God's favor, in the face of a man who has wisdom and understanding within by God's grace. It gives him an inner peace and joy reflected in his face. The face of the wise man reflects that joy and peace and manifests it in a peaceable spirit.

Second, the effect is that the boldness, or fierceness and hardness, of his face is changed. Wisdom works a humbling of pride, yielding a gentle spirit. A sanctifying grace of God, it breaks the power of a sinful human nature that is hard and self-willed. It works a change that bears the fruit of meekness, humility, and submission, leading away from sin into a pathway that lives out of having peace with God.

The way of wisdom is the way of faith in the fear of God that takes heed to his word. "I counsel thee to keep the king's commandment, and that in regard of the oath of God" (v. 2). This verse and the following section have been variously understood. It is possible to understand it, as some do, as referring to the fifth commandment to honor the king as an earthly magistrate. This does not well fit the immediate context nor the full language of the text that follows. It is better to understand the text and what follows as being preeminently of God as the king, in his word, sovereign majesty, and judgment. The thought parallels Ecclesiastes 5: "Keep thy foot when thou goest to the house of God...for God is in heaven, and thou upon earth" (vv. 1–2).

The admonition or counsel (the words *counsel thee* are added) is to keep the commandment, literally, "the mouth of the king," that is, the word that proceeds out of his mouth: his will and judgment, and hence commandment. To keep that word, when it is God's word, is to hold it by faith in the heart, to regard it with respect, and to walk in obedience to it. He adds "in regard of the oath of God," or even in the matter of the oath of God (8:2). This expression is difficult as it may refer to what God has sworn or what man has sworn before God. The latter is perhaps the starting point. For Solomon has spoken in Ecclesiastes 5 of one who is "rash with [his] mouth" and hasty in heart to speak a vow in the presence of God and then seek a way to annul it (vv. 2–6). In his prayer at the dedication of the temple and the bringing of the ark into it as the emblem of God's throne, Solomon prayed,

31. If any man trespass against his neighbour, and an oath be laid upon him to cause him to swear, and the oath come before thine altar in this house:

32. Then hear thou in heaven, and do, and judge thy servants, condemning the wicked, to bring his way upon his head; and justifying the righteous, to give him according to hisrighteousness."—1 Kings 8:31–32

It is that prayer which God declares to Solomon he has heard, appearing to him the second time (1 Kings 9:1–9).

While the house of David, as God's anointed kings, must

judge the people in righteousness in harmony with such an oath, it is God's judgment that is on the foreground in Solomon's prayer. If the text is to be understood of an earthly king, then it is to be limited to the throne of David, the messianic throne, God's visible representative as king, in Solomon as type and Christ in its fulfillment. God speaks his word and maintains it. He judges among men, our words and works. Entering his presence, we enter the place of the judgment of the king, also with our oaths and vows. He holds them. He who keeps the word of God in his heart and walks in obedience, regards his oaths or vows in the light of the majesty and righteousness of the king before whom he speaks.

Thus the admonition follows:

3. Be not hasty to go out of his sight: stand not in an evil thing; for he doeth whatsoever pleaseth him.
4. Where the word of the king is, there is power: and who may say unto him, What doest thou? (Eccl. 8:3–4)

Ultimately it is in the sight or presence of God that we stand. Into that presence of God we consciously come in prayer, in worship, and in all our spiritual activities. Before that presence a child of God would come in the Old Testament when he entered the temple to pray (Eccl. 5:1), and when he entered the throne room of God's anointed king. Careless irreverence before the majesty of the king had no place there then, nor does it now before God in Christ in heaven. God's throne is a throne of righteous judgment.

"Stand not in an evil thing" (8:3). Before that holy throne, sin, especially unrepentant sin, has no place. Yet such is the pride and folly of sin that just as in the case of the Pharisee in Jesus' parable, or as Cain and his sacrifice, men enter God's presence in the arrogance of sin and rebelliously stand before him. "Stand not in an evil thing" is therefore the warning. For the king is *king,* and his will prevails. That will of the holy king of heaven and earth is a holy and sovereign will. He declares: "My counsel shall stand, and I will do all my pleasure" (Isa. 46:10; see also Eph. 1:11).

While an earthly king may manifest a measure of sovereignty as a tyrant, God's sovereign kingship is absolutely holy in power and judgment. Where his word is there is also indeed the power to perform his will, to bless and to curse in judgment and to carry out that blessing and curse in judgment. Of God above all, none may say "what doest thou?" He is truly God, and we are but creatures of the dust and by nature inventors of evil things.

But that means also God carries out his judgment in time, in his providence according to his own counsel, will, and purpose, which are often hidden from us. Judgment may seem delayed in time. This is part of the concern with which Solomon struggles in the rest of the chapter. But he lays here the foundation, in calling us to submission before the king, to a patient waiting upon his will, and in wisdom to a resting in his word which he will surely perform, for his word never returns unto him void.

Thus Solomon arrives at the blessedness of wisdom in the fear of God. "Whoso keepeth the commandment shall feel no evil thing; and a wise man's heart discerneth both time and judgment" (Eccl. 8:5). The words rendered *feel* and *discerneth* in the verse are the same word in the original Hebrew. The word means to know something by experience and thus to be able to discern something with a certain measure of understanding. Keeping the commandments of God guards one from sin and evil; and while trouble and trials do come in God's sovereign providence, yet he makes "all things work together for good to them that love" him (Rom. 8:28). Submitting himself to God's will in wisdom, a wise man knows God as a righteous judge who will, according to his own time and purpose, render just judgment. He will deliver the righteous and judge the wicked. Such understanding works a patient waiting upon the will of God in trial and affliction, giving peace to mind and heart.

Let us then seek earnestly for this blessing of wisdom at the mouth of the king, whose word is pure and whose testimonies restore the soul.

Of Time and Judgment

6. Because to every purpose there is time and judgment, therefore the misery of man is great upon him.

7. For he knoweth not that which shall be: for who can tell him when it shall be?

8. There is no man that hath power over the spirit to retain the spirit; neither hath he power in the day of death: and there is no discharge in that war; neither shall wickedness deliver those that are given to it.

9. All this have I seen, and applied my heart unto every work that is done under the sun: there is a time wherein one man ruleth over another to his own hurt.

10. And so I saw the wicked buried, who had come and gone from the place of the holy, and they were forgotten in the city where they had so done: this is also vanity.

11. Because sentence against an evil work is not executed speedily, therefore the heart of the sons of men is fully set in them to do evil.—Ecclesiastes 8:6–11

The gift of wisdom in the fear of God works both the grace of contentment and a knowledge of God's sovereignty over the life of men that yields a submissive and obedient heart. Thus it is said: "Whoso keepeth the commandment shall feel no evil thing; and a wise man's heart discerneth both time and judgment" (Eccl. 8:5). To underscore this truth Solomon returns to the point made in chapter 3: "To every thing there is a season, and a time to every purpose under heaven" (v. 1). To that idea of a time or season he now also adds judgment, which wisdom also discerns, for therein lies an element of its blessedness.

"Because to every purpose there is time and judgment" (8:6).

The purposes or affairs of life come in time as God disposes. There is a time to every matter that occupies the life of man whether to be born or die, to gather and build, or to scatter and tear down. God's purpose is realized therein. God also "shall bring every work into judgment" (12:14).

This is reality. Man is not the master of his own existence, but man who is fallen strives with the sovereign majesty of God in rebellion, as he is the inventor of evil things (7:29). The result is: "the misery of man is great upon him" (8:6). Misery is that which is evil. The evil of man is great; it multiplies itself in his life, and with it come the wretchedness and misery of his life. Man is not in control of his life. God indeed "doeth whatsoever pleaseth him" (v. 3), but of man such cannot be said. Of man it must be said: "For he knoweth not that which shall be: for who can tell him when it shall be?" (v. 7).

Man may indeed claim to be in control of his life and times, but they are not in his own hand. Though he walk in the pride of his heart, yet he is but dust. He does not know, let alone control, what shall be on the morrow. Wisdom teaches a man to say, "If the Lord will, we shall...do this or that" (James 4:15).

Further, God's sovereign government is characterized by righteous judgment. He not only ordains what will come to pass but does so as one who judges the works of men in time and in eternity. "The wages of sin is death" (Rom. 6:23), and "the soul that sinneth, it shall die" (Ezek. 18:4). There is time and judgment. Nor does man know what shall be or when. Neither concerning his plans and designs, nor even concerning the measure of his own days, is his life in his hand.

Solomon would drive this point home. He says: "There is no man that hath power over the spirit to retain the spirit; neither hath he power in the day of death: and there is no discharge in that war; neither shall wickedness deliver those who are given to it" (Eccl. 8:8). Man's spirit is that breath of life in him. It comes from the word for wind or breath by which the Spirit of God breathed into man at his creation "the breath of life; and man became a living soul" (Gen. 2:7). Death is first described as the departure of that human spirit. It departs, and he dies. He has no power over it to stave off the departure of his spirit. It is in the hand of the Spirit of God. "Thou hidest thy face, they are troubled: thou takest away their breath, they die, and return to their dust" (Ps. 104:29); "neither hath he power in the day of death" (Eccl. 8:8). Man is like the beast that dies. Before the power of death he is frail and helpless. Whether it comes by age or disease, accident or sudden event, the time of it is in the hand of God, and it belongs to the judgment of God upon sin.

Wicked man is particularly described here as being at war and as seeking to deliver himself by his wickedness. He strives with death to gain the mastery over it, to put it from him, to be lord over its power. He would retain the spirit; he would remove the day of death. Sinful man seeks to escape that conflict to gain a victory over it. Much of his labor in science and medicine is directed to that end. So likewise he labors to ease the burdens of life and its hardships, that death may be thrust away from him. He heaps and gathers riches to make himself secure in an evil day. He pursues pleasures of sin and yet seeks to escape the consequences of them. When death becomes inevitable, then he may seek to rule it by taking his own life, but he is not its master.

Death is a relentless enemy of man's life of sinful self-indulgence: "and there is no discharge in that war, neither shall wickedness deliver those that are given to it" (Eccl. 8:8). And yet under the sun it may seem that there is not judgment, for all men die, the righteous as well as the wicked.

Solomon now turns to illustrate this dilemma. As man who works evil does not seem to suffer the consequences, the judgment due to his evil, Solomon says: "All this have I seen, and applied my heart unto every work that is done under the sun: there is a time wherein one man ruleth over another to his own hurt" (v. 9). Among the works of men are the wicked works of oppression, particularly when one has power over others. The rich, the powerful, the cunning man who oppresses his neighbor, passes in review before Solomon's eyes among the works done under the sun. That he has the wicked in view is clear from verse 10. Solomon would have us to see that wicked man as he also sees him in this world under the sun.

What of that wicked man? The viewpoint is similar to that of Psalm 73 and the prosperity of the wicked. The wicked man dies; seemingly there are "no bands in their death: but their strength is firm" (Ps. 73:4). The inspired writer observes: "And so I saw the wicked buried, who had come and gone from the place of the holy, and they were forgotten in the city where they had so done: this is also vanity" (Eccl. 8:10). Did that oppressor die in shame and misery? No, he was buried, no doubt with great men eulogizing his passing. He was profane, though outwardly religious, like the Pharisees who robbed widows' houses yet came and went in and out of the temple and before God's holy presence.

Yes, the wicked man died, but so do the pious and godly. Where then was justice? He lived his days and departed. While it is true that, departing, he also departed from the holy men or godly who were so often the objects of his oppression—an alternative explanation for the place of the holy—yet this explanation does not address the development of the vanity found in the situation. Death is exactly that which is seen under the sun to touch the righteous and the wicked. Rather it is the fact that he did die. There was an end to his wickedness. He did not deliver his own soul from death

This pattern is so familiar in human life. Men come and go. Such a man dies and is forgotten, and the evil works which he did are also forgotten. They are caused to be forgotten, that is put out of mind and remembrance. Therein is the vanity of the matter under the sun. Wicked man takes no instruction from his wicked neighbor's death. It is treated as normal or natural and forgotten. However, death is the judgment of God that he did not escape.

That judgment did come with its horror upon one who did wickedly and profanely, but that judgement is not taken to heart. The life of men in the city goes on. The one forgetting is yet one who from his own death cannot also escape. The sentence or verdict of God is there, but it is not seen by the eye of men. It is only by faith that the wise ponder the matter.

This leads to a certain conclusion: "Because the sentence against an evil work is not executed speedily, therefore the heart of the sons of men is fully set in them to do evil" (v. 11). Evil works bring down upon them the just judgment of God. God's condemnation of these evil works in his law is manifest. His word stands, and his verdict goes forth from his throne concerning them as a divine decree and sentence of guilt in judgment. But the sentence is not carried out speedily. The wicked are not instantly smitten in God's wrath. In the moment of sin, judgment does not immediately fall upon the sinner. Adam and Eve did not immediately drop down dead physically when they sinned, nor did Cain instantly perish when he murdered his brother.

That the sentence is not speedily executed does not mean it is not there, nor that God's judgment is not at work in the life of the wicked. It is the sentence of physical death, which takes a man's name and place under the sun that is under consideration. For God's people this seeming delay belongs to the mercy of God who brings his people to repentance, faith, and forgiveness in Christ. The apostle Paul describes the goodness, forbearance, and longsuffering of God as that which "leadeth thee to repentance" (Rom. 2:4).

But with the wicked it has the opposite effect. They see also that the sentence is not speedily executed. This is the issue the passage in Romans addresses. Natural man thinks or deceives himself into thinking that he shall escape judgment or has escaped it (Rom. 2:3). He despises God's mercy shown to his people in this delay, and it does not lead him to repentance (v. 4). "But after thy hardness and impenitent heart treasurest up unto thyself wrath against day of wrath and revelation of the righteous judgment of God" (v. 5). This is the same concern that Solomon has in Ecclesiastes. That God's judgment is not visibly manifested speedily in death leads men's hearts in the way of their own wickedness. "Therefore the heart of the sons of men is fully set in them to do evil" (Eccl. 8:11). The effect is that described in Psalm 73: "And they say, How doth God know? and is there knowledge in the most High?" (v. 11).

The result in the life of men is that their heart is "fully set to do evil" (v. 11). They develop in sin. Their conscience is hardened. Sin and pride grow in them not only unto the day of their death but unto the day of God's final judgment upon sin, the day of wrath and revelation of the righteous judgment of God. The word of God makes it clear that behind this is the purpose of God that sin appear as sin in the day of judgment. Sin develops in the life of the wicked individual and in a wicked world and its society. It develops under an operation of the wrath of God spiritually, so that the full reality of sin as worthy of eternal judgment is made plain. The individual is treasuring up wrath against the day of wrath. The cup of iniquity in a wicked world is being filled up (Gen. 15:16). Sin grows as a weed that is to be cut down and burnt. This is the organic development of sin under the wrath of God described in Romans 1:18–32.

The result is, therefore, that their heart is filled up in them to do evil, and the sons of men, fallen in sin, pursue sin. They seek out many inventions or devices to sin (Eccl. 7:29). Occasionally the sins of some catch up with the wicked in this life, and they are brought to shame. But often they seemingly stand even above the law of men, buy their way out of difficulty, and continue on in their ungodly way. The full judgment of God is not seen under the sun, with one exception: they die. Death is the norm in human life, but it is not normal; it is the judgment of God upon sin. The wicked perish, and with it their hope ceases: their treasures go not with them, and they stand before the judgment seat of God. They do not escape.

It Shall Be Well with the Righteous

12. Though a sinner do evil an hundred times, and his days be prolonged, yet surely I know that it shall be well with them that fear God, which fear before him:

13. But it shall not be well with the wicked, neither shall he prolong his days, which are as a shadow; because he feareth not before God.

14. There is a vanity which is done upon the earth; that there be just men, unto whom it happeneth according to the work of the wicked; again, there be wicked men, to whom it happeneth according to the work of the righteous: I said that this also is vanity.

15. Then I commended mirth, because a man hath no better thing under the sun, than to eat, and to drink, and to be merry: for that shall abide with him of his labour the days of his life, which God giveth him under the sun.

16. When I applied mine heart to know wisdom, and to see the business that is done up-on the earth: (for also there is that neither day nor night seeth sleep with his eyes:)

17. Then I beheld all the work of God, that a man cannot find out the work that is done under the sun: because though a man labour to seek it out, yet he shall not find it; yea further; though a wise man think to know it, yet shall he not be able to find it.—Ecclesiastes 8:12–17

The word of God now turns to a confession of faith. What is seen under the sun, because God's judgment does not fall immediately on the wicked, is that the wicked pursue their evil course. "Therefore the heart of the sons of men is fully set in them to do evil" (Eccl. 8:11). They arrogantly presume that God does not know and cannot or will not judge.

They are wrong. But this is a matter of faith in the truth of God as a righteous and holy God, who is both sovereign over the affairs of men's lives, and who judges sin in time and eternity. Therefore "though a sinner do evil an hundred times, and his days be prolonged…it shall not be well with the wicked" (vv. 12–13). The word *prolong* is used twice in verses 12 and 13 with a different reference point. The first refers to his evil activity. He walks in his sin and does evil again and again so that the days of his evil activity are extended. His days in that sense are prolonged, a hundredfold in his evil works. It may seem as if he escapes judgment. Wisdom discerns that all is not what it seems. "It shall not be well with" him. There is an end that must be taken into consideration. The sinner shall die and enter into the place of judgment. We may be inclined to see only what is before us at the moment: the pathway of wicked men and their works, or the misery in the wake of their sins. What that wicked man is actually doing is filling up the cup of iniquity unto condemnation; he is not "getting away with it."

Solomon says this pathway of life of the wicked does not truly prosper. "But it shall not be well with the wicked, neither shall he prolong his days, which are as a shadow" (v. 13). The second reference point, in that word *prolong*, is to the measure of his days. His prolonged career in sin does not add days to his life, as Solomon has said, "neither shall wickedness deliver those that are given to it" (v. 8). The sinner is running unto death and judgment. Solomon has made this point before, that though a man live twice a thousand years without good, it profits nothing for he still dies (6:6). He has no peace now, and judgment will come.

Solomon draws a picture of that life of the wicked. It is as a shadow. It is a transitory passing thing, insubstantial like a shadow or a passing vapor. It is also like a shadow that grows longer and longer toward sunset, until it vanishes away with the close of day. As that shadow that grows long and fades, so the lengthening of the wicked in sin does not mean it is well with them. They stand under the wrath of God and descend into eternal darkness. They shall perish. The root of their folly is also set before us: it is so with the wicked "because he feareth not before God" (8:13).

By contrast Solomon says: "Yet surely I know that it shall be well with them that fear God, which fear before him" (v. 12). The fear of God is the beginning and true foundation of wisdom. It is the way of blessing. He repeats the idea: there is the person, the God-fearer; and there is his walking by faith in true wisdom, fearing before God. By implication he turns from the way of evil to walk by faith in childlike obedience. For he is not only a God-fearer, but of them "which fear before him." He lives consciously as one who stands in the presence of God, the king, hearkening to his word, trusting his grace, and walking in that fear before him.

By faith Solomon can say of them that fear God "that it shall be well with them" (v. 12). God's grace and favor shine upon them now, and though their days also are as a shadow in time, under the sun, yet their end is blessed.

Such confidence of faith is needed, for we walk by faith in God's promises, not by our own understanding in what is seen under the sun. Under the sun, what we see may appear contradictory. He declares,

> There is a vanity which is done upon the earth; that there be just men, unto whom it happeneth according to the work of the wicked; again, there be wicked men, to whom it happeneth according to the work of the righteous: I said that this also is vanity." (v. 14)

"Happen" here is not random chance but rather a sudden touch that strikes or brings one to the ground. In the context, it is God's sovereign rule over man's life when death carries him away. The righteous and the wicked both die. The righteous die and suffer affliction, while the wicked go on in the way of their sin. Job is an example of this: who though righteous, yet it happened unto him according to the work of the wicked. It was exactly the error of Job's friends that, as it happened to him according to the work of the wicked, they drew the conclusion that Job himself must be wicked. The same mistake is made when judgment does not fall immediately or quickly upon the wicked.

The mistaken premise is that we can figure out what God is doing and understand his judgment by what we see in the world around us. It belongs to the limitations of wisdom and man's understanding that this is not so. It belongs to the vanity, the transitory character of our life and of the world itself. Solomon explains this more fully in what follows, but first he would draw out a conclusion that he has pointed out before, rooted in that vanity of life, our limitations of understanding, and our calling to walk in fear before God. The right conclusion is not despair, nor the pride of the wicked who do not fear before God. Rather it is to live in the present in contentment of faith with thanksgiving. He says,

> Then I commended mirth, because a man hath no better thing under the sun, than to eat, and to drink, and to be merry: for that shall abide with him of his labour the days of his life, which God giveth him under the sun." (v, 15)

In commending mirth or rejoicing, Solomon is not saying let your heart be in the house of feasting and mirth (7:2–4). He has rejected that impulse as the way of folly. To rejoice in the present daily blessings, one's daily bread, is not only appropriate but the way of wisdom. The morrow is hidden from us. This kind of rejoicing, the rejoicing of the covetous man, the man pursuing evil, can never really do. His bondage to covetousness will not let him rest in contentment and rejoice. His mirth is that of excess, sought as an end in itself. Rather Solomon has in view what abides with us of our present labor under the sun. The word *abiding* has a kind of figure in it, in the original, of a person who comes and lodges for one night and is gone. So also is the fruit of our labor for the day. It is to be received with rejoicing, and the blessings received under the sun for that day. This is the way of wisdom. In that sense we are to "eat, and to drink, and to be merry," or rejoice (8:15).

This includes also a recognition that God himself imposes this limitation upon us in the transitory character of life under the sun. The days of our life and our labor are that "which God giveth [us] under the sun" (v. 15). This rejoicing is part of what God is doing with them that fear God, his blessing upon us. The measure of our days is in his hand. He sends both joy and sorrow. Thus we may see, though it is by faith, that it is well with us for his grace shines upon our way. And the end of that way, though death, is also a matter of faith, and there too "it shall be well with them that fear God" (v. 12).

By faith also we know that it shall not be well with the wicked. God is righteous and a righteous judge. That truth of who God is is not shaken by the transitory character of life or its vanity. Rather, that truth of vanity imposes a limitation upon our understanding from what is seen under the sun. The life of man and the whole creation through the fall is subjected to vanity. Wisdom belongs to the comfort of faith in discerning the will of God and walking in it in fear before him. It has also a limitation. God is God, and his sovereign determination is not revealed to us in the ordinary affairs of life.

God has sent signs of his judgment in history recorded in his word, that we may know that he is a righteous judge over against sin. He showed himself to be such in the flood, the plagues upon Egypt, the destruction of Pharaoh in the Red Sea, the fall of Jericho, and the destruction of Sodom. That he is a righteous judge, God's word and works testify. But that does not mean that we can figure it out day by day in ordinary life by what is present in the world before us. Thus, there is a limitation to wisdom, in that which is hidden in the counsel of God. The very vain transitory character of life, where we do not know what shall be or when it shall be, makes it so. The problem is not in God: the limitation is in us as creatures of the dust.

Solomon therefore addresses further this limitation:

16. When I applied mine heart to know wisdom, and to see the business that is done upon earth: (for also there is that neither day nor night seeth sleep with his eyes:)

17. Then I beheld all the work of God, that a man cannot find out the work that is done under the sun: because though a man labour to seek it out, yet he shall not find it; yea further; though a wise man think to know it, yet shall he not be able to find it." (Eccl. 16–17)

Solomon by the gift given him had applied his heart to know wisdom, to understand with skill and discernment the world around him. This was a matter of applying his heart, not merely his mind. That is, he was seeking a spiritual understanding, not simply earthly wisdom, for the heart is the spiritual center of a man's life. He sought to see the business or travail that is done upon earth, so as to know it, to discern and understand it. He sought not merely the outward form of it but its meaning and purpose. He was seeking to know God's purpose and work therein.

He points us to the intense and prolonged character of his study and reflection. The parentheses added in the next part by the translation would suggest that the all-seeing eye of God and his beholding the works of men is being mentioned. The parentheses could better be dropped, as it is rather Solomon's sleeplessness that is indicated. In seeking to understand, he kept himself awake at night with his reflections so that "neither day nor night" he saw sleep with his eyes (v. 16). He did what many a child of God has done pondering a matter, particularly when it is one of trouble and distress, when the way of God is not clear, or when the burden of the matter weighs upon mind and heart. It is this spiritual struggle that is in view in which one walks the floor over the matter the way one walks with a fussy infant with a fever.

From it he derives his conclusion: "Then I beheld all the work of God, that a man cannot find out the work done under the sun"

(v. 17). The conclusion reached is that behind all "the business done upon the earth," there is the "work of God" (vv. 16–17), that is, God's sovereign disposition and ordering of men's affairs by his almighty power. To that work belongs both that God is righteous in judgment and that yet it happens to the righteous and the wicked in a way that transcends our limited understanding (v. 14). Because behind the works of man is the work of God, "a man cannot find out the work that is done under the sun" (v. 17). This is a matter not simply of frustration with the limits of our understanding. It is rather part of his confession, as the fruit of reflection; and as such, it testifies to a humbling of one who is a child of God in submission to the will of God.

The searching of wisdom in man is limited. What is known is known by faith, not merely by the power of earthly observation and discernment. "Because though a man labour to seek it out, yet he shall not find it; yea further; though a wise man think to know it, yet shall he not be able to find it" (v. 17). This is Solomon's confession of his own activity, of his sleepless nights. The activity was not unfruitful, as the book testifies, but the wisdom derived from it is limited, because the one seeking to understand is himself finite and limited. The work God does is a divine work, transcending the power of man, a mere creature, though a believing child of God, to fully comprehend it. The principles we may know, which God has revealed in his word. The way of God in his holy perfection and his sovereignty over all things is set before us in Scripture. But wisdom, which is given to bring instruction and comfort, is not exhaustive. The works of God are far deeper than our thoughts. Wisdom is not an end in itself. It leads us beyond ourselves into the presence of God, that we should fear before him in all his majesty, power, and glory. It leads therefore to the real comfort of wisdom, which says "thy will be done."

CHAPTER 9

"All Things Come Alike to All"

1. For all this I considered in my heart even to declare all this, that the righteous, and the wise, and their works, are in the hand of God: no man knoweth either love or hatred by all that is before them.

2. All things come alike to all: there is one event to the righteous, and to the wicked; to the good and to the clean, and to the unclean; to him that sacrificeth, and to him that sacrificeth not: as is the good, so is the sinner; and he that sweareth, as he that feareth an oath.

3. This is an evil among all things that are done under the sun, that there is one event unto all: yea, also the heart of the sons of men is full of evil, and madness is in their heart while they live, and after that they go to the dead.—Ecclesiastes 9:1–3

Solomon has reached a certain limitation in the wisdom he sought. He has just said: "Then I beheld all the work of God, that a man cannot find out the work that is done under the sun: because though a man labour to seek it out, yet he shall not find it; yea further; though a wise man think to know it, yet shall he not be able to find it." (Eccl. 8:17). God's works transcend man's understanding and, beholding those works under the sun, there is much hidden from us in God's counsel. The judgments of the righteous and sovereign God are deeper than wisdom can discern from what is seen under the sun.

Now he continues: "For all this I considered in my heart even to declare all this, that the righteous, and the wise, and their works, are in the hand of God: no man knoweth either love or hatred by all that is before him" (Eccl. 9:1). This limitation Solomon considers and spiritually takes to his own heart that he may declare or explain it also to us. The truth is that the righteous and the wise and their works are in the hand of God. God holds his people—for that is who the righteous and the wise are—in his hand. God is indeed gracious and merciful to his people. He governs and directs their works in time under the sun according to his own counsel and purpose. As the objects of his grace and love, they and their works serve the realization of his counsel and purpose. This is known by faith through the promises of God. They and their works are truly in the hand of God, which holds them not simply as sovereign over them, but as the one who upholds, governs, and directs them. That man's wisdom and understanding are limited does not mean we are devoid of comfort. Rather, by this limitation, we are called to a childlike trust and confidence in God and his fatherly care.

This leads to an important conclusion when we contemplate what is seen under the sun: "no man knoweth either love or hatred by all that is before him" (v. 1). The love and hatred spoken of are the love and hatred of God. The scriptural idea of God's love embraces the truth of his grace, mercy, and goodness, while God's hatred includes his wrath, anger, and judgment. The point made is that you cannot and may not by looking at external circumstances—the affairs of life that are before you, before your face—draw the conclusion that God either loves or hates you, your neighbor, or someone else. What you see under the sun does not itself reveal the attitude of God. To know that you must go to his revealed word.

God is no respecter of persons. "He maketh his sun to rise on the evil and on the good, and sendeth rain on the just and on the unjust" (Matt. 5:45). Seeing this, you may not draw the conclusion that all men are the objects of his grace, not even of a "common grace," or find in it a general goodness of God toward men. God is good, all he does is good, and his gifts are good gifts in the creation. But they are not a revelation of a universal favor of God or an attitude of grace toward all. Solomon here rejects such a conclusion as false, for it is based on a mistaken inference from what is seen.

Similarly when calamities come as they did to Job, we may not draw the false conclusion that God's wrath has come in judgment as Job's friends did. The prosperity of the wicked does not mean that God loves them. The poverty of Lazarus, in the parable of the rich man and Lazarus, does not mean that God hates Lazarus and loves the rich man. In the parable the opposite is true (Luke 16:19-31).

The reality is: "All things come alike to all" (Eccl. 9:2). God deals with men and the life of men organically so that in the daily course of life "all things come alike to all." Fruitful and barren years, riches and poverty, sickness and health are so in the hand of God that they come upon men personally and corporately, in such a way that, in themselves, you may not draw from them the conclusion that God loves or hates this person or that person, this nation or that nation.

Sin manifestly has consequences, but all have sinned. All deserve the consequences of sin. But from what can be seen, the wrong interpretation may not be drawn. Jesus takes this up in its negative aspect when confronting the Jews:

1. There were present at that season some that told him of the Galilaeans, whose blood Pilate had mingled with their sacrifices.
2. And Jesus answering said unto them, Suppose ye that these Galilaeans were sinners above all the Galilaeans, because they suffered such things?
3. I tell you, Nay: but, except ye repent, ye shall all likewise perish.

4. Or those eighteen, upon whom the tower in Siloam fell, and slew them, think ye that they were sinners above all men that dwelt in Jerusalem?

5. I tell you, Nay: but, except ye repent, ye shall all likewise perish. (Luke 13:1–5)

The word of God guards us from the erroneous conclusion, which we are inclined by nature to draw from what we see. We would infer God's love or hatred from external circumstances or from things seen under the sun. But grace and wrath are not in things. The point is both important in the practical circumstances of our own life as well as important for our doctrinal understanding. "No man knoweth either love or hatred by all that is before them. All things come alike to all" (Eccl. 9:1–2). It is exactly our natural tendency when things go well with us to feel that God loves us and when things go badly that God is against us. The knowledge of God's love, his chastening hand of correction for sin, the burden of a troubled conscience belong to the knowledge of faith by the word. God may use the circumstances of life or the consequences of our behavior to drive us to that truth revealed in his word and to repentance, but we may not make a false inference from things in themselves. The same is true doctrinally for the theories of some universal favor or goodness of God in rain and sunshine. Such an inference is here repudiated by the text, so that it is well worth repeating: "no man knoweth either love or hatred by all that is before them. All things come alike to all" (vv. 1–2).

This truth Solomon demonstrates in the rest of verse 2: death comes upon all. "There is one event to the righteous, and to the wicked; to the good and to the clean, and to the unclean; to him that sacrificeth, and to him that sacrificeth not: as is the good, so is the sinner; and he that sweareth, as he that that feareth an oath" (v. 2). That one event to which all are subject no matter whether they are good or evil, righteous or wicked, is death. This contrast of good and evil, where yet one event comes upon all, means also that God's righteous judgment is largely hidden from our sight under the sun. By faith we know that God is righteous and judges in time and eternity, but that does not mean that we may ourselves see this work of God with our earthly sight under the sun.

This fact, that all are subject to one event, namely death, brings out the truth that God is no respecter of persons and underscores the limitation of our understanding by what we see before us. All die and through death are subjected to vanity in this world and to a judgment hidden from us in that which is to come for an individual at the moment of his death. It is by faith in the light of God's promises and his righteousness that Solomon confessed in the preceding chapter: "Though a sinner do evil an hundred times, and his days be prolonged, yet surely I know that it shall be well with them that fear God, which fear before him: but it shall not be well with the wicked" (8:12–13).

Further, Solomon points us to a certain fruit this reality has in the life of men. That no one knows love or hatred by all that is before him, that one event comes to all, that all are subject to vanity and death, all work a certain spiritual fruit in the life of man as he is fallen by nature. He says: "This is an evil among all things that are done under the sun, that there is one event unto all: yea, also the heart of the sons of men is full of evil, and madness is in their heart while they live, and after that they go to the dead" (9:3). The evil of which he speaks is not in that which God does, but in the effect God's work has upon the heart of wicked man because he is a sinner.

Verse 3 speaks of the "sons of men," which may well have here the original sense for the word *men*, which is of sons of the man, that is Adam. For it is man as he is fallen in Adam and under the judgment of death who stands before us. Fallen man's heart is "full of evil, and "madness;" the folly and blindness of sin is "in his heart" (v. 3). The root of the problem is that man through the fall into sin has become totally depraved by nature. Evil is not only in his works and deeds, but it is in his heart. The heart is the spiritual center of man's life out of which arises the activity of his life in thinking and willing, working and doing. The folly of sin resides there, in the heart of the fallen, unregenerated sinner.

Sinful man sees that there is one event to all: that all die and leave this life. He is confronted by the transitory vanity of this present life. He beholds the appearance, from what is seen with the eye, that there seems to be no difference between the good and the evil, the righteous and the wicked, because all leave this life. He draws the false conclusion: What difference does it really make as to what I do? He denies the judgment of God. He concludes as in Psalm 73:11: "And they say, How doth God know? and is there knowledge in the most High?" The effect of this is that the evil conclusion is drawn that I should live it up now, take from life what I can get in pleasure and excitement, and live for myself. It works the spiritual fruit in the heart of sinful man that he gives himself over unto the lusts of his flesh and is held in bondage to sin, both because he is fallen and yet also willingly as one who serves sin.

Sin works through also in this way: fallen man through fear of death is in his lifetime subject to spiritual bondage. Sin and bondage to sin reign over him and in him, in his heart. Solomon describes this sad state: evil and madness in his heart "while they live, and after that they go to the dead." They leave this life and go to the grave, and all they have in this life, their portion in the things of this world, is taken away. They die and depart forever from the earth. They wrongly conclude, Get it now! because God is not in their thoughts.

It belongs to the wonder of our salvation that Jesus Christ assumed our human nature from Adam to overcome and destroy death and its power to enslave us, so that, having redeemed us unto God, he might transform us from being sons of Adam to being sons of God.

14. Forasmuch then as the children are partakers of flesh and blood, he also himself likewise took part of the same;

that through death he might destroy him that had the power of death, that is, the devil;

15. And deliver them who through fear of death were all their lifetime subject to bondage. (Heb. 2:14–15)

Joined to the Living

4. For to him that is joined to all the living there is hope: for a living dog is better than a dead lion.

5. For the living know that they shall die: but the dead know not any thing, neither have they any more a reward; for the memory of them is forgotten.

6. Also their love, and their hatred, and their envy, is now perished; neither have they any more a portion for ever in any thing that is done under the sun.

7. Go thy way, eat thy bread with joy, and drink thy wine with a merry heart; for God now accepteth thy works.

8. Let thy garments be always white; and let thy head lack no ointment.

9. Live joyfully with the wife whom thou lovest all the days of the life of thy vanity, which he hath given thee under the sun, all the days of thy vanity: for that is thy portion in this life, and in thy labour which thou takest under the sun.

10. Whatsoever thy hand findeth to do, do it with thy might; for there is no work, nor device, nor knowledge, nor wisdom, in the grave, whither thou goest.—Ecclesiastes 9:4–10

One event, namely death, comes upon all, both the righteous and the wicked without distinction. This shapes the lives of the sons of men, fallen in sin, who shall die. The reason it shapes the lives of men lies in the finality of death and the contrast between the living and the dead. In setting forth this truth and its implications, Solomon turns to a description of this contrast in its various elements.

This is similar to his approach in Proverbs, where he frequently makes various observations before drawing a conclusion.

"For to him that is joined to all living there is hope: for a living dog is better than a dead lion" (Eccl. 9:4). The text sets before us the sphere of human activity, the road of life in which a man walks under the sun. It embraces all his earthly existence as he interacts with other men and the life of the creation. He is united or joined to it. It is his allotted place under the sun. God, his creator, gave him that place, uniting him to all the living in a bond of earthly life.

In that life there is hope or confidence that arises out of being joined to the living. The hope or confidence spoken of is not here the eternal hope of the believer but the daily expectation, planning, and activity of a man as he goes about his life under the sun. It is something we tend to take for granted, though as believers, we make it also a matter of prayer (James 4:15). The wicked live out of the same form of confidence of life, but their hope is rooted in themselves and their plans and desires. Though outwardly the earthly lives of believer and unbeliever are similar, the internal spiritual principle is markedly different.

But death coming suddenly, often without warning, hovers over that life of men as a dark cloud. That union with the living is in reality very tenuous, for men are creatures of the dust and like the grass of the field that passes away (Ps. 103:14–16). Nor does man have power over death. Solomon has said: "There is no man that hath power over the spirit to retain the spirit; neither hath he power in the day of death: and there is no discharge in that war; neither shall wickedness deliver those that are given to it" (Eccl. 8:8).

"For a living dog is better than a dead lion" (Eccl. 9:4). To draw out the comparison, Solomon uses what may have been a colloquial proverb with a contrasting picture. The dog mentioned is not a household pet but a scavenger who slinks down dark streets and across the fields, much like a coyote. Its character here is not so much its cunning, but that it is an animal that shies away from danger, having a strong sense of self-preservation and caution. By contrast, the lion is bold and fierce, ready to stand its ground, roaring its presence. The term *better* here does not have a moral connotation. The figure applied to people is one of the contrasts between shrinking self-preservation and brave courage. The one admired, the lion, however, is dead; his boldness leads to his destruction. The slinking dog lives, for he knows when to run away. The dog's lot is better because he abides among the living; he yet has hope in the world. The lion is a rotting carcass and has ceased from the earth.

Solomon then states the point more plainly: "For the living know that they shall die: but the dead know not any thing, neither have they any more a reward; for the memory of them is forgotten" (v. 5). The living have yet a portion under the sun, though with the knowledge that this present life shall end. They can still plan and carry out the activities of life. For the dead the door of life has closed, and that closing is final. The rewards or present benefits of life, its fruitful activity, has ceased. Their place and portion under the sun is taken away by death, and even their name in the world departs and is forgotten.

Solomon expands this latter thought: "Also their love, and their hatred, and their envy, is now perished; neither have they any more a portion for ever in any thing that is done under the sun" (v. 6). This is the grim reality of death under the sun. It is exactly this also which makes the life of man one of transient vanity. Death takes everything in this world from him in a moment. Solomon uses vivid language to drive home his point: his love, his hatred, his envy perish. All his plans and purposes, desires for good or evil, are ended. He has no more any portion under the sun. Death shuts the door of this present life forever. As we contemplate what the text is saying, we must keep in mind that the viewpoint is that which can be seen under the sun. Solomon is not rejecting the higher reality of judgment and salvation and eternal life and death. But that cannot be seen under the sun, as he has said previously, "Who knoweth the spirit of man that goeth upward?" (3:21).

In contemplating this, we must keep in mind that God is sovereign over the affairs of life. God brings us into this world and appoints our place and calling, our portion under the sun. God gives life, but God also is sovereign over death to close the door of life and take us from this world under the sun. This reality of death described, Solomon sets before us the first conclusion he would draw and does so by exhortation. He would address the believer, particularly in his youth, as he walks the pathway of life. He is still leading us to the conclusion he will make in chapter 12: "Remember now thy Creator in the days of thy youth" (v. 1).

Therefore, he comes with the exhortation: "Go thy way, eat thy bread with joy, and drink thy wine with a merry heart; for God now accepteth thy works" (Eccl. 9:7). The calling to enjoy the things of this present life is a point Solomon has made before. They are good gifts of God to his people by the labor of our hands as our daily bread. That enjoyment is also a privilege, for the wicked are in bondage to covetousness, as he has shown.

He adds here a basis for that exhortation, that our works are accepted with God, or already pleasing in his sight. The picture is of one who, remembering his creator and covenant God, serves God in his labor and his work as a sacrifice of thankfulness pleasing to God. This thought Solomon develops more fully, for it comprises the believer's response to the reality of death and the present purpose of his life. That response is one of present joyful thanksgiving before God in the things of this life, because we know that although they shall also end, being transitory, they are the portion which God has given us in his grace (v. 9).

Solomon gives us a number of injunctions in connection with this exhortation. He says first: "Let thy garments be always white; and let thy head lack no ointment" (v. 8). The picture is one of joy and rejoicing, of celebration and thanksgiving, both in the color white and in the anointing of the head with oil. While the figure refers to our daily earthly life, it has also an underlying spiritual connection, for white is also the picture of cleansing from sin, of the white robes of salvation and righteousness. Likewise, the refreshment of oil poured upon the head in a hot climate, making the face to shine, is a picture of the anointing of the Spirit and his blessing.

This rejoicing with a merry heart is the rejoicing of one who walks in covenant fellowship with God, in his forgiving mercy and with a good conscience before the Lord. The believer's inner spiritual blessings come to expression in his joyful daily walk in the things of his life. To this walk Solomon then adds a second element, namely, the blessing and gift of marriage.

"Live joyfully with the wife whom thou lovest all the days of the life of thy vanity" (v. 9). "Live," or more literally, "look upon life with the wife whom you love," again draws a picture of daily life through which we walk under the sun. In that life under the sun God has set the blessings of marriage that we may walk together in communion of life. Marriage is for this life. It too belongs to the things that pass away. By it God enriches the life of his people and works the blessings of his covenant.

This thought Solomon further develops: "live joyfully with the wife whom thou lovest all the days of thy vanity, which he hath given thee under the sun, all the days of thy vanity: for that is thy portion in this life, and in thy labour which thou takest under the sun" (v. 9). Food and drink, rejoicing in this present life, and marriage, all belong to the transitory nature of this life. The days of our life are the days of that transitory vanity—a point made twice in the text to emphasize that truth—but they are also our portion from the hand of God. They are God's gift to his people who walk in the fear of his name. Rejoicing in them with contentment and thanksgiving belongs to that portion.

Third, Solomon then adds the labor we take under the sun. For that too is given of God, by his design. Yes, that labor is one of toil in a passing thing that does not abide. We are not to cling to it, nor to earthly riches, for they shall end in death. But our labor is also that which God has given and therein lies the real foundation for the meaning and purpose of our life. By our labor we serve him. The calling is therefore to stewardship, to diligent and faithful labor, which is fruitful, not in itself, but in the service of God. Thus he concludes: "Whatsoever thy hand findeth to do, do it with thy might; for there is no work, nor device, nor knowledge, nor wisdom, in the grave, whither thou goest" (v. 10). Now in this present life is the time of work, of planning and carrying out those plans or devices. Death will close that door, and with it make and end of that which belongs under the sun. When we serve the Lord, that labor is not in vain, for it is accepted of God in his grace.

Further Conclusions

11. I returned, and saw under the sun, that the race is not to the swift, nor the battle to the strong, neither yet bread to the wise, nor yet riches to men of understanding, nor yet favour to men of skill; but time and chance happeneth to them all.

12. For man also knoweth not his time: as the fishes that are taken in an evil net, and as the birds that are caught in the snare; so are the sons of men snared in an evil time, when it falleth suddenly upon them.

13. This wisdom have I seen also under the sun, and it seemed great unto me:

14. There was a little city, and few men within it; and there came a great king against it, and besieged it, and built great bulwarks against it:

15. Now there was found in it a poor wise man, and he by his wisdom delivered the city; yet no man remembered that same poor man.

16. Then said I, Wisdom is better than strength: nevertheless the poor man's wisdom is despised, and his words are not heard.

17. The words of wise men are heard in quiet more than the cry of him that ruleth among fools.

18. Wisdom is better than weapons of war: but one sinner destroyeth much good.—Ecclesiastes 9:11–18

In this section of Ecclesiastes, Solomon draws a series of conclusions from the truth that death closes the door of life as the one event that comes to all, whether to the righteous or the wicked. In natural man it stirs him to sin (Eccl. 9:3). For the believer, it means that his life in this world is shaped by the transitory vanity of being under the sun. The first conclusion therefore is that our focus must be to serve God with thanksgiving, rejoicing in marriage and in our daily bread and labor as our portion under the sun (vv. 7–10). We are not to set our heart upon the things of this life.

This brings us to the second conclusion the inspired writer would draw, so that he leads us to return and again ponder what we see under the sun:

> I returned, and saw under the sun, that the race is not to the swift, nor the battle to the strong, neither yet bread to the wise, nor yet riches to men of understanding, nor yet favour to men of skill; but time and chance happeneth to them all. (9:11)

This conclusion might at first seem counterintuitive. Has Solomon not said that we are to labor with all our might? Surely the logical conclusion is that the swift win the race, the strong the battle. These are not denied as such, but Solomon points us to what is seen in that "time and chance happen to them all." The Authorized Version uses the word *chance* here, in this connection, to describe what appears to be (to us under the sun) a random occurrence, which man could not anticipate. It happened, and descended upon someone in the midst of his activity. The idea is that our works "are in the hand of God" (v. 1).

Man's life under the sun is governed by God's providence, his almighty sovereign purpose or counsel. Man's strength is not in himself nor his life in his own hand. God sets the time and boundaries of our lives and circumstances which "chance" upon us or occur when we do not look for them. Therefore, "the race is not to the swift…nor yet favour [in the presence of men] to men of skill" (v. 11), except the Lord will. He is the God "who worketh all things after the counsel of his own will" (Eph. 1:11). By the Lord's appointment the race is won, the battle victory achieved. He gives bread, riches, and honor to men under the sun.

As God is no respecter of persons, and all things come alike to all under the sun, so also time and chance occurrence happen to them all. Man is not his own master. This is true generally of God's providence, but especially when we contemplate it in the light of the truth that we shall die. Solomon points therefore to our finite character and how it works out in our lives under the sun: "For man also knoweth not his time: as the fishes that are taken in an evil net, and as the birds that are caught in the snare; so are the sons of men snared in an evil time, when it falleth suddenly upon them" (Eccl. 9:12). Our life and times, the measure of our days and our circumstances, are in the hand of God. We know not that which is hidden from us in God's counsel, so that man "knoweth not his time."

Solomon uses the figure of fish caught suddenly in a net and birds in a snare. They swim and fly freely in the activity of life when suddenly the net and snare come upon them, and they are caught and taken. So is the life of man under the sun generally with trial and affliction, in an evil time, but particularly when death falls upon him and takes him, as it were, in the midst of his activity from this life. "When it falleth suddenly upon them" (v. 12)—man too is caught unawares, though he knows he shall die. This sober reality underscores the calling to labor as sojourners in the world while it is day.

There is also another consideration or illustration brought forth. It arises in part out of what Solomon has said, that the dead have no more "a reward; for the memory of them is forgotten" (v. 5). It also arises out of what he has just said about the battle not being to the strong (v. 11).

13. This wisdom have I seen also under the sun, and it seemed great unto me:

14. There was a little city, and few men within it; and there came a great king against it, and besieged it, and built great bulwarks against it:

15. Now there was found in it a poor wise man, and he by his wisdom delivered the city; yet no man remembered that same poor man." (Eccl. 9:13–15)

While the form of the narrative of verses 13–15 approaches that of a parable, Solomon is evidently describing or drawing upon international events of his day in the kingdoms of the nations about him. His court was an international court, and he also studied the events of his day. He describes therefore what "I have seen also under the sun" (v. 13): events which, while he does not give us the specific details, he has observed. He says, "It seemed great unto me" (v. 13). What he saw appeared important for the lesson it taught about life and the place also of wisdom.

A strong and mighty king is defeated in battle by one weaker through the wisdom of one poor man. God's providence set the poor man and his wisdom in the city, and by his wisdom the poor man brought the strength and might of the great king and his siege of the city to nothing; "Yet no man remembered that same poor man" (vv. 14–15). The works of the poor man and his wisdom, which wrought a great deliverance for the city, passed away. He himself was not remembered. This again underscores that under the sun, all that is of man is a passing vanity. Even man's wisdom passes away.

Solomon then concludes: "Then said I, Wisdom is better than strength: nevertheless the poor man's wisdom is despised, and his words are not heard" (v. 16). The illustration of the besieged city leads to further reflection. Wisdom overcame strength, physical strength and power, in the illustration just given. Wisdom is the better portion, but this also was seen: it was not remembered, nor the man who possessed it.

Wisdom encounters a certain problem to which the illustration points, in that it is not regarded or remembered, and the poor man to whom it was given is despised. He and the memory of his deliverance are forgotten, not only in death, but also in life, so that the problem is broader. For even in life, the wise man and his wisdom are not listened to; his words are ignored. The problem is rooted in the pride of men, so Solomon speaks of despising the wisdom of the poor man. The word *despise* here has the idea of one lifting the head in proud disdain for something beneath one's notice. The man who is wise in the illustration is of no account. He is a "poor man," a beggar. Who would notice him? Though in the illustration he delivered the city, his words are dismissed, "his words are not heard." This may have been the case up until he delivered the city. But after delivering the city, he is again ignored, and his wisdom is forgotten.

While God is no respecter of persons, man who shall die is a respecter of persons. In pride he disdains his neighbor who is poor. He will not turn his ear to listen; the poor man's words are not heard, which is to the proud man's own hurt and ruin. His own folly is his undoing. As the believer is often set forth in Scripture as the poor, and wisdom that of faith, the text also illustrates the place of a believer and his witness in the world.

To the subject of wisdom itself, Solomon now begins to turn his attention. This leads him to the conclusion of this chapter and into the subject of the next. He brings up the contrast between wisdom and folly which has occupied much of Ecclesiastes. When we consider this, the wise man and his wisdom go hand in hand. Despise the one, and you despise the other. Verses 17 and 18 still draw on the illustration just given, but they could also well go with the next chapter.

"The words of wise men are heard in quiet more than the cry of him that ruleth among fools. Wisdom is better than weapons of war: but one sinner destroyeth much good" (vv. 17–18). Wisdom is the ability to put knowledge and understanding to use. While there is a certain practical wisdom in the world, true wisdom is founded in the fear of God, in acknowledging him in all our ways and works. The truly wise man is one who walks by faith as a child of God. It is to the words of that wisdom and the hearing of them that our text turns.

Proud natural man cannot hear nor retain the words of wisdom because they are contrary to his sinful flesh and his old man of sin. But those are also learned, not in the midst of a world of shouting, noise, and tumult, but in quiet. Preaching, mediation on God's word, hearing and receiving instruction, require focused attention and spiritual reflection. "The words of the wise men are heard in quiet more than the cry of him that ruleth among fools" (v. 17). The cry and shouting of the world is set before us by way of contrast. Men rule by might and power over others. They exercise dominion by lifting up their voices. Such is the governance among men who are here called fools. The word and the will of the ruler is driven home, as it were, by force. Wisdom cannot be acquired that way. The way of the world is one of force and contention of earthly strength and the power of the arm of the flesh.

Thus, Solomon says: "Wisdom is better than weapons of war: but one sinner destroyeth much good" (v. 18). The illustration of the poor man delivering the city shows this. Spiritual wisdom in the needs and cares of life and death gives a strength that weapons of war in the hand of a great king cannot. But this leads to an additional sober thought: "but one sinner destroyeth much good." This is Solomon's own trouble in certain respects.

CHAPTER 10

Of Sin and Folly

1. Dead flies cause the ointment of the apothecary to send forth a stinking savour: so doth a little folly him that is in reputation for wisdom and honour.
2. A wise man's heart is at his right hand; but a fool's heart at his left.
3. Yea also, when he that is a fool walketh by the way, his wisdom faileth him, and he saith to every one that he is a fool.—Ecclesiastes 10:1–3

"Wisdom is better than weapons of war: but one sinner destroyeth much good" (Eccl. 9:18). In the preceding verses the difference between wisdom and strength was set forth. Wisdom is the better portion, for it has a greater strength than earthly might. But now the text sets forth a contrast: "one sinner destroyeth much good" (v. 18). Sin is destructive. It is folly. It works the corruption of that which is profitable under the sun as well as moral evil. It destroys that which is wrought with wisdom.

Yet man is a sinner who walks in the way of sin by nature. Man by nature is a fool because of sin that dwells in him, a fool who seeks his own way and will not have God in his thoughts. Psalm 14:1 draws the connection: "The fool hath said in his heart, There is no God. They are corrupt, they have done abominable works, there is none that doth good." Sin and its folly cleave also to one who is a believer. Rooted in his flesh by nature, sin works not only guilt before God but also the sorrowful consequences of sin in this life. Yet Solomon does not simply say sin destroyeth much good, but "one sinner destroyeth much good" (Eccl. 9:18). It is the person he would have us to see, not merely his activity.

This is our problem, for we are sinners. This was Solomon's problem. For all his wisdom, he was still a sinner, as would be the one after him who inherited all his works. Solomon, in the folly of his old age with his heathen wives and idolatry, would sow the very destruction and decline of the kingdom. In the days of his son the kingdom would be divided. This leads to the sober reflection in the next verse.

"Dead flies cause the ointment of the apothecary to send forth a stinking savour: so doth a little folly him that is in reputation for wisdom and honour" (Eccl. 10:1). This observation is a warning and at the same time an indirect confession on the part of Solomon of his own downfall into sin and folly. The picture is that of a fragrant ointment compounded by the apothecary or perfumer. This ointment is like wisdom and honor, which form the reputation of a person. Such were the gifts of wisdom and attendant honor compounded, like an ointment, in Solomon's life. They were like a fragrant smell in the life of the church and in the world. He was one lifted up to high estate in glory and honor.

Yet he was also a sinner with the root of folly in his flesh. Age did not eliminate that presence of indwelling sin. His long honor and majesty in the world bore the fruit of pride in his old age. He uses the figure of dead flies corrupting the ointment. The idea is not simply that of the bodies of fallen insects but of the effect flies have on something exposed to their presence. They carry disease, pollution, and corruption. Where they land, walk around and also die, they work contamination, so that the ointment in the figure sends forth a stench instead of a sweet smell; hence the warning, so does a "little folly" (v. 1) in the life and walk of one held in honor for his wisdom and dignity.

Rather than a direct personal confession, for that is not the purpose, Solomon sets this figure before us as a warning. He has in view the instruction of the young starting out on the path of life. His personal history and experience confirm that warning and its seriousness. "Wherefore let him that thinketh he standeth take heed lest he fall" (1 Cor. 10:12). We are of like flesh and blood, sinners and by nature foolish. Sin, like the flies in the ointment, works corruption in our lives. Sin seems a small matter when we start down its pathway, a little thing. But it contaminates and works through when given place. It brings one to shame and reproach. So it was with Solomon and his heathen wives. He did not marry them all at once. It took place over time as did his catering to their desire for temples to the idols (1 Kings 11). What was a "little folly" in the beginning, out of a desire to please his wives, became great folly, which sowed the seeds of idolatry in the kingdom. It is for good reason therefore that we are taught to pray at the end of Psalm 119: "I have gone astray like a lost sheep; seek thy servant; for I do not forget thy commandments" (v. 176).

Setting that warning before us, the text turns again to the nature of folly and of the unbelieving fool to underscore it. Solomon has said before in Ecclesiastes 2:13–14: "Then I saw that wisdom excelleth folly, as far as light excelleth darkness. The wise man's eyes are in his head; but the fool walketh in darkness." Now he uses a similar figure. "A wise man's heart is at his right hand; but the fool's heart at his left" (Eccl. 10:2). The contrast draws perhaps on the fact that physically one covers his heart with his right hand. The heart is the spiritual center of man's life, while the hand, particularly the right hand, is the normal instrument of the body for human activity. The point of the fool's heart being "at his left" is that the fool is backward spiritually in his heart and activity, backward because he is turned from God in sin and folly, and therefore from the way of wisdom under the sun. He is a fool within his heart, blind and in darkness, without understanding, and the fruit of his hand is the folly of sin.

Sin is both a striving with God and his law, a moral evil, but it is also a striving with the boundaries of life that God has set and maintains in the creation. Man is a fallen rational, moral creature. He can think and make choices, but he does so out of the folly of sin. Striving against God's holy law, he also strives with the order of things under the sun. Sin in that sense is unreality, a striving with God's imposed limitations on man's natural life under the sun.

The Canons of Dordt summarizes this fact:

> There remain, however, in man since the fall, the glimmerings of natural light, whereby he retains some knowledge of God, of natural things, and of the difference between good and evil, and discovers some regard for virtue, good order in society, and for maintaining an orderly external deportment. But so far is this light of nature from being sufficient to bring him to a saving knowledge of God, and to true conversion, that he is incapable of using it aright even in things natural and civil. Nay farther, this light, such as it is, man in various ways renders wholly polluted, and holds it [back] in unrighteousness; by doing which he becomes inexcusable before God.[1]

Considering the person of the fool and the folly of his heart and activity, the text would have us take warning by having us to see this folly in his walk and speech. The corrupt tree brings forth corrupt fruit (Matt. 7:17), while out of the abundance of his folly, in heart, the fool also speaks.

"Yea also, when he that is a fool walketh by the way, his wisdom faileth him, and he saith to everyone that he is a fool" (Eccl. 10:3). This is the effect of folly in the heart. His wisdom, more literally his heart, fails or is lacking. It is devoid of understanding spiritually and, in large measure, practically. His walk is the pathway of his life. His heart being full of himself and estranged from God, he walks the broad way to destruction (Matt. 7:13). Thus, as Solomon has earlier pointed out, the fool heaps and gathers to himself earthly riches, without asking whose shall these things be,

---

1 Canons of Dordt, 3-4.4, in Schaff, *Creeds of Christendom*, 3:588.

for he shall die. This characteristic has been illustrated in this and other forms over the course of the book. The fool is a sinner that destroys much good (Eccl. 9:18).

His speech also reveals what lives in his heart. This is so, whether it be the hard speeches of ungodly men against God and his law, or the foolish talking and mockery of men. Man proclaims himself to be as God, and his hard rebellious speech resounds through the earth. He makes transparent excuses for his folly and justifies his sin. He seeks to change times and laws and seasons. He will even claim the right to determine his own gender, as if the boundaries of life are in his hand. The vain notions of his heart come out of his mouth, and he declares to everyone that he is a fool. Other fools will follow, because they too are at enmity with God.

This warning the text would underscore, so that we see it and flee from the foolishness of sin that cleaves to us also as children of God. The word of God has a multitude of examples of children of God who stumbled in sin and pride and fell into folly to their sorrow. The spirit of an unbelieving world around us affects our discernment too, for we have the same root of folly in our own sinful flesh. We are not untouched by the propaganda of a sinful world that says right is wrong and good, evil, of a world that daily justifies its depravity.

The way of wisdom is one of daily conversion. That way of daily conversion is one of daily repentance and turning to God in prayer and humility. To underscore this need to take heed, the text turns in much of the rest of the chapter to illustrate both folly and its fruit.

Of Folly Manifested and the Ruler

4. If the spirit of the ruler rise up against thee, leave not thy place; for yielding pacifieth great offences.
5. There is an evil which I have seen under the sun, as an error which proceedeth from the ruler:
6. Folly is set in great dignity, and the rich sit in low place.

7. I have seen servants upon horses, and princes walking as servants upon the earth.—Ecclesiastes 10:4–7

The folly of sin becomes manifested in the world under the sun as it strives with the boundaries God has set in this life. To show this, Solomon, who was himself king, turns first to the sphere of earthly government. But before turning to the folly, "which proceedeth from the ruler" (Eccl. 10:5), he begins with an admonition in the text to one standing under the ruler as the servant, citizen, or counsellor of the king. Both king and servant are sinners inclined to folly.

"If the spirit of the ruler rise up against thee, leave not thy place; for yielding pacifieth great offences" (v. 4). The picture is that of one who has offended or is perceived to have offended, so that the spirit of the ruler rises against him in anger and displeasure. As the text speaks of great offences, we may assume here that the displeasure of the ruler is just. It is the folly of the counsellor or servant who has a place in the ruler's presence. What is the way of folly, the way of sin, in such a situation? The temptation is to justify oneself out of a spirit of rebellion, to strive, to make excuses, to blame the ruler. In the figure, it is to rise up and leave one's place.

The calling of those under authority is the opposite:

1. Let every soul be subject unto the higher powers, For there is no power but of God: the powers that be are ordained of God.
2. Whosoever therefore resisteth the power, resisteth the ordinance of God: and they that resist shall receive to themselves damnnation. (Rom. 13:1–2)

The calling of those under authority is submission in all lawful things, according to the word of God. The word of God does not command cowardly action nor false compromise but a lawful submission to authority.

When that spirit of the ruler rises in displeasure against one, especially for just reason, the way of wisdom is not the way of our sinful inclination to rebellion and stubbornness, but to yield and submit. In doing so we keep our place, yield to authority to receive rebuke, and accept judgment. This is the way of meekness before authority and before God. Pride would lead us in the opposite direction. But the ruler is set there by God, and his authority is derived from the one who placed him in his office. Rebellion is therefore also a striving against God. It is folly.

The way of wisdom, of yielding, "pacifieth great offences" (Eccl. 10:4). Yielding quiets the anger, prevents the quarrel from escalating, and seeks to restore peace. It is the way of laboring to remove the offense, that it should not become greater still. Thus we read: "A soft answer turneth away wrath: but grievous words stir up anger" (Prov. 15:1). We live in a world where the striving of those in power, among themselves or with those under their authority, predominates in civic life. The tongues of men are given to slander and contention. Men come with grievous words with the goal of mastery over one another and stirring up strife. This works violence and disorder in society. It is the way of the fool who "saith to every one that he is a fool" (Eccl 10:3). As sin develops under the sun unto the day of final judgment, the way of a child of God, to which we are called, which is that of wisdom, becomes increasingly difficult. Our calling is still: "If it be possible, as much as lieth in you, live peaceably with all men" (Rom. 12:18).

With that admonition and instruction, the word of God turns to the ruler, for he is also a sinner and by nature given to folly.

5. There is an evil which I have seen under the sun, as an error which proceedeth from the ruler:
6. Folly is set in great dignity, and the rich sit in low place.
7. I have seen servants upon horses, and princes walking as servants upon the earth. (Eccl. 10:5–7)

The ruler in Solomon's day, whether in Israel or among the nations surrounding them, were sovereign monarchs, hereditary kings. Our more democratic and republican forms of government did not exist in the Middle East. The principle issues, however, are the same whatever form the role of the ruler and those in authority may take. Nor is it to the personal lives of kings to which we are pointed here in this description, but as they stand in positions of power under the sun, to their rule and government. Solomon is again directing us to what he has observed. Where a human ruler in authority is to be found, a sinner is found, and with him the folly of sin by nature. Even a good ruler, held in reputation and honor like a good ointment, is subject to folly (vv. 1–3).

The "error" mentioned that proceeds from the ruler is one of wandering out of the way. That is, it is a departure from wisdom and judgment, a turning from the order of things that rests upon what God has ordained. God gives men gifts of wisdom and prudence, judgment and discernment. It is in that positive sense that we must understand the "rich" here in the text. They are rich through such gifts, not out of covetousness and greed but by wisdom and prudence under the sun. They are therefore men of discernment who should be honored and received as counsellors. The fool is self-willed, a profligate waster, a man without good sense. When the ruler sets such a fool in a place of great dignity and honor while the rich are set in a low place, the order of things is turned upside down.

The long-term result is the destruction of the kingdom. The monarch is to seek the welfare of the kingdom and its citizens. His authority is to be exercised for the good of those under him and not for his own grandeur and glory. The error is no different when in our democratic context fools are elected to govern in the world rather than those who are sober and have discernment.

At issue in the text is the error of setting such fools in a position of power and influence. It is the ruler who has power to appoint them, to select them in preference to wise men, and to give them honor. It is the ruler who is out of the way. In our context of voting men into office, one would have to say, that in many respects the error proceeds from the voter as well as those in direct power and authority. When the vain and foolish, the workers of iniquity, rule, the end is destruction. God is against them that do evil. Because "righteousness exalteth a nation: but sin is a reproach to any people" (Prov. 14:34), wickedness destroys a nation. Behind what can be seen under the sun is the working of God's almighty power and judgment, his wrath against sin which gives men over to folly. The text does not dwell on this, though it assumes we understand it.

Rather the text points us to the effect of this state of affairs under the sun. "I have seen servants upon horses, and princes walking as servants upon the earth" (Eccl. 10:7). This is the result of the folly of sin. Princes in the text are not the spoiled nobility of a corrupt kingdom but those who are raised up to rule and judge with equity, while the servant is not. The picture is again of folly that turns good order upside down, so that things are out of their proper place. Those qualified to rule and exercise authority are rejected, relegated to a low place, and made to walk on foot, while the fool and the servant are exalted and ride on horses. They have power and influence, which is unfitting and for which they are unqualified. They have an honor and dignity, which only fuels in them pride and more folly.

Yet what Solomon says is what he has seen in the earth; it is what happens. Nor is it something that works anyone's good. The folly involved will not end well for the kingdom. What is seen is sin and folly working through in the lives of men. As it is from the hand of God also, it is a token of his judgment upon sin.

Since we also see these things under the sun, we are called to contemplate them and understand what we are seeing. The same principles and warning the word of God applies to other spheres of authority, to marriage and family, to employer and employee, and to the life of the church. Also in the rule of the church when there is a spiritual decline, the same working of folly leads the church in the way of worldly-mindedness, an unwholesome respect of persons, and doctrinal drift. Walking circumspectly in a sinful world and having a regard for God-ordained authority, while confronting the reality of sinful folly seen before us, is a sober calling. As the fool lurks in our own sinful flesh, it must needs lead us to prayer and watchfulness in the battle of faith.

Of the Order of Things and Consequences

8. He that diggeth a pit shall fall into it; and whoso breaketh an hedge, a serpent shall bite him.
9. Whoso removeth stones shall be hurt therewith; and he that cleaveth wood shall be endangered thereby.
10. If the iron be blunt, and he do not whet the edge, then must he put to more strength: but wisdom is profitable to direct.—Ecclesiastes 10:8–10

Having set before us the folly and disorder of affairs in civil life, the word of God turns to a series of natural or organic connections. The intent is that we should contemplate them, discern the reality of things, and by that reflection be pointed to the way of wisdom and warned against folly. We need therefore to consider the illustrations in their natural context first.

"He that diggeth a pit shall fall into it; and whoso breaketh an hedge, a serpent shall bite him. Whoso removeth stones shall be hurt therewith; and he that cleaveth wood shall be endangered thereby" (Eccl. 10:8–9). On the foreground is the person and then his activity, the "whoso" of the text.

The person digging a pit is by that very activity the one most likely to slip and fall into the pit or be injured by a cave-in in its excavation. Similarly, poisonous snakes hide in the thick underbrush to ambush their prey. The one clearing brush or cutting down a hedge, which may be used as a fence, is engaged in a dangerous project: "a serpent shall bite him" (v. 8). The same is true for the one removing stones, whether clearing a field or removing his neighbor's landmark; his activity endangers himself physically, whether by dropping stones on himself or some other aspect of the toil in which he is engaged. The cutting of wood with an axe is a potential source of self-injury whether from the axe, flying wood chips, or something slipping in the process. All of these things are the reality of life and set forth the dangers of someone engaging in these projects in physical terms.

Solomon has said this before in Proverbs: "Whoso diggeth a pit shall fall therein: and he that rolleth a stone, it will return upon him" (Prov. 26:27). It is also used figuratively: "Whoso causeth the righteous to go astray in an evil way, he shall fall himself into his own pit: but the upright shall have good things in possession" (28:10). It is used in the psalms as the consequence of an evil plot and God's judgment upon the wicked: "He made a pit, and digged it, and is fallen into the ditch which he made" (Ps. 7:15; see also Ps. 35:7; 57:6.). The hedge is used as a barrier, a defense and protection for the field. It is used figuratively to describe God's protection of his church, which is then broken down in his judgment upon a people who have departed in the way of sin (Pss. 80:12; 89:40). Here the figurative idea is that of one breaking through a hedge, similar to the thief and hireling of John 10.

While Scripture uses these activities in a variety of figurative senses, we must not overlook the natural point. Even in things under the sun, physically, the way of folly is manifested in carelessness or heedlessness of man in such activities. The natural inclination of man is to go about such activities with the pride of heart that says, "I can do this; others may be injured, but I will not." Man is so often revealed as a fool even in such natural activities. He denies that there may be consequences to what he is doing. God has joined together the things of this world with boundaries, such as gravity or other elements of physical laws, which shape our activities in doing them. God has made, sustains, and upholds both the things that are made and what we call natural laws governing them. This reality under the sun is

God's work of upholding and governing the universe. It is not a matter of a mere organic process, which the heathen might call karma, but it is God's work. Attributing it to the creation as a mere mechanical process is idolatry and a denial of the Creator and Sustainer of all things.

We need to contemplate this description somewhat. That there is a connection between man's activities and consequences, that there is cause and effect, is a work of God undergirding the creation. Moreover, that there is danger of physical harm in them is not a matter of accident, as we so often speak of it, but a certain judgment of God, the working of his curse in the creation by which all things wear away, are corrupted, and lead to death. Thorns and thistles grow, weeds multiply under the judgment of God upon us in a fallen world (Gen. 3:18).

The folly of sin leads man to the notion that he controls or can control the elemental principles of creation as if he were God. He claims to be able to control disease when God sends pestilence—and fails. He claims to control the climate, to determine his own gender, to cure human nature's violence, racism, and other ills. Instead, he works the evils he claims to cure. Man's dominion over the creation was given in the beginning before the fall. He is now fallen, and the creation is under the curse upon sin. That curse is an active power and work of God's judgment. Man fails and must fail, for God is against him. It might seem for a season as if he has solved a problem, but eventually it is clear he has only formed another problem. When the consequences of man's proud experiments manifest themselves in disaster or failure, he labels them mistakes or accidents. The results are, after all, unintentional, or so he would describe them. Man makes excuses for his folly. These failures do not work a turning from pride or repentance but a persistence in folly.

Yet this is not the whole picture, for it is sin in fallen man that ignores God and the boundaries he has set and maintains. It is the carelessness of the folly of man, a sinner, who heedlessly does himself an injury or injures others. It belongs to the working of God's curse in the creation that it is so. It is in that connection that we pray for God's fatherly care and provision in our activities, for we know that without his blessing they will not profit us. The fool, heedless of this reality and of God its author, passes on in sin and is punished.

While it is this physical reality which is on the foreground here in Ecclesiastes, the word of God in many passages, as was noted, also takes up these pictures and uses them in a variety of figurative senses to describe the willful activity of sin and God's judgment upon it. Man digs a pit for his neighbor to ensnare him with guile, to rob and to kill. He breaks down a hedge, the barrier fence, that he may break through and steal. He moves the stone, the landmark of his neighbor, out of covetousness to take what is not his. If the physical activity is subject to God's judgment and the working of the curse upon the ground, how much more that which is described as wickedness in the figurative application. If God's judgment is manifested in these activities physically, how much greater is the fool who thinks he will escape that judgment of God when he walks in these sins described by the figurative picture. He will fall into the pit he devised for others, and as he breaks through the hedge, a serpent will bite him.

Pursuing the figurative application of these figures further will lead us away from the point of the text being made here, that God sets the bounds of man's life in such a way that our activity stands always within the bounds he has set. The way of wisdom is the way of discernment of those boundaries and walking in submission to them. He has said of the fool: "Yea also, when he that is a fool walketh by the way, his wisdom faileth him" (Eccl. 10:3). The fool strives with those boundaries in sin and rebellion. The judgment of God upon him is not immediately apparent as he digs his pit, and he keeps digging. His wisdom is self-confidence in himself and his own will. God is not in his thoughts. We read a similar idea in James,

13. Go to now, ye that say, To day or to morrow we will go into such a city, and continue there a year, and buy and sell, and get gain:

14. Whereas ye know not what shall be on the morrow. For what is your life? It is even a vapour, that appeareth for a little time, and then vanisheth away. (James 4:13–14)

The text in Ecclesiastes makes the application of this in this way: "If the iron be blunt, and he do not whet the edge, then must he put to more strength: but wisdom is profitable to direct" (Eccl. 10:10). The description is clear: a dull axe does not cut; the way of wisdom is to sharpen it. The idea of *direct* in the original is that of a successful or fruitful outcome.

This requires discernment and thought. The one who does not sharpen his axe wastes his strength. He is striving with the order of things under the sun. He is being foolish. This is more than the practical wisdom needed in earthly things, though that is included. Sin is foolishness. It is without direction, and it strives with God, who confronts man on every side with his presence and government. The fool spends himself in his folly and does not truly prosper. He is adrift in the world without God, without true knowledge and understanding. He is in darkness. That darkness makes him as dull-witted as the dull axe.

Wisdom in the fear of God gives direction and therefore profit under the sun. It works a fruitful walk that is successful in its outcome for good. That good is both the prospering of our earthly way, which is in harmony with God's design, and profitable spiritually. It yields both our daily bread, contentment, and our rejoicing in the Lord who gives it. This belongs to the better portion of the child of God in his days under the sun who walks in the light. The man who seeks God's care and blessing in his activities seeks also discernment in the needs of life.

The Tongue of the Fool

11. Surely the serpent will bite without enchantment; and a babbler is no better.
12. The words of a wise man's mouth are gracious; but the lips of a fool will swallow up himself.

13. The beginning of the words of his mouth is foolishness: and the end of his talk is mischievous madness.

14. A fool also is full of words: a man cannot tell what shall be; and what shall be after him, who can tell him?

15. The labour of the foolish wearieth every one of them, because he knoweth not how to go to the city.—Ecclesiastes 10:11–15

Earlier in Ecclesiastes 10 we read: "Yea also, when he that is a fool walketh by the way, his wisdom faileth him, and he saith to every one that he is a fool" (v. 3). The walk of the fool has been found among rulers. That walk is also found by ignoring God's ordering of things under the sun. It is with that in view that the text now turns to the speech of the fool and his tongue: "he saith to every one that he is a fool."

This consideration begins by pointing out another thing that belongs also to the ordering of things. "Surely the serpent will bite without enchantment; and a babbler is no better" (v. 11). The figure drawn is of a swaying serpent, rising up and moving its head and body to strike. The charmer by the swing of his body, and often with his swaying reed instrument, charms or masters the snake, semi-hypnotizing it, holding it under control. Such a scene would not have been uncommon at the time in the Middle East, as it is still found in parts of Asia.

The figure is applied to a "babbler" or, more literally and clearly, the tongue and its master. The tongue is like a swaying serpent, full of poison. To master it requires the powers of a snake charmer. The owner of the tongue has no advantage, is no better than the serpent and the snake charmer. In James 3 the point is made using other figures for the tongue and its influence. James there speaks of the tongue: "For every kind of beasts, and of birds, and of serpents, and of things in the sea, is tamed, and hath been tamed of mankind: but the tongue can no man tame; it is an unruly evil, full of deadly poison" (vv. 7–8).

A believing child of God with the spiritual gift of wisdom understands this infirmity of his flesh and struggles with it, seeking by the grace of God to tame his tongue. Hence the contrast now introduced: "The words of the wise man's mouth are gracious; but the lips of the fool will swallow up himself" (Eccl. 10:12). Gracious words are more than pleasant or beautiful. They are words spoken soberly in truth, rooted in the truth of God, and therefore, just. And yet they are beautiful, for they edify and build up the hearer in the fear of God. Thus Jesus' words are described, when he was in the synagogue in Nazareth, in Luke 4:22, "And all bare him witness, and wondered at the gracious words which proceeded out of his mouth," though the response of his witnesses was one of unbelief.

The fool in his speech, which is the focus here in the text, swallows up himself, that is, he works his own self-destruction by his words. "He saith to every one that he is a fool" (Eccl. 10:3). His speech is that of a poisonous serpent, evil, dissembling, full of arrogant folly. His mouth is an untamed serpent. The result is: "the beginning of the words of his mouth is foolishness: and the end of his talk is mischievous madness" (v. 13). The text describes both the "beginning of the words" and the end of the speech of the fool, and in doing so all the content in between; his entire speech. It is characterized by the folly of sin, by that which is evil or mischievous, which works evil. It is the madness of sin that strives with God, with his word, and with his providence.

The text implies a warning to discern our own speech, as the folly of sin cleaves to us after the flesh. It also calls us to consider what we hear and to whom we give much ear. The speech of the fool is poisonous; it leads one to further folly. It has the character of being arrogant, proud, and boastful, so that the speaker is full of himself: his will, his plans, his profane language.

James speaks of this as something inconsistent and sinful in the life of a believer, who should have wisdom:

10. Out of the same mouth proceeded blessing and cursing. My brethren, these things ought not so to be.
11. Doth a fountain send forth at the same place sweet water and bitter?
12. Can the fig tree, my brethren, bear olive berries? either a vine, figs? so can no fountain both yield salt water and fresh.
13. Who is a wise man and endued with knowledge among you? let him shew out of a good conversation his works with meekness of wisdom." (James 3:10–13)

In like manner Solomon points us to the way of wisdom in godly speech, which also flees the speech of the unbelieving fool of this world and seeks not its company or imitation.

This is further illustrated: "A fool also is full of words: a man cannot tell what shall be; and what shall be after him, who can tell him?" (Eccl. 10:14). The idea of the text is the reality that a man cannot determine what shall be, the immediate future, nor can he tell or predict what shall come to pass after he dies. The future is simply unknown to man both for tomorrow and into the distant future. God alone, who has ordained the end from the beginning, can tell us what shall be. But man cannot find it out by his own reasoning. His plans are subject to God's sovereign will.

Yet the fool is "full of words" (v. 14), that is, in connection with his plans and expectations. In his pride the fool speaks not only endlessly of himself but of what he will do and what he will accomplish. He speaks as if the future is in his own hand, under the government of his will and thought. His trust is in his own prowess. Such is the speech of the world we hear on a daily basis, both regarding the immediate future and its long-term expectations. The wise man speaks of these things in the consciousness, even if not always expressed, that the future is in the hands of the Lord and that we ourselves do not determine this or that, but as the Lord wills.

James, who may have much of this section of Ecclesiastes in mind in James 3 and 4, says:

13. Go to now, ye that say, To day or to morrow we will go into such a city, and continue there a year, and buy and sell, and get gain:
14. Whereas ye know not what shall be on the morrow. For what is your life? It is even a vapour, that appeareth for a little time, and then vanisheth away.
15. For that ye ought to say, If the Lord will, we shall live, and do this, or that.
16. But now ye rejoice in your boastings: all such rejoicing is evil. (James 4:13–16)

It is that self-confident boasting and rejoicing (v. 16) which applies particularly here in Ecclesiastes. This forms the multitude of words of the fool (Eccl. 10:14). He trusts in himself. He is like the fool in the parable of the rich fool who will build bigger barns but regards not God (Luke 12:15–21).

The result of both his walk and words (Eccl. 10:3) is that he fails. He pursues what is vain as an end in itself. "The labour of the foolish wearieth every one of them, because he knoweth not how to go to the city" (v. 15). The fool spends his life and strength in vanity, driven by the lust of his own flesh, heedless of God and his government, and boasting in himself. He accomplishes nothing of value under the sun but wearies himself. He lacks spiritual common sense. "He knoweth not how to go to the city," that is, he lacks the basic sense of direction and purpose in his life and labor. He cannot read the signposts in the world around him, which would direct him in the way. Of the word of God he wants nothing; and even the ordinary boundaries of life, which God has ordained, he sets aside in his pride. He will dig a pit and not fall into it. And his tongue boasts thereof, particularly when for a season it may seem as if he gets away with his folly and that consequences do not immediately befall him. Instead of not knowing how to go to the city, we would probably say of the fool that he does not know enough to come in out of the rain and rather gets soaked. From beginning to end he is a fool, and that folly is in his heart, therefore it is "because he knoweth not how to go to the city" that he wearies himself. The cause lies in his heart.

To his people God shows the way in his word, which is gracious, gives wisdom in the walk of life and guards our speech in the way. He also shows us the way to an eternal city which he has built in Christ.

The Woe and Blessing of the Land

16. Woe to thee, O land, when thy king is a child, and thy princes eat in the morning!
17. Blessed art thou, O land, when thy king is the son of nobles, and thy princes eat in due season, for strength, and not for drunkenness!—Ecclesiastes 10:16–17

Solomon as the Preacher has been describing the way of the fool in his walk, talk, and inability to know the way of wisdom under the sun. That foolishness of man is rooted in the fall and in the folly and depravity of sin. He turns now to a description of two contrasting states, the one rooted in folly, the other in wisdom.

This contrast comes with woe or blessing upon the land (Eccl. 10:16–17). The land is the earth, viewed from its division into territories or countries. The woe and blessing are not upon the people only but also upon the whole realm or kingdom. The description is first of all a general one.

Woe is that which causes distress and grief, which has its source, in earthly terms, in the character of the rulers. The land is not well governed. The rulers rule for their own pleasure and not for the welfare of the land. The blessing by contrast is that which is straight or right, fitted to the need of the land and therefore works tranquility and happiness or prosperity under the sun. The land of woe is in decline, and those who should keep it work its destruction. The happy land is flourishing under good governance. Such in general is the principle even of the kingdoms of this world seen under the sun.

But we must inquire further. The land of woe has a king who "is a child" (Eccl. 10:16), one who is young, immature, and inexperienced. His princes are self-indulgent rather than wise counsellors. They eat or feast in the morning. As is clear from the end of verse 17, they feast for drunkenness. They drain the kingdom of its riches and increase to profit themselves and not the kingdom. They rule for their own pleasure. The ruler as a child is contrasted with one who is a son of nobles. The idea is not that of European nobility, or of a higher caste of person distinguished from lower classes, but of one of noble character; that is, the issue is one of maturity, not necessarily of chronological age.

The Spirit speaking through Solomon, prophetically, may well have Solomon's son Rehoboam in view, whose folly with that of his companion princes and their counsel would be part of the occasion for the division of the kingdom (2 Chron. 10). Rehoboam's son, King Abijah, in his confrontation with Jeroboam describes his father at the time of the revolt and division of the kingdom as "young and tenderhearted" (13:7). As Rehoboam was 41 years old when he became king, he was young or a child only in the sense of his immaturity, and tender (like the young shoot of a plant) in heart only by inexperience. To be 41 years old and a child in character is a matter of the foolishness of sin, of pride and self-indulgence, not a matter of age.

It is that immaturity, which ultimately is a spiritual problem in both the childish king and his profligate princes; that is the point at issue. It brings woe upon the land under their rule. The happy land, by contrast, has one who is trained and mature to govern, with princes who are devoted to the needs of the land as a whole. The officials or princes of the prosperous kingdom eat for the proper reason, "for strength" to labor "and not for drunkenness" (Eccl. 10:17). The land is therefore well governed, in good order, and those over it look to its welfare and that of its citizens. Ultimately this requires discernment or natural wisdom. The description therefore also contains a general truth concerning kingdoms and nations under the sun.

Yet foolishness and wisdom are essentially spiritual realities, and the word spoken in Ecclesiastes was delivered for the church's instruction. What is said must therefore be applied not simply to lands in general but to *the* land, which was Canaan, the land of promise, the type of the kingdom of God. The history of the kingdoms of Judah and Israel is the spiritual history of the church of the Old Testament. That history as it is unfolded in Scripture makes clear that the principle stated in these verses would be repeated again and again. Only under godly kings in Judah would the land have spiritual peace and be genuinely prosperous, as a blessing.

In that connection, Psalm 144 describes the blessings of that typical kingdom in terms of earthly prosperity, as a figure of the spiritual blessings of God's covenant with his people and a godly seed, and it is a prayer for those blessings. It concludes: "Happy is that people, that is in such a case: yea, happy is that people, whose God is the Lord [Jehovah]" (v. 15).

The true blessedness can come only in the way of such spiritual blessings within. In like manner the word of God describes the woeful land, the church corrupted, in terms of God's judgment upon a sinful and profligate people:

4. And I will give children to be their princes, and babes shall rule over them.
5. And the people shall be oppressed, every one by another, and every one by his neighbour: the child shall behave himself proudly against the ancient, and the base against the honourable. (Isa. 3:4–5)

Woe and blessing are divine works in God's sovereign government of all things. He sets up childish, self-indulgent rulers in judgment and chastening where there is need for reformation and renewal.

He gives men of noble character to rule in his blessing in the life of his church and kingdom. As the psalmist in Psalm 144, we are to earnestly seek and pray for God's blessing upon his church. When God gives this blessing, we should thank and praise him for it.

This sovereign government of God sending woe and blessing is a sobering thought, for what is said of the Old Testament church applies likewise to the New Testament church, to both individual congregations and denominations, as is clear, for example, in the letters to the seven churches in Revelation (Rev. 2–3). When the foolishness of sin, of pride, of self-indulgence, and of vanity enter the church, both in the pew and in the councils of the church, God sends this woe upon the church or congregation. When the church departs in the way of worldliness, spiritual drift in doctrine, or the hypocrisy of Phariseeism, he may give his church over to woe in its government, so that the foolish rule in the church. Many a denomination has been given over through its departure from the word to the rule of the hireling, to men-pleasers as elders who are sustained by a people with "itching ears" (2 Tim. 4:3). Folly begins to pervade the life of the church, so that the rulers as fools and the parishioners, also foolish, labor and walk in vanity. Solomon has just said in the preceding verse, "The labour of the foolish wearieth every one of them, because he knoweth not how to go to the city" (Eccl. 10:15). When that city is the city of God in heaven, of which the church in the world is an imperfect manifestation, the matter is spiritually destructive.

There is a reason why the apostle in Acts 20:28 says: "Take heed therefore unto yourselves, and to all the flock, over the which the Holy Ghost hath made you overseers, to feed the church of God, which he hath purchased with his own blood." The order is important. First take heed "unto yourselves," the pastors and elders, then the flock. The reason given in verses 29–31 is the threat of spiritual corruption from within and without. It is God's church. He bought it; he keeps it. Faithful rule in wisdom is the rule of Christ, the noble king of the church, over his blood-bought flock. Those who rule under him are to be spiritually the sons of nobles and princes who eat "for strength, and not for drunkenness" (Eccl. 10:17), who serve the king of the church, and who seek the welfare of the flock. Blessed, happy is such a church, such a congregation, such a denomination—the land. "Happy is that people, that is in such a case: yea, happy is that people, whose God is the Lord" (Ps. 144:15). There God commands the blessings of his covenant.

Observations Calling for Discernment

18. By much slothfulness the building decayeth; and through idleness of the hands the house droppeth through.
19. A feast is made for laughter, and wine maketh merry: but money answereth all things.
20. Curse not the king, no not in thy thought; and curse not the rich in thy bedchamber: for a bird of the air shall carry the voice, and that which hath wings shall tell the matter.—Ecclesiastes 10:18–20

Ecclesiastes 10 concludes with three further observations or warnings which we are called to ponder. They belong to the reality of life in a fallen world under the sun. They draw on the way of the fool in his walk and talk (vv. 12–15), that folly illustrated in the rulers among men (vv. 5–6; 16–17), and the inclination to folly rooted in the flesh (vv.1–2). These observations serve to summarize elements of the chapter and its lessons, call us to a certain measure of discernment over against folly, and lead into the next chapter concerning our labor under God's providence and the way of wisdom.

"By much slothfulness the building decayeth; and through idleness of the hands the house droppeth through" (v. 18). The text draws a familiar picture of a building decaying and falling through. The rafters sag, the roof leaks, and the structure begins to fold in on itself. The old house or barn in the country, left and neglected, is such a building. Old buildings in the city are no different. The temple itself would need to be maintained and repaired in the course of its history. The reality in a fallen world is that moth and rust corrupt so that all the works of men decline and decay.

The figure must first be taken in its plain sense. It is a calling to diligence in our earthly labor and toil, in the vanity of this world. Labor is required if the house is to be kept and maintained. The fool who strives against God's will ignores such warnings and folds his hands in idleness. Much slothfulness, here, is a pattern of indolence that will not lift the hands to the task and work. This is, spiritually, a striving with the curse of God upon a fallen creation. It is the walk of one who expects to prosper without work, seeks temporary pleasure as an end in itself in self-indulgence, and is devoid of discernment. Such a one runs on heedless of the ruin he brings upon himself and his house. The familiar judgment of God, in the curse upon the ground (Gen. 3:17–19) makes this life of indolent self-indulgence an unsustainable folly.

At the same time the picture is also a figure that has broader implications. As it is with a building that must be maintained by much labor while much slothfulness destroys it, so also the life of the home, of marriage, of one's daily business all require diligence. As the building decays so does a household, a kingdom, and also the church. The kingdom, whose princes "eat in the morning... for drunkenness" (Eccl. 10:16–17), is a kingdom in decline; like a house, that kingdom will fall through. Where the keys of the kingdom are not faithfully exercised, the church will not prosper. Where spiritual diligence in the believer is not found in his spiritual life and in the covenant home, he and his house will suffer from neglect.

All the things to which the figure may apply involve the use of means, whether of grace or earthly tools. The use of these means is not automatic. It requires care and attention of thought: study, labor, exertion and toil under the sun. It requires diligence, whether it be putting a roof on a house, maintaining discipline in the home, order in the civil state, or preserving the heritage of the gospel unto the next generation in the church. The temptation of sin leads to the deceitful notion when things go well that we have arrived and can now let go and indulge ourselves. The Lord himself, his judgment and providence, does not allow man to walk in idleness. Our calling is to labor while it is day, the more so as we know that we are stewards in every aspect of life and that the Lord will come again (Matt. 24:42–51).

"A feast is made for laughter, and wine maketh merry: but money answereth all things" (Eccl. 10:19). Labor and toil do not mean that there is no place for rejoicing. Solomon has pointed out that we are to "rejoice in [our] own works" (3:22), to take our portion from the labor of the day with thanksgiving and to eat and drink of it (5:18–20), to do so also with merry heart (8:15). The purpose of a feast is laughter, and wine maketh merry. God made it so. The use of these activities and things in their proper order with thanksgiving before God is itself "the gift of God" to the believer (5:19). It comes by diligent labor under the sun.

Sin, however, corrupts the life of man, so what is transitory or temporary, of feasting and rejoicing after labor, becomes a curse to him. Seeking feasting and wine as an end in themselves is destructive. The world lives for partying, for food and drink, for the pleasures of the moment. These things become the goal of a man's life, like that of the rich fool who would possess himself in idleness and pleasure (Luke 12:16–19). The idleness of rulers who eat and drink for drunkenness in the morning works the ruin of the house of the kingdom (Eccl. 10:16). Seeking to dwell in the house of laughter is the folly of sin: "It is better to go to the house of mourning, than to go to the house of feasting: for that is the end of all men; and the living will lay it to heart" (7:2). Sin corrupts the good gifts of God; the use of them is not the problem, but the man who uses them in the service of sin.

Discernment in our labor and calling keeps these gifts of God in their proper place. They are the fruit of diligent labor and are a transitory blessing. This is put in perspective in the latter part of verse 19, "but money answereth all things." The contrast is between *a* feast and *the* money, or the silver. The one is a fleeting thing, the other is an answer, a response to all things, that is, to all the things needful. Under the sun the fruit of our labor and increase, the resulting money, corresponds to all the needs of life. It is the means to meet those present needs.

The point has been made that covetousness, the heaping and gathering of riches, is bondage. The fool heaps and gathers, hoards his silver, without understanding its purpose or his own end. This has already been termed vanity. The love of money has been warned against (5:10), but it is the necessary fruit of labor and diligence. In its proper place, as a means to serve the needs of our earthly life under the sun, it is an answer to all those things. It is not *the* answer to life itself, for that is the fear of God. But it is a necessary servant that comes by way of hard work and toil.

The Scriptures promote neither idleness nor covetousness. All our activity finds its central reference point in the service of God and thanksgiving for his gifts and the means of life under his providence. But that requires walking by faith under God's care: "In the morning sow thy seed, and in the evening withhold not thine hand: for thou knowest not whether shall prosper, either this or that, or whether they both shall be alike good" (Eccl. 11:6).

Solomon has said: "for wisdom is a defence, and money is a defence: but the excellency of knowledge is, that wisdom giveth life to them that have it" (Eccl. 7:12). Money is a present defense, answering the needs of life under the sun. It cannot give life. Only grace in Christ, the knowledge of God by faith does that. But money is a defense under the sun, addressing our present passing needs. It is to be a servant and not a master. It comes by way of diligent labor and toil in the things of this life, in our work and calling.

"Curse not the king, no not in thy thought; and curse not

the rich in thy bedchamber: for a bird of the air shall carry the voice, and that which hath wings shall tell the matter" (10:20). The thought of verse 20 is still rooted in the design and government of God over all things. It is he who sets a king in power and gives riches unto men. It is God who ordains "the powers that be" (Rom. 13:1). At the same time the text draws on the speech of the fool in contrast to the words of the wise (Eccl. 10:12–13). Discontent with God's way with us and covetousness lead to a spirit of rebellion and anger with God's disposition in the affairs of life. That wicked men rule, that the rich oppress the poor (5:8), that there is evil among the powers that be (10:4–7) has already been addressed.

We have been warned: "Also take no heed unto all words that are spoken; lest thou hear thy servant curse thee: for oftentimes also thine own heart knoweth that thou likewise hast cursed others" (7:21–22). In the mouth of the fool "the beginning of the words…is foolishness: and the end of his talk mischievous madness" (10:13). We are warned not only to heed not all that is spoken but also to guard our own thoughts and tongue. To curse men in enmity is a striving with God's providence.

There is a holy anger with sin, which is to be given over to God, that the "sun go [not] down upon" it (Eph. 4:26). God says: "Vengeance is mine; I will repay" (Rom. 12:19). But the curse in view here in Ecclesiastes 10:20 must be understood primarily of a sinful anger and its imprudent expression in both thought and word. The warning concerns yielding ourselves to such anger and its curse of others in private thought or uttering it in what we deem secret, the bedchamber.

The warning not to yield to this sinful impulse is needed. One's attitude reflects his thought, and it works its way out. The world around us is full of the raging speech of wicked and rebellious men, who curse their neighbor, their boss, the rulers, and the rich. A curse is a word of power, a verdict. When God utters the curse, it works judgment. Man's word is that of a creature. To curse thus is to usurp a divine prerogative, unless it be in the service of God, which condemns what God condemns as anathema.

The text describes the imprudence of such a curse from its consequences: "a bird of the air shall [or may] carry the voice, and that which hath wings shall tell the matter" (Eccl. 10:20). God judges the works of men in time as well as eternity. Such cursing is not harmless venting. It is a foolish yielding to a sinful impulse. Given what has been said before, "For oftentimes also thine own heart knoweth that thou hast cursed others" (Eccl. 7:22), it is a sobering admonition.

We live in a world where men curse in their rage against one another, lie about their neighbor, and slander one another. The point of the text is that it will come back upon their own head. The way of wisdom is to flee from it. The bedchamber today is as much an email, or some other social media, as it is venting to oneself when seeming alone. Discernment guards us from the inherent folly of our own sinful tongue and pulls us back from it. While present with us in our sinful flesh, our tongue is not to have dominion over us. This in part brings us again to the beginning of the chapter. "Dead flies cause the ointment of the apothecary to send forth a stinking savour: so doth a little folly him that is in reputation for wisdom and honour" (10:1).

The way of wisdom is to walk under God's government, under his sovereign disposition in the affairs of men, and to leave the rendering of judgment in God's hands where it belongs.

21. For even hereunto were ye called: because Christ also suffered for us, leaving us an example, that ye should follow his steps:
22. Who did no sin, neither was guile found in his mouth:
23. Who, when he was reviled, reviled not again; when he suffered, he threatened not; but committed himself to him that judgeth righteously:

24. Who his own self bare our sins in his own body on the tree, that we, being dead to sins, should live unto righteousness: by whose stripes ye were healed." (1 Pet. 2:21–24)

This involves humbling ourselves in repentance before God, seeking and putting away the impulses of the flesh, and walking in newness of life.

CHAPTER 11

Going about Our Calling

1. Cast thy bread upon the waters: for thou shalt find it after many days.
2. Give a portion to seven, and also to eight; for thou knowest not what evil shall be upon the earth.
3. If the clouds be full of rain, they empty themselves upon the earth: and if the tree fall toward the south, or toward the north, in the place where the tree falleth, there it shall be.
4. He that observeth the wind shall not sow; and he that regardeth the clouds shall not reap.
5. As thou knowest not what is the way of the spirit, nor how the bones do grow in the womb of her that is with child: even so thou knowest not the works of God who maketh all.
6. In the morning sow thy seed, and in the evening withhold not thine hand: for thou knowest not whether shall prosper, either this or that, or whether they both shall be alike good.—Ecclesiastes 11:1–6

The need for discernment over against the folly of sin having been addressed, the text now turns to our going about our calling in the labor and activity of this life. In harmony with the boundaries God has set in our life and his government over all undertakings, we are to labor conscious of our dependence upon him in every outcome.

"Cast thy bread upon the waters: for thou shalt find it after many days. Give a portion to seven, and also to eight; for thou knowest not what evil shall be upon the earth" (Eccl. 11:1–2). Verse 1 contains a principle which joins together the activity of sending forth and the return or finding of it as its fruit. It has been used as a legitimate reference for both Christian giving and the sending forth of the preaching of the word and its fruit. However, its immediate reference is more concretely to our labor and enterprise.

The casting or sending forth under the figure of sending forth "bread upon the waters" in verse 1 has caused some difficulty. The figure has been understood of sowing an inundated field, while yet under water, with a view to the eventual springing of the grain as the water recedes. While this makes some sense in the context of sowing in verse 4, it does not fit with verse 2, which continues the thought of verse 1. Furthermore, that farming technique is one used in Egypt with the annual flooding of the Nile, not in Canaan which depended on the falling of the rain.

Rather we should turn to Solomon's history.

26. And king Solomon made a navy of ships in Ezion-geber, which is beside Eloth, on the shore of the Red sea, in the land of Edom.
27. And Hiram sent in the navy his servants, shipman that had knowledge of the sea, with the servants of Solomon.
28. And they came to Ophir. and fetched from thence gold, four hundred and twenty talents, and brought it to king Solomon." (1 Kings 9:26–28)

Additionally, "the king had at sea a navy of Tharshish with the navy of Hiram: once in three years came the navy of Tharshish, bringing gold, and silver, ivory, and apes, and peacocks" (1 Kings 10:22; see also 1 Kings 10:11–12; 2 Chron. 9:21.) While Tharshish was originally a place name for the area near Gibraltar in the Mediterranean, it became a term for a large cargo ship of which Solomon had a large fleet. Solomon's ships were sailing out of a port on the Red Sea along the coast of Africa and obtaining gold and ivory. The word of God also references bringing almug trees, a form of sandalwood, for making pillars and musical instruments (1 Kings 10:11–12), and peacocks. Both of these are native to India, so that Solomon's navy was sailing across the Arabian Sea on extended three-year voyages both to Africa and India.

The figure, then, is of Solomon's commercial enterprises sending forth upon the surface or face of the waters his ships, selling grain in exchange for the riches that were brought back. Not all of Solomon's wealth came in the form of gifts; rather, most of it came in the form of trade and commerce. This makes the concrete reference in Ecclesiastes 11:1 of sending and returning clear. It also makes the next verse clear: "Give a portion to seven, and also to eight; for thou knowest not what evil shall be upon the earth" (v. 2).

The calling therefore to the believer is to go about his work, to engage in enterprise, building a business, undertaking the affairs of life in buying and selling. He is not to be timid, fearful, or sloth-ful, but industrious and diligent. Solomon has in view the young man building a business or career who labors in the fear of God. But that fear of God also guards him from the pride of the world, which thinks its life is in its own hand. Therefore, Solomon counsels prudence: you do not know "what evil shall be upon the earth" (v. 2). The times and seasons of life are in the hand of God; "If the Lord will, we shall live, and do this, or that" (James 4:15). "Give a portion to seven, and also to eight" (Eccl. 11:2) is the way of wisdom and prudence. Not every enterprise will succeed; the world lies under the effects of the fall and the curse. Solomon's ships could be driven by storms, attacked on a hostile coast, or miscarry in some form. Solomon did not put all his grain in one ship. The calling to undertake our labor is given us. It is limited by the fact that we do not know the outcome, which is in the hand of God. The qualification "for thou shalt find it after many days" (v. 1) makes clear that the fruit of our enterprise or undertaking will not always be immediately apparent. As the future is unknown to us, prudence is called for, but beyond that we are to leave it in the Lord's hand.

"If the clouds be full of rain, they empty themselves upon the earth: and if a tree fall toward the south, or toward the north, in the place where the tree falleth, there it shall be" (11:3). The fact that all is in the Lord's hand is further underscored. A cloud full of rain will empty itself. This we can discern. While prudence takes note of these facts, it is limited. When that rain will fall, exactly where or on what field, and how much rain there will be—these things are unknown to us. The principles inherent in the creation we can discern in a limited way, as cause and effect. But the time and seasons of them are not ours to determine or judge. This is not a fatalism which shrugs its shoulders but a recognition of our limitation as creatures under the hand of God who works all things for good to his people.

He is God, and under his dominion, where the tree falls, south or north, there it shall be. "O Lord, I know that the way of man is not in himself: it is not in man that walketh to direct his steps" (Jer. 10:23). Man's life is circumscribed by the power and government of God his Creator. God governs all things. This calls us not only to a humble recognition of his sovereignty but also to a childlike trust in his provision in our labor and activity.

Man in sinful pride wants to be in control: "He that observeth the wind shall not sow; and he that regardeth the clouds shall not reap" (Eccl. 11:4). But he is not in control, not of the weather nor of the climate, not of sickness nor disease. Man wants to figure out the future, as if it were his to discern and judge. He tries to model it as if he could predict the result—whether to plant or reap in the illustration of the text. But this ability is not his. He goes astray as some unseen circumstance enters in. His efforts are vain. God himself makes them vain, for he will not give his glory to another. Man wants to cover all eventualities, to protect himself, to make the outcome according to his will. He is either timid in his fears or proud in himself in his pretended knowledge. His predictions are no different from those of the soothsayers and diviners of the heathen, though they be clothed with computer sophistication. He is not able to predict the future. This limitation leads to prudence in the fear of God for the believer. It does not lead to timid paralysis but rather to a just discernment in his activity of his dependence upon God's providence. We are called to sow and reap and to labor with prayer, for "without thy blessing neither our care and labor nor thy gifts can profit us."[1]

"As thou knowest not what is the way of the spirit, nor how the bones do grow in the womb of her that is with child: even so thou knowest not the works of God who maketh all" (Eccl. 11:5). The knowledge of man is a finite knowledge; the text now underscores this fact. While the word translated *spirit* can be the human spirit of a child growing in the womb physically, it is perhaps better to take it here as the basic meaning of the word, which is "wind." The movements of the wind are unseen except in their effect. The growth of a child likewise was completely hidden in the womb in an era when there was no ultrasound. Even now, how the bones grow is still an unseen wonder. Both the wind and the growth of the bones are hidden and unseen. Man's understanding, not just his power and control, are limited. God's government, on the other hand, is almighty. He works all things under the sun according to his eternal counsel and wisdom. Not a sparrow can fall to the ground nor a hair of our head but by the will and wisdom of God (Matt. 10:29–31). He maketh all, that is, he does all his good pleasure, realizing his counsel and purpose in and through all things and bringing to pass all things under the sun. Before that majesty of God, man's limited knowledge and understanding, which has the emphasis here, are that of a creature of the dust. Man is finite, dependent; the works of God are beyond his comprehension. We are to walk in what God has revealed in his word for our understanding. That is to be a walk by faith and trust in our heavenly

---

1   Heidelberg Catechism Q&A 125, in Schaff, Creeds of Christendom, 3:353.

Father's wisdom and disposition of all things. The fool strives with this in rebellion. It is by grace that we walk in the fear of God,

Hence the conclusion to which the word of God brings us: "In the morning sow thy seed, and in the evening withhold not thine hand: for thou knowest not whether shall prosper, either this or that, or whether they both alike shall be good" (Eccl. 11:6). God's provision and blessing are the real fountain of that which is good for us. He knows what we do not. Going about our work and calling in the fear of God, we may rest, for God's way with us is right. This is not pessimism but the way of peace in contentment.

The Days of our Years

7. Truly the light is sweet, and a pleasant thing it is for the eyes to behold the sun:
8. But if a man live many years, and rejoice in them all; yet let him remember the days of darkness; for they shall be many. All that cometh is vanity.—Ecclesiastes 11:7–8

Turning from our calling to labor under God's providence in the preceding verses, the text turns to a similar subject, but from a more subjective viewpoint. We are to sow our seed and labor, not knowing what shall prosper in God's providence. We labor under the sun in a transitory world. Our works and labors, as has been shown over the course of the book, do not abide. God gives us, in our labor, seasons of light and joy in this present life, when our works prosper. Hence the point is raised: "Truly the light is sweet, and a pleasant thing it is for the eyes to behold the sun" (Eccl. 11:7).

The word of God draws on our natural response to a bright and beautiful day. It is a delight; we feel energized. The tasks of the day do not seem burdensome. As we go forth to sow in the morning, the light of the day seems to charge the day with promise, and our hands are ready to work. As the text says: "Truly the light is sweet" (v. 7). We, as it were, drink in the sweetness of the light. God created it to be so in the beginning, when "God saw every thing that he had made…it was very good" (Gen. 1:31), and the mark of that goodness as a work of God is still impressed upon the creation. Ecclesiastes 11:7 continues: "And a pleasant thing it is for the eyes to behold the sun." The light brings a certain joy to the eyes; it dispels the dark of the night, the gray, and the gloom. It warms the earth, and the beauty of the creation unfolds before our eyes.

Yet the figure refers to more than the sensation of light, for the text has a figurative idea underlying the idea of the light. For the description is not just for the moment, leading not only to a day, a month, a year, but to "many years" in the next verse (v. 8). There are phases of life when things go well, when the sun shines upon our labor and activity, when life is rich and fruitful. This is especially the case when we are young, and the possibilities of life unfold before us. Solomon would turn our attention in the following verses particularly to the time of youth in contrast with the time of old age.

Beholding the sun and enjoying the privilege of living under the sun, particularly when our strength is full and the power and activity of life given us is strong within us, is after all a good gift of God. For a child of God, that is indeed a blessing when he walks in the way of the fear of God and remembers his Creator in his youth.

The fool, however, takes such times in his days under the sun as if they were his due, holding on to them as if he owned them, or as if they were under his power. God is not in all his thoughts. To the fool, these good gifts of God work his condemnation. For he receives them in the service of sin and folly and is unthankful for them.

Therefore, setting that figure before us, the text continues: "But if a man live many years, and rejoice in them all; yet let him remember the days of darkness; for they shall be many. All that cometh is vanity" (v. 8). The text moves from the light of the day to the years of life. The portion of each one is not the same in this life, but to some there are given many years, and the text envisions one who seemingly rejoices in them all. Whether he be a believer or a fool is not on the foreground directly; rather it is what he considers and holds in mind. The question is what he keeps in remembrance in his life in the passing of the years, what he holds in the light of the sun, and on what his rejoicing is founded.

How so? The purpose is not to introduce a despondent or morbid note, to be a gloomy voice in the light of the day. Rather it calls us to a certain spiritual sobriety and discernment. The fool will not listen, for when dark days come, he is bitter; his joy in himself is marred. His life is of the earth and tied to this world. Its pleasures and treasures are his only possession. He strives with the hand of God when the sun is veiled.

We need a spiritual sobriety which puts the pleasant time in perspective. That spiritual sobriety consists in a true understanding brought about exactly in the way of remembering the "days of darkness" (v. 8). The days of darkness belong to the trials and troubles of this life. They are the days when the good in life seems to depart, and we have trial and sorrow, when it seems as if all is dark and the way full of burdens that are heavy to bear. To these belong also times of weakness and care.

These things, too, come from the hand of God and under his providence. The word of God repeatedly addresses our heavenly Father's purpose in them for our comfort in chastening, trial, and affliction. Here, what is on the foreground is the fact that it is God who sends them as days of darkness in our life. And their purpose is to work a sober assessment of the meaning of our life under the sun. The remembrance of them is to give us to see the days of light and rejoicing under the sun as good gifts of God and to work a thankfulness for them.

But the dark days serve also to draw us away from this present life under the sun. They lead us to set our priorities aright, for this present life is not where our hope lies nor where our abiding treasure is to be found. That treasure belongs to the things that are above, to our eternal salvation and communion with God. To learn daily to seek the things that are above, to labor in the joy of this present life, yet with an eye to its eternal end and where our true hope is to be found, is the purpose of this remembrance. Then we can also rejoice in the midst of affliction and trial, for we have a light that is beyond the sun of this world and earthly days. It is a light that does not fade away.

That remembrance leads us to the conclusion set before us more than once in Ecclesiastes, and found here again: "All that cometh is vanity" (v. 8). Both in days of light and days of darkness, in days of rejoicing and in days when, in an earthly sense, rejoicing is difficult, "all that cometh is vanity." They are passing things of this life under the sun; they do not abide. The very transitory character of the days of our life makes it vanity; it gives to life under the sun a certain emptiness. That emptiness lies in a world subjected to vanity because of sin. The days pass, the years flee away. If our hope is only in this life, we have nothing that endures, and we ourselves pass away.

For one who walks as a sojourner in this life, seeking his life out of himself in God, there is a meaning and joy in this present life. This is true when the sun shines, but also in the days of darkness, the believer finds there is consolation and light from above in the presence of God's sustaining care. All that cometh under the sun is indeed vanity. But what God has wrought in his saving work in Christ alone answers that reality of the present vanity under the sun. The light of the sun points to it. The days of darkness press upon us the need for that light of God's Son and his salvation.

In the midst of the truth that "all that cometh is vanity," we have hope. But it is not of this world under the sun but from God who is above and works all things for the glory of his own name.

A Godly Rejoicing in One's Youth

9. Rejoice, O young man, in thy youth; and let thy heart cheer thee in the days of thy youth, and walk in the ways of thine heart, and in the sight of thine eyes: but know

thou, that for all these things God will bring thee into judgment.

10. Therefore remove sorrow from thy heart, and put away evil from thy flesh: for childhood and youth are vanity.—Ecclesiastes 11:9–10

The Word of God now turns from the natural joy of life under the sun and its spiritual implications to a similar reality, the joy and strength of youth.

"Rejoice, O young man, in thy youth; and let thy heart cheer thee in the days of thy youth, and walk in the ways of thine heart, and in the sight of thine eyes" (Eccl. 11:9). The word of God here comes with an exhortation to rejoice, which is perhaps easy to overlook, given the warnings which follow. That calling to rejoice, however, is important. It sets before us the work of God in our human nature, as God made us, and in which we are given to walk in our youth. We grow from childhood into adulthood with a strength of life and energy that are the natural design of God and a good gift of God in itself. Though this gift is not given to all in the same manner because the afflictions and sorrows that touch the life of man in a fallen world touch children also, yet it is the normal pattern of life in childhood and youth under the sun.

Youth is a time of discovery of the world which God has made and upholds. It is the time to plan and seek out the things of this life, one's place and calling. The world which God has made opens itself in opportunities, paths of life to walk, of work and labor. In youth, the eye is young, sees the things of this life with an anticipation that the clouded eye of old age no longer has. Childhood and youth are a gift of God.

The word of God here addresses this reality of childhood and youth. Rejoice in it. "Let thy heart cheer thee" (v. 9), or make good thine heart, with that which is right and fitting to its joy. The text exhorts the young man to do this in the days of "thy youth," and continues to encourage him to "walk in the ways of thine heart," that is, explore his talents, gifts, and interests; follow them with the enthusiasm of youth. The text speaks likewise of walking "in the sight of thine eyes," which is what Solomon did.

He described in Ecclesiastes 2 the works which he did in his strength of youth: "I made me great works; I builded me houses; I planted me vineyards: I made me gardens and orchards" (vv. 4–5). He was engaged in all the labor and activity of life. He says also: "And whatsoever mine eyes desired I kept not from them, I withheld not my heart from any joy; for my heart rejoiced in all my labour: and this was my portion of all my labour" (v. 10).

This activity arises out of the heart, figuratively, just as the physical organ pumps blood throughout the body. Out of the heart "are the issues of life" (Prov. 4:23), and it is fitting that we enter into the activities of life in our youth and rejoice in them. The joy in the activity itself, of laboring and building, as well as the sense of achievement, are its proper fruit and our portion. Solomon says "this was my portion of all my labour" (Eccl. 2:10), for the things which are made do not themselves abide.

The activity and joy belong to God's design of man's life. Even in the garden of Eden man was to work, "to dress it and to keep it" (Gen. 2:15). But sin has also entered the world, and through the fall that same heart has become corrupt so that "the heart is deceitful above all things, and desperately wicked: who can know it?" (Jer. 17:9). We are totally depraved by nature, and out of the heart of fallen man issues forth the pollution of sin.

That same heart, figuratively, is thus the spiritual and ethical center of man's life, the spiritual center of our activity. It is also the fountain of sin in our nature, and its stain cleaves to all our activity. In the deepest sense, in a regenerated heart, that spiritual center is made new and becomes the fountain of a new life in Christ lived by faith under the word of God.

But we live by faith through the presence of the flesh and indwelling sin. Thus, the warning comes: "but know thou, that for all these things God will bring thee into judgment" (Eccl. 11:9). It is the young man or woman, the sinner, that shall be brought into judgment for his works. The spiritual principle in that calling to rejoice, therefore, is importantly a calling to walk consciously before the Lord in all that activity of life. In our planning and delight in the creation under the sun and in the joy of youth and its energy and works we are called to "remember now thy Creator in the days of thy youth" (Eccl. 12:1).

The fool walking after the folly of his own heart labors in the service of sin and his own lust. God is not in his thoughts. This is not the rejoicing to which the text calls us. Rather we are called to a godly joy in the strength of our life in the service of God, which is the rejoicing to be sought and which must shape our walk. Not any desire of heart, but that which genuinely cheers it, or makes good the heart in that which is right and fitting before God, is to be the way of our heart in our walk in our youth. For it yields the testimony of a good conscience before God.

The same thought is addressed to the son in Proverbs concerning the heart and its activity:

23. Keep thy heart with all diligence; for out of it are the issues of life.
24. Put away from thee a froward mouth, and perverse lips put far from thee.
25. Let thine eyes look right on, and let thine eyelids look straight before thee.
26. Ponder the path of thy feet, and let all thy ways be established.
27. Turn not to the right hand nor to the left: remove thy foot from evil." (Prov. 4: 23–27)

We will be brought before God in the hall of judgment to stand and give an account. A believing child of God whose sins are covered in the blood of Christ and his righteousness also so labors in the fear of God, knowing that this fact is not a threat but rather a sobering life-transforming truth. Serving to keep us from a heedless walk of sin and the way of the world, it calls us to a conscious walk after that fear of God in the way of godliness. It calls us to remember the Creator as we walk in his creation.

That is the intention of this warning here, as is clear from its intended fruit: "Therefore remove sorrow from thy heart, and put away evil from thy flesh: for childhood and youth are vanity" (Eccl. 11:10). Sorrow is that which vexes and angers. It is that which provokes God to anger because of sin. It therefore works grief, sorrow, and shame in the heart of one walking therein, who walks consciously before God. It works condemnation and sorrow to one who is heedless, walking in the folly of sin. Out of the heart this sorrow arises; and the calling is to mortify it by putting sin and its sorrow away from our heart, to "keep [our hearts] with all diligence" (Prov. 4:23).

Similarly, Ecclesiastes 11:10 says, "put away evil from thy flesh," or, as we find elsewhere, "flee also youthful lusts (2 Tim. 2:22). The calling is both an internal one—to pass from it in the heart—as well as an external one in our walk, to keep ourselves in body as well as soul from evil.

The reason given is also to be noted. "Childhood and youth" belong to the transitory reality and character of life. They "are vanity" (Eccl. 11:10): vanity, not in the sense of emptiness, but of a fleeting state of life that quickly passes away. This time of life is momentary, and eventually we grow older and the infirmities of age come. Just as the purpose of the previous verses was to set before us the contrast between the light and the days of darkness, so the following verses contrast the strength of youth and the infirmity of age for the same purpose. Therefore remember thy Creator, remember him *now*, at the time of youth and in the days of thy youth.

CHAPTER 12

Remembering Our Creator

1. Remember now thy Creator in the days of thy youth, while the evil days come not, nor the years draw nigh, when thou shalt say, I have no pleasure in them;
2. While the sun, or the light, or the moon, or the stars, be not darkened, nor the clouds return after the rain:
3. In the day when the keepers of the house shall tremble, and the strong men shall bow themselves, and the grinders cease because they are few, and those that look out of the windows be darkened,
4. And the doors shall be shut in the streets, when the sound of the grinding is low, and he shall rise up at the voice of the bird, and all the daughters of musick shall be brought low;
5. Also when they shall be afraid of that which is high, and fears shall be in the way, and the almond tree shall flourish, and the grasshopper shall be a burden, and desire shall fail: because man goeth to his long home, and the mourners go about the streets:
6. Or ever the silver cord be loosed, or the golden bowl be broken, or the pitcher be broken at the fountain, or the wheel broken at the cistern.
7. Then shall the dust return to the earth as it was: and the spirit shall return unto God who gave it.
8. Vanity of vanities, saith the preacher; all is vanity.
   —Ecclesiastes 12:1–8

The preceding chapter contained an exhortation to the young in the days of youth. Our text continues that thought and completes it. "Remember now thy Creator in the days of thy youth, while the evil days come not, nor the years draw nigh, when thou shalt say, I have no pleasure in them" (Eccl. 12:1).

The calling is to remember, not in the sense of looking at what is past, which belongs to the elderly, but in the sense of holding in mind. Hold in mind, as constantly before your mind, thy Creator. Do so now, in the present, daily, while you are yet young. In all the activity of life and joy of youth as life unfolds before you, consider him who made you, in whose creation you walk, and whose works your eyes behold. Do so knowing "that for all these things God will bring thee into judgment. Therefore remove sorrow from thy heart, and put away evil from thy flesh: for childhood and youth are vanity" (11:9–10).

Childhood and youth are vanity, a fleeting transitory state or phase of life under the sun. They do not endure. Days will come which are evil, full of trial, affliction, and chastening from the Lord. Thus, Moses prays in Psalm 90: "Make us glad according to the days wherein thou hast afflicted us, and the years wherein we have seen evil" (v. 15).

The days come when the joys of life fade because of the infirmities of age and its increasing limitations. What follows in Ecclesiastes 12 is the contrast between youth and old age, which further explains "when thou shalt say, I have no pleasure in them" (v. 1). The purpose is to underscore the reason for the exhortation given: "Rejoice, O young man, in thy youth" (11:9). Old age comes with its limitations but also with a looking back at that which is past, a remembrance of days gone by. Remembering our Creator in the days of our youth keeps one from sins of youth, which are a burden in old age. The psalmist prays: "Remember not the sins of my youth, nor my transgressions: according to thy mercy remember thou me for thy goodness' sake, O Lord" (Ps. 25:7).

In harmony with the viewpoint of Ecclesiastes, the text focuses on the physical infirmities of age, when one says of one's days, "I have no pleasure in them" (Eccl. 12:1). The delights and physical joys of seeing and hearing, the activities of taste and sound fade away.

"While the sun, or the light, or the moon, or the stars, be not darkened, nor the clouds return after the rain" (v. 2). In youth the sight of the eyes is clear and bright; with aging comes a decline in vision. The purpose in this description is not to introduce some hidden symbolic figures but to describe the infirmities of age in contrast to youth. The time comes when vision is blurred and dimmed. Cataracts, for example, the clouding of vision, dim the light, and in Solomon's days some surgical relief was not to be found. The decline does not stand still. Clouds return after the rain; so it is to one whose vision is clouded, and one who goes through successive trials like rain. The point is that these infirmities do not yet touch the young, but they follow in the course of life. The result is old age: "In the day when the keepers of the house shall tremble, and strong men shall bow themselves, and the grinders cease because they are few, and those that look out of the windows be darkened" (v. 3). The picture, while figurative, is not difficult. The body wears out, arms and legs lose their strength, they tremble and bow. The strength of youth is gone, and that which was once strong now bows and becomes weak. The grinders, the teeth, cease; they fall out or have to be removed because of decay. The windows, the eyes, become darkened, so that one slowly becomes blind. We have canes, walkers, hip replacement surgery, dental care, dentures, glasses, eye surgery, and other means to compensate for the decline of old age, though they are only easing of the decline, not cures. Solomon had more limited means in his time.

Similarly old age is the time when "the doors shall be shut in the streets, when the sound of the grinding is low, and he shall rise up at the voice of the bird, and all the daughters of musick shall be brought low" (v. 4). The picture in the verse is essentially one of old age hearing loss. The doors of the ears are shut; they cannot any longer hear the sound from the street or from the kitchen of grinding the flour for a meal. Conversation therefore becomes difficult. Yet, the higher pitch sound of a bird is still heard and awakens one or causes one to rise early as sleep departs. The pleasure of rest in sleep diminishes as a result. Music and its enjoyment likewise depart because the hearing can no longer distinguish its sound and melody. Solomon had both singers and instruments in his court; it was part of the splendor of his kingdom (2:8). Yet in old age he tells us indirectly: "I have no pleasure in them" (12:1). This affects the joy of life and fellowship with others at the same time. It isolates the elderly.

"Also when they shall be afraid of that which is high, and fears shall be in the way, and the almond tree shall flourish, and the grasshopper shall be a burden, and desire shall fail: because man goeth to his long home, and the mourners go about in the streets" (12:5). With the infirmities of age and a loss of strength come also fears of heights and of walking, unknown when one is young. One's grip, balance, strength to stand, and walk are not the same. The limbs become stiff, the strength and balance are not there. One totters and needs support.

The almond tree blooms white or a pinkish white. Here, the flourishing of the tree aptly represents the hair turning white with age, the hoary head. The figure of the grasshopper or locust is probably to be understood of the insect when it crawls along, rather that hops or flies. Its creeping motion represents then the burden of movement in old age. The picture is that of the fading of the powers of life and the slow decay of the body which age brings. "And desire shall fail" (v. 5). The same decline is found internally in wanting and willing, as the natural desires for the things of this life fade.

The cause is set before us: this decline is unto death and the grave. The grave and death, the long or eternal home, await us and claim the life of a man or a woman, putting an end to his or her place in this world. We die, and the mourners go about in the street. We would say, the funeral procession goes by. Such is the lot of all men under the sun.

6. Or ever the silver cord be loosed, or the golden bowl be broken, or the pitcher be broken at the fountain, or the wheel broken at the cistern.

7. Then shall the dust return to the earth as it was: and the spirit shall return unto God who gave it. (vv. 6–7)

The pictures or series of pictures in verse six are intended to present a pattern of death as a sudden separation; the cord is loosed, and the bowl, possibly that of a lamp, falls to the ground and is broken. The bowl hangs by a silver chain which is slipped off and the bowl falls, spilling its contents and perhaps the light it once gave is extinguished. It is broken, damaged. The silver and gold are loosed. So also is the life of man, precious in our days under the sun, but suddenly cut off by death, and the beauty and glory depart.

The pitcher and the wheel present a similar idea. The pitcher of clay is fragile. It is suddenly shattered to pieces at the fountain and can hold no more water. Its place and use—its life—is done. The wheel which drew water out of the cistern collapses. Worn out and weakened, it falls and is broken. It will draw water no more.

Death comes suddenly, irreversibly, as far as this world is concerned, and takes us from this life. The point is to remember thy Creator now, especially in thy youth "or ever," or before, this comes, this death and separation from the things of this life under the sun. For "God will bring thee into judgment" (11:9).

Death itself is the judgment of God upon sin; old age is the expression of the working of God's curse upon fallen man. "For dust thou art, and unto dust shalt thou return" (Gen. 3:19). Man is dust; such is the meaning of the name Adam or man. From the dust of the earth he was formed, and at death "shall the dust return to the earth as it was" (Eccl. 12:7). The word for dust used here is slightly different from the word used in Genesis. It is a synonym, which emphasizes the earthy character of that dust as a clod of earth. "Man is of the earth, earthy" (1 Cor. 15:47). He has no power over death, nor can he by his activity, which is earthly, find an answer to it. The spirit or breath of life which God breathed in him also returns to God who gave it. Thus, the word of God returns to the basic observation of the book: "Vanity of vanities, saith the preacher; all is vanity" (Eccl. 12:8). Vanity, a transitory thing which does not abide or endure, is empty in itself, a passing moment under the sun. Such under the sun is the life of man and man himself who dies. Man has no power to retain the spirit. Only in God the Creator who in Christ is God our Redeemer is there an answer. That requires the work of grace from above. It cannot arise from man who is of the earth below and returns to his earth.

Words of Truth

8 . Vanity of vanities, saith the preacher; all is vanity.

9. And moreover, because the preacher was wise, he still taught the people knowledge; yea, he gave good heed, and sought out, and set in order many proverbs.

10. The preacher sought to find out acceptable words: and that which was written was upright, even words of truth.

11. The words of the wise are as goads, and as nails fastened by the masters of assemblies, which are given from one shepherd.—Ecclesiastes 12:8–11

The word of God in Ecclesiastes now moves to the conclusion of the book. But first it sets before us the objective theme and the inspiration of the book. That theme is: "Vanity of vanities, saith the preacher; all is vanity" (Eccl. 12:8).

The transitory character of life under the sun has been the object of contemplation. We labor and toil under the sun. The world presents itself as rich and beautiful, for God made it, and his handiwork is revealed by the things which are made. But that world also lies under the curse and judgment of God upon sin, which has subjected the whole creation to vanity: "For the creature was made subject to vanity, not willingly, but by reason of him who hath subjected the same in hope" (Rom. 8:20). The result is that all things under the sun wear away, decay, and decline in corruption. The works of man crumble and fall. Man himself ages and decays unto death and the grave.

The unbeliever, the fool in Ecclesiastes, as we have seen, strives with that reality of vanity, seeking to find his treasure and joy in this life. The result is the folly of sin, the heaping and gathering of the wicked to his own hurt. The Preacher, Solomon, has sought to set before us the truth of the matter for the spiritual instruction of God's believing people, that we might see with the eye of faith the world and its vanity, so as to understand what is good and profitable for a child of God under the sun. This purpose he now sets before us as the book draws to a close.

"And moreover, because the preacher was wise, he still taught the people knowledge; yea, he gave good heed, and sought out, and set in order many proverbs" (Eccl. 12:9). The course of the book has been one of a serious discerning study of things under the sun, to know their meaning, purpose, and value. He "gave good heed and sought out" wisdom. The book of Proverbs, with its gathering of observations of the world and resulting wisdom, was the same endeavor. Ecclesiastes, forming as it were an appendix to Proverbs, builds on the wisdom found there. Solomon, laying hold of the wisdom God gave him, sets in order many proverbs, not only in the book of Proverbs but in this book as well. The design of a proverb, as well as this material in Ecclesiastes, is that we take up that word of God in our minds, reflecting upon it as we live our day-to-day lives, contemplating what it means for us in every situation of life. That word is like a searchlight shining upon the world around us to give spiritual understanding of the states of life and their meaning. It is intended to warn and guard us from the way of sin and its folly.

With that purpose in view, the Preacher calls to mind the gift of wisdom given him. Wisdom is both the gift of discernment and the ability or skill to put that knowledge to use. Having that wisdom, Solomon walked in the calling to teach knowledge and wisdom to the people. That Ecclesaistes 12:8–10 is in the third person, as speaking about the Preacher, rather than as the Preacher directly, does not necessarily mean we have a different writer, though that is not impossible. God used Solomon to write. He also used other men by his Spirit to collect and set in order that which was written by divine inspiration. Thus, we read in Proverbs 25: "These are also the proverbs of Solomon, which the men of Hezekiah king of Judah copied out" (v. 1). His purpose is rather to call to mind God's work in him and the grace of wisdom which he received. We have been dealing with a work of God and his word by Solomon. The wisdom in Ecclesiastes and Proverbs is not the natural fruit of a gifted human mind but a work of God in Solomon of divine inspiration.

Inspiration of the Scriptures is an organic work of God in which the prophet, or Preacher in this case, is who he is, with the gifts given him, and is led by the Spirit of God to speak and teach, not his own human wisdom, but the word of God. "Holy men of God spake as they were moved by the Holy Ghost" (2 Pet. 1:21). The result is that no Scripture is of "any private interpretation" or opinion (2 Pet. 1:20). The Bible is not a document of human philosophy or of worldly discernment and wisdom. Ecclesiastes is here laying a claim to divine inspiration for itself and for the book of Proverbs to which it is joined. This is necessary. There was then and still are many books of wisdom written by men with advice, common sense, and human thought. Divinely inspired wisdom, God's wisdom ministered to us by the Preacher, is in a wholly different category.

Hence the argument continues: "The preacher sought to find out acceptable words: and that which was written was upright, even words of truth" (Eccl. 12:10). Under that inspiration and by means of the gift of wisdom, the work of God in inspiration extended even to the words chosen and used. That holy men "spake as they were moved by the" Spirit of God (2 Pet. 1:21) means more than just that the concepts and observations were of God. The work of God extends to the very words chosen and set down in the Scriptures. The work of God also in Proverbs and Ecclesiastes is verbally inspired. Therefore, "that which was written was upright, even words of truth" (Eccl. 12:10). What is given, therefore, is upright as to its moral character; it is the holy word of God. As Jesus said of the Scriptures, "Thy word is truth" (John 17:17). This is the same declaration given here; what is written are "even words of truth." In this and in the other Scriptures is God's own counsel and instruction. Receiving it by faith, we may rely upon it as truth, a light in a world darkened by sin and unbelief.

The text broadens its scope further in its consideration of the Scriptures and their divine inspiration, saying: "The words of the wise are as goads, and as nails fastened by the masters of assemblies, which are given from one shepherd" (Eccl. 12:11). "The words of the wise" and the "masters of assemblies" belong together as parallel thoughts. The word *assemblies* can have the idea of that which is assembled or collected together. The reference would then be to "the words of the wise," the men by whom God gave his word, such as Solomon, and the authoritative gathering of that word, the collection under the leading of the Spirit by the church. The men of Hezekiah's kingdom gathering the proverbs of Solomon into the book of inspired Scripture would be an example of this. The gathering, collection, and preservation of the word was also a work of God by men. One finds a similar process when Baruch must transcribe the word of God revealed to Jeremiah and set it down in writing (Jer. 36:27–28, 32; Jer. 45). Many of the New Testament epistles were likewise spoken by Paul or Peter but written and set down by others as scribes (Rom. 16:22; 1 Pet. 5:12). When Paul did this he would also sign the epistle to assure its authenticity (1 Cor. 16:21; 2 Thess. 3:17).

The point is that that word, spoken and set down in writing has only one source: namely God as the God of our salvation in Jesus Christ. It is from one Shepherd, the Lord. While the process of revelation involves the activity of men, its organic character, both of the writing and of gathering it together, is of the Lord. The Bible is God's divinely inspired and infallibly written word, the word of God in every part of it.

That word is described as coming to us "as goads, and as nails fastened" (Eccl. 12:11). A goad is a pointed stick or pole used to prod cattle. Its function is to rouse a sluggish ox and keep it moving. It also serves to direct and keep in the way one who wanders out of the path. The word of God has the same spiritual function for a believer, to keep him in the way, and to lead and move him along to walk in the way he should go.

At the same time the figure of a fixed nail, fastened, which does not move, sets before us the reliability and certainty of the word of God. It is truth, not of man's speculations but of God's own word to us. Truth is not relative, a matter of my opinion and your opinion, which is how the world views it. We are given to know the truth, possess it, and rest upon it in our life. The authority and trustworthiness of the Scriptures are thereby underscored, including its assessment of life set forth in the book of Ecclesiastes. It is "even the words of truth" (v. 10).

The End of the Matter—Found

12. And further, by these, my son, be admonished: of making many books there is no end; and much study is a weariness of the flesh.

13. Let us hear the conclusion of the whole matter: Fear God, and keep his commandments: for this is the whole duty of man.

14. For God shall bring every work into judgment, with every secret thing, whether it be good, or whether it be evil.—Ecclesiastes 12:12–14

The preceding verses in Ecclesiastes 12 set before us the word of God as truth. It is divinely inspired, infallibly written, and, as the word of God, to be relied upon. God is our faithful shepherd. In that connection the text continues: "And further, by these, my son, be admonished: of the making of many books there is no end; and much study is a weariness of the flesh" (Eccl. 12:12). The concern of the text is not to disparage books and study in themselves, but to contrast that divinely inspired word of God over against the writings of men. "And further, by these" could better be read, "More from these;" that is, Solomon warns against what goes beyond the Scriptures, further or more than that word of God, which comes from men, their writings of human wisdom outside of Scripture. Man labors to obtain wisdom, learning, and understanding. Such knowledge is necessary for labor and skills needed in the world. The text is not disparaging education or learning. Math, science, history, the technology of the earth have a necessary and useful place. But it is of man, fallen man.

A limit must be drawn, a warning or admonition must be given. Of these books and the making of them there is no end. They may not supplant the word of God, the word of truth. Nor where they depart from that infallible rule in unbelief, with the vain philosophy of men, are they to be received. They belong to this world and the vanity of man who walks after his own imagination. They may accurately describe some state or process in the creation. But such learning in the wisdom of men can never arrive at spiritual truth, for it is corrupted by sin.

For the same reason, much study of the wisdom of this world and its learning "is a weariness of the flesh" (v. 12). It is like all other toil of man under the sun. It is rooted in the vanity of this present life. As with any labor under the sun, it wears out the laborer. It may hold the promise of great things, but in the end, it too shall pass away with the world. The truth which God has given abides forever.

"Let us hear the conclusion of the whole matter: Fear God,

and keep his commandments: for this is the whole duty of man" (v. 13). In verse 8 the objective observation or theme of the book was set forth again, "Vanity of vanities, saith the preacher; all is vanity." Now the word of God addresses the subjective conclusion or spiritual response to that observation, the subjective theme of the book. God as the Lord of the whole creation governs all things according to his counsel and wisdom. The creation shows the beauty of God who made it but also his judgment, for the whole of the creation has been subjected to vanity because of sin.

The conclusion addresses us with a universal calling, literally: "God fear. And his commandments keep." The emphasis falls upon where one stands before God. The fear of God is the reverence of faith that acknowledges God and his word, trusts in him, and walks humbly before him. In that fear we also keep his commandments by faith, holding them in our hearts and walking in them as before his face. We are to remember our Creator in the light of his word of truth and his works under the sun.

That calling is the whole duty of man or, as the word *duty* is in italics, the whole of man. It is his fundamental calling. The calling to fear God, holding his word by faith and walking in obedience to his will, is the calling which confronts all men and all mankind. It is the call to repent and believe. That calling, which is proclaimed with clarity in the gospel, also confronts man under the sun through the creation now subjected to vanity.

The manifest truth that all is vanity under the sun renders unbelieving man, the fool, without excuse, testifying as it does of God, his work under the sun, and his judgment.

19. Because that which may be known of God is manifest in them; for God hath shewed it unto them.
20. For the invisible things of him from the creation of the world are clearly seen, being understood by the things that are made, even his eternal power and Godhead: so that they are without excuse." (Rom. 1:19–20)

The very nature of that truth, of vanity under the sun, the transitory character of life where no treasure abides and man himself dies, stands as a warning to fear God. Man is not in control; God governs the life of man. He will also judge.

"For God shall bring every work into judgment, with every secret thing, whether it be good or whether it be evil" (Eccl. 12:14). This concluding word of God also gives a reason for that exhortation. It is both a warning and a comfort. God will bring every work of man into judgment, including that which is secret or hidden. The fool will not hear this. He thinks God does not know. Walking after the imagination of his own heart, he strives with God and the boundaries of life set by God in the creation. Spiritually a fool who will not have God in his knowledge, he is given over by God in sovereign wisdom and judgment to the folly of heaping and gathering, to a walk after the folly of sin. Standing under the wrath of God, he foolishly works his own destruction and brings himself into judgment. That which is secret is not hidden before the eyes of God. God is the one who evaluates what is good and evil. Man is not the arbiter of judgment nor the standard, but God who is righteous. Not only that which is external but that which is hidden in the heart will be judged.

Concerning Ecclesiastes 12:14, we may note that the text speaks of "every work" that is, it has in view each one particularly or individually. The more normal expression in Scripture is "works," plural, viewed as an organic body of works which are the fruit of one's spiritual life and walk (Matt. 16:27; Rom. 2:6–8; Rev. 20:12). "Every work" includes "every idle word that men shall speak" (Matt. 12:36). "Every work," therefore, is not just deeds and undertakings but all our activity as it proceeds from the heart, out of the mouth, and is found in the labor of our hands.

Concerning this judgment of every work, we must note that it is God in Christ who renders judgment and that the standard is God's righteous judgment revealed to us in the principles of the law of God, which we as sinners imperfectly apprehend. It is not our self-assessment of our own work but God's judgment. That judgment includes not only the external but the secret or hidden things (Eccl. 12:14), that is, the internal root of our activity, our motives, thinking, and willing, as well as what is done out of the sight of others.

It is a judgment of "whether it be good, or whether it be evil" (v. 14). The question is not whether it be part good and part evil, a matter of percentages or degrees. The word of God does not divide our works into parts. They are either good or evil in God's sight. In themselves all our works, as they are wrought through the flesh, also in our seeing and hearing, and therefore thinking and willing through the flesh, are all stained with sin. Hence the Heidelberg Catechism says,

> But why can not our good works be the whole or part of oar righteousness before God?
>
> Because the righteousness which can stand before the judgment-seat of God must be perfect throughout, and wholly conformable to the divine law; whereas even our best works in this life are all imperfect and defiled with sin.[1]

Good works are imperfect works, individually and as a body of works. Because of this defilement, in that sense, all our works are evil works. That God judges works to be good is a matter of his saving grace in Christ, founded in Christ's imputed righteousness to the believer. "Which works, as they proceed from the good root of faith, are good and acceptable in the sight of God, forasmuch as they are all sanctified by his grace."[2]

> But what are good works?
>
> Those only which are done from true faith, according to the law of God, for his glory; and not such as rest on our own opinion or the commandments of men.[3]

---

1 Heidelberg Catechism, Q&A 62, in Schaff, *Creeds of Christendom*, 3:327.
2 Belgic Confession 24, in Schaff, *Creeds of Christendom*, 3:411
3 Heidelberg Catechism Q&A 91, in Schaff, *Creeds of Christendom*, 3:339-340.

Ecclesiastes 12:13 points us in the same direction. The one doing good is one who fears God in the reverence of faith, holds God's word in his heart to keep it, and seeks to walk in it. Good works are works that are acceptable to God by Jesus Christ and that are the fruit of faith wrought in the love of God. The wicked do nothing but evil works in the sight of God, and, when the believer walks after his own sinful flesh and not out of faith, he also walks in sin in evil works. Such was David's walk in his sin of adultery and murder (2 Sam. 11). These were evil works for which he was called to repent.

To one who walks, therefore, in the fear of God and holds his word by faith, the promise of the gospel, the forgiveness of sins, and the grace of God shines upon his pathway. Living before that judgment of God now in repentance and forgiveness, not only for his evil works but also for the sin which defiles his good works, he has assurance in that day of judgment, an assurance which is not in himself but in the mercy of God. His way is blessed, as has been repeatedly shown in the course of the book of Ecclesiastes. Even in this life under the sun, in the midst of the present vanity, the child of God's portion in this life is a good gift of God and a blessing to him. Though he is oppressed in a world of sin, his treasure is not in the things of this world that passes away. Although walking in the way of God's commandments does not seem good in the eyes of the world under the sun, for it is mocked and persecuted by a wicked world, yet doing so by faith is the way of true spiritual blessing and contentment.

The vanity of things under the sun cannot give an answer to sin and death. They can only show the need to be reconciled to God. In the grace of God, the way of a child of God is one lived as before the face of God who is his heavenly Father for Christ's sake. Better is a little, a small portion in this life, with the fear of God. (Ps. 37:16).

Ecclesiastes is a book written by one who is old and who in his course of life has explored every work of man under the sun and weighed its meaning and fitness before God. The Preacher "still taught the people knowledge" (Eccl. 12:9). It is a book to be pondered. It addresses in particular the young person who is starting on life's pathway, as instruction from one who has been there, so to speak, and can give wisdom and counsel from experience. It is the light of the word of God upon the things under the sun.

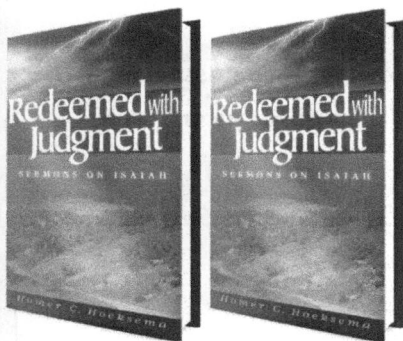

Redeemed with Judgment: Sermons on Isaiah
(2 volumes)
by Homer C. Hoeksema

Why did Jesus and his apostles quote from Isaiah as often as they did? What did the author of this book see in the prophecy of Isaiah that made him concentrate much of his preaching on this book for some thirty years? The answer lies in the messianic characteristic of the book; Isaiah speaks of Christ. Sometimes the prophecy is indirect, vague, and difficult to understand. At other times clear, literal, and straightforward. In either case, Isaiah always speaks of the coming of the Messiah implying both the judgment of the wicked world and the salvation of Zion.

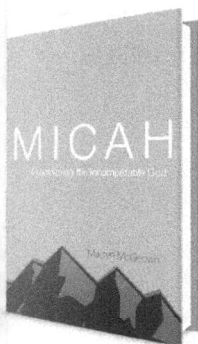

———

Micah: Proclaiming the Incomparable God
by Martyn McGeown

Christians want to know Christ from the Old Testament, from Micah, and the other minor prophets. And yet for many of us the minor prophets are like a sealed book. The inspired writing of the minor prophets are addressed to the people of God and addressed to us also in the New Testament church. As inspired scripture they indeed speak of Christ: Micah does so extensively, and not only in the obvious reference to Bethlehem in chapter 5:2. The prophet Micah proclaims the incomparable God of judgment and mercy. This God is our God, the God of all who believe in Jesus Christ. And this prophecy has vital lessons to teach us today.

All books available at **rfpa.org**,
or by calling the Reformed Free Publishing Association
at **616-457-5970** or emailing **mail@rfpa.org.**

REFORMED
FREE PUBLISHING
ASSOCIATION

Our Mission

To glorify God by making accessible to the broadest possible audience material that testifies to the truth of Scripture as understood and developed in the Reformed tradition.

Reformed Free Publishing Association
1894 Georgetown Center Drive
Jenison, MI 49428-7137
Website: rfpa.org
E-mail: mail@rfpa.org
Phone: 616-457-5970

www.ingramcontent.com/pod-product-compliance
Lightning Source LLC
Chambersburg PA
CBHW060753100426
42813CB00004B/797